Voices from the Corner

Poverty and Racism in the Inner City

voices
from
the corner
poverty and racism
in the inner city

Raphael S. Ezekiel

TEMPLE UNIVERSITY PRESS
PHILADELPHIA

Temple University Press, Philadelphia 19122
© 1984 by Temple University. All rights reserved
Published 1984
Printed in the United States of America

Library of Congress Cataloging in Publication Data

Ezekiel, Raphael S., 1931-
  Voices from the corner.

  1. Afro-Americans—Michigan—Detroit—Interviews.
2. Afro-Americans—Michigan—Detroit—Economic conditions.
3. Detroit (Mich.)—Race relations.   4. Detroit (Mich.)—
Economic conditions.   I. Title.
F574.D49N438   1984   305.8'96073'077434   84-2637
ISBN 0-87722-358-0

for Daniel, for Margalete, for Joshua

for Tish, for Nathaniel,

and

to the memory of

Navah

contents

acknowledgments

I am indebted in a way that cannot be repaid to the people of the Corner, who allowed me into their midst and treated me with gentleness. It is my hope that this product of our time together will aid the next generation that is rising on the many Corners of our land.

Many people have helped in the course of this project; not all of them can be listed here.

The Ford Foundation played a major role with two grants (Nos. 68-26 and 680-0026A). Nancy Dennis, my desk officer at Ford, became a close friend; I am richer for her wisdom, energy, and good humor.

Numbers of people have worked at one time or another transforming material from tape to type, including Joanne Berke, Camille Buda, Vivian Chen, Mary Lee Edgren, Deborah Eisberg, Donna Harsch, Elizabeth Hertz, Gayle Penley, Dorothy Robohm, Elizabeth Schwartz, and Nancy Steege. I am grateful for their good-natured persistence at a demanding task. Gerald Wiggins helped me to start and to keep going, and Mary Radke Cain has lent me repeatedly her industry, good spirit, and intelligence.

I have discussed this material with classes for some years, both at the University of Michigan's campus at Ann Arbor and at the University's extension classes in Detroit. Hundreds of students have helped me with their reactions and their reflections.

A good deal of thinking in the book originated in long, hard arguments with my good friend Susan LeVan, a fine artist and a tough-minded lady.

A number of friends sustained me through personal sorrows early in this work. Lois Hoffman was my rock. She was joined by a lonely band: Dave and Joanna Gutmann, Joe and Jody Veroff, Bill and Zee Gamson,

Marty Hoffman, Becky Mullen, and the late and deeply beloved Al Mullen.

Michael Ames at Temple University Press has been a marvelous editor; I am pleased by the careful and delicate work at Temple of Candy Hawley. Earlier, David Brent at the University of Chicago Press and Elliot Liebow at the National Institutes of Health gave me priceless encouragement and aid.

My attempts to understand persons owe everything to my teachers (not all of whom I worked with in the classroom)—M. Brewster Smith, John Clausen, and David Hamburg. Let me also acknowledge from an earlier period Bert Hoselitz, Christian Mackauer, Hans Rothfels, Joseph Schwab, and Milton Mayer.

Finally, there is the debt to those who are closest, Tish and our children, those with whom I have shared the joy of exchanging nurturance. We have grown in our tiny community and rejoiced in one another's growth. Like all the parents and children whom you will meet in these pages, we wish this happiness for the greater community as well.

part one

introduction

Lame Catherine's house stood at a corner in one of the poorest sections of Detroit. That house, and those alongside it, has since been leveled, but during the last years of Johnson's administration and the first years of Nixon's, a small community was located in those houses and on that corner. I lingered there, visiting among the members of the community, for long stretches of time, two or three days a week for several years, talking with the very poor Black men and women who lived on that corner or who hung out on that corner. Periodically, one of the men or women agreed to tape-record a discussion with me, and we would talk about the person's life and the meaning he or she found in it.

The research took place during a time of intense re-evaluation for many of us in this country. During those years and for a number of years afterward, I puzzled over the reactions and the thoughts that marked my part of the research interactions. I became more and more interested in looking at the way that I and other whites thought about white and Black interactions. My examination of my own actions and thoughts, when in the field and when talking about the field, led to insights about the nature of white consciousness.

The present book attempts to present the feel of that poverty-stricken Black corner *and* the emotions and thoughts I experienced from my time there. The focus of the book is two-fold. What is it like to be Black and poor, like the people who are being interviewed? What is it like to be white and middle-class, like the author and most likely the reader? I want to convey the sound and look of a piece of underclass life and to communicate my reactions to it. I also want to move beyond my immediate personal reactions to the underlying social and psychological forces that lead large numbers of us into similar responses. Dealing awkwardly with my own role as the purveyor of a portrait, I have tried to make this work pivot on questions of white reactions as well as on Black oral histories. My hope is to lead readers to a greater awareness of their own thinking.

The Author and His Research

This study had its immediate stimulus in the fall of 1966. I was doing pilot work on conceptions of life and the future held by eighth- and eleventh-grade boys, comparing middle-class to working-class children. I received a visit from a student I had taught at the University of Michigan, where I am employed as a faculty member in social psychology. She wanted to tell me how her life was going (I had counseled her through some crises); among other things, she told me about her work, teaching in a Black high school in Detroit. I asked to come and visit her eleventh graders.

I went to school and taught several classes with her. I was accompanied by Navah Ezekiel, my first wife, who died a few months after this study began. The school was in an all-Black neighborhood, and Navah and I had several surprises. Initially, we were frightened when we walked from our car to the school. This disturbed us. We had forgotten how alien one could feel. Later, however, after having a wholly enjoyable time in the school, we found ourselves smiling and easy when we walked back to our car—and found ourselves smiling happily at friendly people on porches, who greeted us with warmth. Finally, the students were a pleasure. They were bright, intelligent, warm, and intact. We thoroughly enjoyed working with them. This particularly surprised us, and the surprise gave us pause.

We realized we had expected a world of shattered souls rather than brisk students who played chess and warm neighbors who liked us. Recent descriptions of broken lives in the ghetto had led me to very different expectations. I needed a good, hard look, close up. Here was the world I wished to understand. What was the experienced life of these people in their own words? I proposed to hang out in a working-class setting and in a lower-class setting and to spend a long time with a very few people in each place. I visited Detroit weekly for a few months, trying out my skills, and then began to write for grants.

Census data were used to orient the choice of research sites. The underclass (lower-class) location had to come from one of the tracts in which the median family income for 1960 fell below $3,000, a level that placed families in the lower third of Detroit Black families.

My original grant proposals spoke of studying the ways that competence was socialized, the ways that a hard-pressed people passed on confidence and skill across generations. I soon found my ignorance of Black life too deep to allow any such sophisticated goal, and settled for trying to understand the rough shape of life in each setting. Since the working-class setting was more familiar to me, I put the greater energy into the underclass location, the place that I call the Corner, the community that is the subject of this volume. All interviews in this book come from the Corner, but my thinking is informed by simultaneous work I carried out on a Black working-class street, and on a Black street where there was fast action, and on a white Appalachian street.

The field work was carried out formally from 1967 to 1972. Return visits since then indicate that the nature of underclass life has not altered; it is still "a hell of a thing." The book is probably not dated as a description of that piece of society. Unfortunately, it may be old-fashioned or premature as a piece of white self-examination; fashions have changed, whether conditions have or not.

In general I carried out the field work alone. A young University of Michigan undergraduate who was a friend of mine and came from a Black working-class family joined me in some of the visits in the first few months. Occasionally I brought in members of my office staff or a friend or one of my children. A generous grant from the Ford Foundation gave me time to hang out on the Corner for those years and paid typists who turned our recorded interviews into print. I studied the transcripts at my office in Ann Arbor, thirty-five miles west of Detroit. I have reflected on the material alone and with my family, with classes in Ann Arbor and extension classes in Detroit, and with personal friends.

Although there was much talk in those days that whites could no longer work among Blacks, with a great deal of determination and some confrontation I rather quickly gained acceptance. Research on the Corner was agreeable. I enjoyed the easy quality of living, the premium on relaxed talk, the disinterest in the pretensions and schedules of the aspiring middle class. The ease I felt among a warm and accepting people took on a special meaning with the loss of my wife. The timeless ebb and flow of Corner life was a comfort; we rocked like kelp in the tide. Later my life regained shape and direction, and Corner life began to chafe. I wished for more to happen. But these people had little power to shape events, and individuals could deal, generally, only with what came their way.

As observer and questioner, visitor and sojourner, I underwent considerable transformation. In Detroit, I absorbed to some degree a serious sense of Black life as it was lived. Driving back to the University, I heard on the radio news a version of that life that I couldn't recognize; back at the University I listened to a variety of people who claimed to other unrecognizable versions. These various portraits served the needs of the speakers.

These disjunctures made me a more skeptical person and more radical. At the same time, the long exposure to the nature of daily life in poverty made me more pessimistic about our society.

Throughout this process, I experienced fundamental changes in the way I taught and the way I did research. Most recently, I became active in electoral politics, winning a seat on Ann Arbor's city council; angry at the smugness of the new conservatism, I campaigned bluntly for a progressive approach. I have continued my field research in groups ranging from pacifist to neo-Nazi.

During my years on the Corner, I spoke with everyone who lived there and most of the people who visited there or hung out regularly. The interviews were usually held in someone's living room, but sometimes on someone's front steps or in a car. The typed transcripts came to more than 3,700 pages.

The selection of interviews for inclusion in this book is my attempt to present that combination of voices that most nearly re-creates for the reader the experience as I understood it. In that calculation, I have depended upon such awareness as I possess as an artist.

The interviews in Part Three are slices from longer interviews; the interview with Jackie Rahlins is explicitly a collection of segments, while the other interviews in Part Two (the Stones, Miller, Foreman, Coolidge) are presented almost in their entirety, except for deletions of thematic repetitions. The interviews have also been transformed slightly to avoid the choppiness of a question-and-answer format. Relatively little of this has been necessary, since my respondents tended to give extended monologues once they were interested in a topic. I have spared the reader the hundreds of times that I said "yeah" or "uh huh" or "you mean ..." in order to help a person keep talking. I have also inserted into the text bridge words to tie back together respondent sentences that were previously joined by questions of mine that are now deleted. From all of these causes, a few words have been eliminated from many pages and a few (three or four) have been added now and then. I have tried to make sure that my invented words do not introduce some new element.

In transcription and editing, no attempt has been made to represent pronunciation: "gettin' " has become "getting," "runnin' " has become "running," and—with more loss—"hongry" has been flattened to "hungry" and the angry, definite sound of "nuthin' !" has become merely "nothing!" Those familiar with the rhythm and the pitch of the spoken language should be able to hear it as they read, since I have preserved the word order of the original, with its strong meter and rich imagery.

All names of persons have been changed, and some additional editing has been necessary to protect anonymity, particularly when respondents have discussed unconventional behavior. This editing has usually involved changes of location, and atlases and city directories have been employed to ensure that fictional locations are the social and economic equivalents of the real locations.

I have excluded tapes from several respondents who seemed to me to have a weak capacity to distinguish personal observation from hearsay. This exclusion was not easy; I had to give up colorful material on the Vietnam war and on police brutality that pampered my biases. Despite the omissions, I still may have believed accounts that a wiser person would have rejected. I hope it has not happened.

The Corner

We discovered the Corner on our first day of looking. A student and I had driven to the first of the low-income tracts that I had identified from the 1960 census. We parked at its extreme southern edge and began to walk toward its northern boundary. The first blocks were strange: the houses were extremely old and large with extensive lawns, the tall brick mansions of some long-extinct rich clans. All of this changed quickly, however, as we walked northward. In a block or two we were passing by much more modest houses. Now began another Detroit—the sagging wooden houses with strips of peeling paint, two-story homes where balconies had broken rails and missing uprights, houses with boards over the windows to keep out the wind, houses whose front doors had an iron hole where the door knob used to be. Motown.

We walked on, one block, two blocks, among these houses; slowly, a third block. The homes seemed right for my venture, but how to know where to start? I stood at a corner, irresolute. Across the street from us a man opened a door and came out onto a front porch. He stood just above his steps and sniffed the chill wind, alert and hunting. His small hat rested confidently on his head; his jacket nestled tightly about his lean body. I looked, across the street, at his face.

It was the meanest, toughest face I had ever seen. The high cheekbones framed a planed African mask that glistened with hatred and evil.

My heart twisted with fear: surely this was the place and the time. We walked across the street.

I stood below him at the bottom of the stairs. He turned his impassive face to me. We looked at each other.

"May I talk to you a minute?" I said.

He nodded and walked down two stairs, halfway to me.

"Yeah," I said. "My name is Rafe. Rafe Ezekiel." I put out my hand. He took it. "Rafe. I'm a teacher at the college in Ann Arbor. This gentleman is Mr. Wiggins, one of my students."

I paused. "I'm looking around in Detroit at different neighborhoods."

I paused again. "I'm looking for some places where I can talk with people about their neighborhoods and how their lives are going."

He looked at me and said, "Rafe, huh?"

I smiled and said, "Yeah, that's my name. I was wondering if someone was around, and then I noticed you come on out." I paused. I went on, "I do want to be able to talk to people in different places. I think maybe I can write a book after a while about some of the ways different people feel in Detroit."

"Rafe," he said again.

He smiled. We shook hands again. He had sized me up. I looked at his eyes. His face was tender and warm. I liked him enormously. "Well, Rafe," he said, "my name is Hawk. You can talk to these people up here." He went in the door and called up the stairway: "Hey, you-all! I'm bringing up a guy wants to talk to you-all!"

And that was how it began. Hawk took me upstairs to Lame Catherine's flat, where she and another woman and three men were drinking and talking. The only heat came from the kitchen stove; all the burners were on. A bare bulb hung from the ceiling on a cord. The ashtrays and liquor were on a metal-topped kitchen table; the people sat around the table on wooden chairs or leaned, paper cup in hand, against the sink. The drink was cheap blend whiskey, with water.

New people drifted in and out, as the afternoon wore on. People came to drink and to gossip. To kick in money for a new bottle. To go out to buy more paper cups. I explained the project a couple of times. I tried to figure how thin the linoleum on the floor was. I answered questions a couple of guys posed me. A few were rhetorical issues about characters in the Bible. I showed by my answers that I had read the Book, but I couldn't solve the riddles I was being asked. Lame Catherine wanted to know about my wife and children. Then they posed new questions: why do white people hate Black people? I told the truth as I saw it: white people hate Black people because they are afraid of them. They are afraid of them because they have done wrong to them.

Mostly, though, I said, white people *and* Black people hate each other because they *don't know* each other. I want to write a book where they can start to get to know each other. And so on.

White people spend their lives far away from Black people, I said. We get funny, I said. We lose touch.

Yeah.

The talk was sober and interesting. I tried to say serious things. I was struck by the depths of the hurt the guys would express: "Why do they hate *me*?"

Damn, I thought. Can it hurt this much, so close to the surface?

So it all began, there on the Corner. I knew that afternoon I had found my place to work.

The Corner was in truth more a street than a corner, though they called it the Corner in their own conversation. "It's been eleven years I've been coming down on this corner," Hawk would say. "I've lived on the Corner eight years," Will would say. By the Corner they meant a stub street that extended five car lengths to a deadend at a group of storage sheds that served a nearby housing project. The Corner was Black. No one came by who was white, except policemen and insurance collectors.

To say "the Corner" was to refer to a social group. The group had two kinds of members. First there were all the families that lived in the four homes on the street. This meant, when I arrived, nine families. Second, it meant all the people who came regularly to the Corner to drink and to talk. Some of these people had lived on the Corner previously and had recently moved further uptown. Others lived nearby. Both residents and non-residents had known each other for years. Many people had known each other since childhood, had grown up in the same two towns in the South (one in Mississippi, one in Alabama), and had lived in each other's homes when they first moved north. Some of the people were related to each other.

The people on the Corner were a time capsule from the South of decades ago. They believed in ancient American virtues.

For example, they believed seriously in human equality. Because we are all God's children, we are all the same: "I don't care what you is, you treat me right, I'm going to treat you right." "You treat me as a man, I am going to treat you as a man."

Many people, probably most people, had the most grave reservations about whites *as a group*. Nevertheless, almost every person on the corner was ready to treat the *individual* white purely as that individual merited.

What was judged? Basically the issue of being "for real," being what you seemed to be. "Not coming out of no trick bag." Being honest, not pretending to be who you were not. Perhaps this egalitarianism is an expression of the less defensive position of those with less to lose. The Corner is a more expressive place than my block at home. We middle-class people are busy spinning webs that reach forward and backward in time, sidewards to left and right in space. We build *careers*. Everything seems to us to depend upon the webs not being broken. We do not have energy to spare to be expressive. And we fear to present in simple form our feelings, to say, "There, that is it, that is me." For what if that is wrong? One needs to be able to say, "There, that is a part of me." And then to add, if the first contact doesn't sell: "But here, here is another part. Do you like that better?" Little wonder we do not seem "for real."

The men and women of the Corner were mostly in their early or middle thirties. Children were mostly of late elementary school age, although some were older or younger. A number of the men worked as maintenance men in nearby industral shops or large bakeries; a few of the visitors had jobs in the auto plants. None of the women worked outside the house; about half drew ADC or disability. There was pre-cious little money on the Corner (as one would suspect from the thin clothing, the battered houses, and the lack of cars), but one was looking at the world of the working poor or the almost-working poor, not at a world of derelicts.

John Rahlins, for example, was a maintenance man at a bakery. He went to work every morning, year after year. Ultimately they asked him to be a foreman, but he didn't want the responsibility. After a while he told them no. He spent the late afternoons bending over the front of his car, working on the engine. He seldom said much. One day he told me that in school he never talked. He had thought to go further in school and study radio or engineering, but was afraid. He always seemed to me the most sensible man on the Corner. It may have been an illusion based on his silence, but I remain convinced. He had been a demolitions expert in the Army and valued in his outfit. He had thought of re-enlisting, but they broke the outfit up and so he didn't. He had wanted to stay with the guys.

When he got out, his sister tried to get him to go to college. She was a schoolteacher. He wanted to go, in a way, but was afraid he'd have to talk. Rahlins is uneasy when he stands out.

David Wainwright was the smallest man around. He always said the same thing: "I have no complaint." He worked every day at a bakery, where he, like Rahlins, did maintenance. He worked in all weather, he raised his children, he kept them company, he avoided the dangers of the fast life. He took lessons downtown in electronics, after his regular job was over. At the end of three years, he got a new job and could have moved, but lacked money for a down payment on a house. He raised that money by running an afterhours joint, a "blind pig" in his home. For two years he went to his job, went to his classes, and stayed up into the early hours to manage the business. He told me none of this except the news about the job, but ultimately he took his family off the Corner.

□ □ □

Will Stone worked from the day he came north. He worked as a janitor and claimed he loved it: "I near about have my own way, I'm my own boss." Will stayed at Rawson-Monroe because he felt secure; he had his time in, they wouldn't lay him off. He had been laid off too often at the auto plants, and things got tight then. They had five kids to feed. All the same, Will did get laid off at Rawson-Monroe and things got tight again, until they took him back. His wife, Rebecca, reminds herself that steak and beans don't feel different once you've swallowed them.

Will really doesn't make enough at maintenance to make things work. How come he doesn't get a better job? Because he is untrained, his job provides no new training, and he is afraid, with five kids, to risk change.

Life is dull for Will. He drinks a while in the early afternoon and kids around with the guys outside. He rides up to work in his car pool and works 'til late at night. Then he comes home and watches late-night TV with Rebecca and eats the supper she has saved him, after which they sleep.

□ □ □

The man I liked least on the corner was Haskell. Haskell was a sour-looking man who talked white hatred. "Hey, I would just like to see one of the sons of bitches in front of my car," he said to his buddy Cleveland. "I would like to see just one. I would run him over. Run a kid over just as soon as a grown one." Haskell meant it. He spoke truths—"They chained us, they stole us"—and in his mouth they turned to lies—"These are my brothers, mister. I love all these men"—a lie because he gave the Corner nothing and preyed on the men at random. He bullied men at pistol point over petty matters.

Haskell made my head ache when we argued. I was young and tried to say honestly why I was there. I understood at last that I was foolish to believe he was sincere, but that was headaches later.

Haskell tried to finish me on the Corner late one night. He egged Cleveland on to get me as Runner and I walked out of a house.

"Whitey-lover!" Haskell hissed at Runner from the darkness. "Running with the peckerwood!"

Runner pulled me toward the car, but I turned about and walked out toward them to confront the voices. "Show him your gun," Haskell said to Cleveland. I marched between the houses to face them down. Then I stopped: Wait, I thought, I'm just a guest; I have no right to let them get in trouble. I turned and slouched into the car.

We drove five yards and I suddenly recalled: "Jesus Christ, these guys don't play. They never bluff." I became sick with fear, after the fact.

Months later I asked Haskell, why did you try to kill me? "Because you need it," Haskell said. "All of you."

Much later I realized that Haskell and Cleveland had been as frightened as I.

□   □   □

Luther pushed refrigerators onto warehouse trucks, until he strained his back and took a rest on workmen's comp. The lawyer got him a check after a long wait and Luther bought three cars in a row and drove each one into the ground. He drank his money up in sixty days. His legs grew numb and then more numb and four years later he was dead.

Luther worked thirty years, beginning in boyhood on a sharecrop farm. He ran away to end the beatings from his pa and found a home in Detroit. He married young and raised two kids, the oldest one brain-slowed. He worked to feed the family, but then his wife found Messenger Smith, a Sanctified preacher, who took her money week after week, money Luther earned. Messenger was holy and told the flock to pray—to pass the cash to the side of the aisle and close their eyes and pray. She knelt and prayed. Sunday, weekdays. "Stay all night," the preacher said. "Look at me," he said. "I can stand here and pray and never leave the pulpit to relieve myself. I can go all day and night. Need is weakness and faith has made me strong."

She listened and saw that he stayed in the pulpit. She believed and stayed all day, all night, half the week, taking the kids with her.

"You can't raise kids like that," said Luther. "Feed them children, take care of them."

Luther left the wife whom he had married when she was thirteen, and wandered to the Corner. He began to live with Lame Catherine. He tore a ligament, drank, worked, and sat brooding. He took work every few months—casual labor—lifting, hauling, grunting, shoving goods around—for a week or two, then stopped, drank, and stared.

Luther took me to see his family once. They smiled shyly to see him—"How are you, hi, Daddy," they said very softly. We drove back to the Corner. I rested my hand on the steering wheel at a red light and glanced over at him. He was looking half to the side; his eyes were wet; he was silent.

The man called Jamaica worked at the foundry and moved his sad-eyed skinny body through red dust air all evening long. Years before, Jamaica had thought to be a doctor or a nurse. He had taken nurse's training for a while but couldn't pass the tests. Then he had apprenticed to an undertaker for a spell. He told me step by step how autopsies were done, just to show me that he knew.

West Indian-born, he thought himself the butt of prejudice. "See, Rafe, they all turn quiet when I come in." He was in fact an isolate, but not because of origin—his speech was pure Detroit. Guys feared him as a Jonah. "We ran him off the Corner," Luther said. "He was giving guys TB." He looked it.

He ran an afterhours place with Dog Man for a while. Their sales were fairly private, just to each other by and large, but Jamaica liked to see himself as someone who was tied to the folk by love, and he liked to feel that the liquor was a service he gave out.

Uptown, he had a home, wife, and kids. They stayed there, he floated to the Corner, in and out, gambling, drinking, purveying, wanting some friendship.

☐ ☐ ☐

Carl Foreman worked on the line at a Ford plant. Carl was twenty-nine, and it was the first straight job he had ever held. The job drove him crazy but he hung on.

Carl wasn't a worker by training. His skill was running con. He played con games on people—found ways to let people think they were cheating him, and took their money, and went away. Or perhaps Carl's whole tale of playing con was a con. Maybe all he did was write bad checks; that's a thing they jailed him on.

I have liked Carl a great deal and I have disliked Carl a great deal. He is very effective in jail. He flashes signs: "I have great potential; you can save me." And the doctors and the nurses line up to save him. "Jesus, this guy Carl is intelligent—and sensitive!" And then he tells them how he lost his mother as a child. It is a box-office smash.

Yet, if Carl has been a shape changer and has often let down those who needed him, he has also offered warmth and energy and in later years moved past the limitations we see in the present interviews.

As a teenager, Nathan Coolidge started boxing. He did big-time stuff in amateur leagues (Golden Gloves and the service) and it may have gone to his head. He had a taste for heroics.

He did extra stuff to pull in cash, and possibly to get excitement: he fooled with bad checks and stolen money orders, and may have messed around somewhat further.

He made excitement for himself with little wars on in-laws. (When weapons have been outlawed, only in-laws will have guns.) He tells us how he charged at in-laws' rifles, threw the rifles in the air, and threw the in-laws with them. And it's probably mostly true: I saw a little of his action.

Nathan took if for granted that he was supposed to work most of the time. He gave himself breaks, periods after being laid off before he got new work. "I've never yet seen any work that really called on much of me." His phrases meant: "The jobs only need a strong back and sticking to it." He is close to bitter when he says it—as close as he can get, because he's too much an outward-going man.

He has charm and several women cluster close. Some of his children live with him. His woman helps support the bunch with ADC. He is glad to have the help and feels it is his due—he's paid taxes every year since his teens.

☐ ☐ ☐

Runner worked too, but not so often. Nathan said that Runner was the sweetest semi driver that he knew, but his basic skills were in construction. He could roof, lay brick, mend walls, fix wiring, do anything a house could need. He had worked on every house on the Corner. The landlords called him in to do repairs—Jack-of-all-trades, non-union, and cheap. But he didn't work often. I don't know why.

Research was different on the Corner. You didn't simply ask men what they did. Work was not the neutral topic you used to get talk started. Men dropped you hints if you listened hard.

People hardly ever talked about their jobs. Once in a long while they might talk about an incident years ago, never what happened today, nor what was likely to happen. Men brought nothing home from the job but money.

The only exception was talking about guys at work. "You know Carter, the guy who works with me at Tacoma's? He pulled the plow off the front of the D-10, that big new blade? He pulled that off by hisself and pulled it to the rack alone, to show us that he could. That is a *big* cat!"

This obscurity about work had its peak with Haskell, who kept it secret that he had a steady job. Nathan stumbled on him at an auto plant one night. Haskell tried to duck, but Nathan saw him. Nathan figured Haskell wanted folks to think he got his money by his wits and wasn't just another working man.

☐ ☐ ☐

The Corner drinks all day. But the Corner isn't bums. The Corner is a station between the derelicts and the workers. Looser and louder than a steady working-class block but no skid row; a place for the in-betweens.

"You are going to talk to other folks, aren't you?" they asked. "You're not going to tell people that *this* is how Black folk live!" *This* meant: less than respectable, out of work sometimes, drunk sometimes.

"You're going to talk to some Black folks that are regular, aren't you? There's white folks live like this, too, you know. I could take you over to Second Street now and show you guys barefoot, barefoot on the street and drinking Thunderbird. And these are white guys. And their kids without no clothes, running on the porch. White guys.

"So it ain't all just Black. Don't you forget it."

part two

interviews

jacqueline rahlins

Jackie Rahlins, smart, tough, and sardonic, looks you in the eye and talks straight. In an early conversation, while she attacked a large load of ironing, I learned that she was busy day in and day out taking care of three young children and an older teenaged boy; that she liked going fishing in the summer; that she did her mending by hand, dried her clothes on a line in the basement, and washed them in a semiautomatic with hand rollers; that she had come up from Alabama when twenty to join her husband, who had come to find work; that he had held several jobs, working for the past eight years as maintenance man in a large bread company; that she would enjoy being out of the house and working but did not feel that someone else would take adequate care of her kids; that she liked visiting several houses over with a girlfriend from her old hometown.

That early conversation was reserved. The more spirited excerpts below come from an impromptu afternoon gathering some three months after we met. I was talking and drinking with a small group on a winter afternoon in an apartment upstairs from Jackie's. She came to join the gathering and greeted me with gaiety, telling me that she had been to jail just a few nights before.

Jacqueline Rahlins

Hey, Professor, I've got a surprise for you, I stayed locked up all Friday night in jail!

I come to visit my friends upstairs and in comes the police, and we all go to jail. And we went to jail and stayed all night.

And Saturday morning, they were just talking, talking, talking, and the judge just read the files. And after he read his complaints off—the

19

policeman read his thing—that he had a call to come to 4547 Aberdeen Road because there's an afterhours joint. Which, Professor, you know they were referring to the apartment where we all talked last week, next door to mine. But when the police came, everybody was upstairs in Crandall's apartment playing cards, because he had thrown a birthday party for himself, and everybody was there, and so naturally enough the police assumed that this was the afterhours joint.

So when he had read that he had a call to come to 4547 Aberdeen Road, because there was an afterhours joint, I asked the judge, "I understand you to say for him to read off that he was called for an afterhours joint. But he didn't get the afterhours joint, he went to a private home that was upstairs."

I had merely came from downstairs upstairs to get me a plate of chittlins, and in comes the police and they grabbing people up. And I said, "Can I get my coat?" I had an old sweater there. And the police said, "Nope." And I ask, "Can I see about my kids?" And he said, "No." He wouldn't even let me see about my kids; they'd been there by themselves downstairs, I wasn't coming up but just a few minutes. He wouldn't even stop, he wouldn't let me go in there and even see about my kids.

There was a million cops. Everywhere you looked there was at least one. And I said, "My kids is downstairs, I came up to get me a plate of chittlins. Can I stop to see to check on my kids." And he said, "Naw." And I said, "Please, my kids is by theirself. Let me just talk to them." But he wouldn't even stop to let me get my coat or check my kids. I wanted to check on my kids, you know, to see and make sure somebody's there with them, and get my coat. I said, "You can send one of your officers down there with me." He could have gone on in the house with me, I wouldn't have cared about that, because I knew we was going to jail anyway. But he wouldn't even do that. He said, "No," and I had to go right downtown.

At first they took us to the station down the street for writing everything about how old you is and where you was born. And then from there downtown. And that's where we stayed all night. But I'm gonna tell you what exception he made, he let one girl go with her baby. I said, "I don't see why her baby is so much more than mine. I've got three downstairs and you won't even let me stop to see about how they are." She had her baby with her and they let her go home.

She's the only one who didn't go to jail. And I want to know why is it that her baby supposed to be so much more important than mine. I wasn't lying that I had three babies downstairs; they could have gone there with me to see.

I had to go right on by the door. All he had to do was knock on the door and see if either one of my other girlfriends was in there to see about the kids. See about them and pass my coat out the door. He wouldn't even let me do that. He wouldn't even let me knock on my door. He told me I could knock on *their* door, across the hall, not mine.

But you know what, from then on he called me Mrs. Rahlins. "Mrs. Rahlins, are you alright?" he says. Because that was wrong, you don't do nobody like that.

I felt like he was wrong. Because I knew I was going to jail. I wasn't trying to get away from them, because I knew I hadn't did nothing. Even if they locked me up there, they couldn't charge me with nothing anyway because I wasn't doing nothing, but the only thing that I had against them was that he wouldn't let me stop and see about my kids. What if the house had caught afire?

They said we were charged for loitering. For loitering in an illegal place of business. But the judge throwed the charges out. See, it was a private birthday party thing that was going on and they had got a call to come to the afterhours joint that was downstairs. He got the wrong place; wasn't nobody at the afterhours joint, you know. And so when he heard the talking going on upstairs where we was having a party, and they came upstairs and then they wanted to put it that it was a afterhours place and we was loitering in a place of business, was operating without a license. And so I told the judge, everybody was talking, he said, "Raise your finger when you want to talk." You know.

He said, "What's your name, just for the record?" I said, "Jacqueline Rahlins." I said, "I understand him to say that's what he read on his complaint, that he was called to 4547 Aberdeen Road to raid a blind pig in the building. It wasn't up there," I said. "We was having a private party. They were upstairs, I live downstairs." I said, "He had the wrong place."

The judge said, "I've got my doubts about it." He told the police officer that he was at the wrong apartment, say "I dismiss the charge."

I didn't completely get it out about how he wouldn't let me go down and see about the kids. But I was so glad he said, "No charge." Because I hadn't done nothing. I didn't come upstairs until twelve o'clock, I left the house at about five minutes after twelve. Because I had said before, "I ain't going upstairs." They had asked me, I said, "I ain't going upstairs, I ain't got no money anyway." Then I came up and then in comes the police. But they came in in disguise, you know, two came in with plain clothes.

Now Jesse, he telling a lie. Jesse telling everybody he was sitting there, said, "I got you, I got three eights!" And the man say, "I got *you*, I got a badge!"

But that wasn't the way it went, that wasn't it. Jesse lie. The truth is, that nobody didn't know that that man was a policeman. Until they knocked on the door and came in, when the sergeant came and stood in the door. He did not let nobody out.

The ones that had come in, in the plain clothes, they were snitches. Or the short one was. The tall one was a policeman. Didn't nobody know. The short one, we didn't see him for a while, but the tall one, he came in at the station and take down, "What is your name, when was you born, where were you going on this date, that date," all this, down at the station. He came in and wrote some of them up.

The little short one stayed out of the room. Jesse told him to come here a minute. He say, "No, no." Jesse said, "If it ever snows, I'm going to snowball you. Snowball you to death." And told the sergeant, say, "I hope it snow and you have a flat!" The sergeant couldn't help but laugh. He just laugh, you know, 'cause I guess he say, "Well, I don't give a damn what you say, you know, I got you down here locked up."

And well, we didn't get the point across to them that it *was* a birthday party until the next day in court. Wouldn't nobody listen to us all night. Nobody paid us any attention. They just thought we was crazy.

But when those two men had come in, big old Bernard here, he shook hands with them. That was the reason. Everyone figured that Bernard knew them. The tall one came up to Bernard and said, "Hey, big man, drunk again, eh?" And shook his hand. And then he bought Bernard a beer.

But you know, I got skeppy about them. I looked at them, and thought, you know they look too clean-cut. And then I thought, well, maybe Bernard knew them. Must be somebody that I didn't know where he lives. Then I said maybe it's somebody from out where Jesse works at. Because they spoke to him.

But I figured Jesse or Bernard knew him. But when he first walked in the door, I thought that he was too clean. You can tell a policeman. He was too clean-cut. I thought, who is this? I kept looking at him. Then he came over and sit down and play poker.

Jesse telling a good story. The way he tell it, Jesse say, "Bet eleven dollars!" And the man say, "Bet!" And he say, "What you got?" He say, "I got two aces." And Jesse say, "Well, I've got you, I got three eights!" And the tall one say, "I got *you*, I got a badge!"

So Jessie say, "Couldn't you have done it on the next hand, man?"

But Jessie telling a lie. That man did have ace, and he have three eights, but the man didn't say, "I've got you, I've got a badge!"

The sergeant knocked on the door. And he stood at the kitchen door, and he stood there all the while he was there, he never came out!

Somebody beat on the door. I don't know whether he had a special knock or what. He probably did. But he knocked on the door, he opened the door. And then this little guy came from in the kitchen and put his hand on the table and said to leave all the money on the table. Just like that. Then that's when we knew that they both were policemen. The one that was playing cards with us and the little one that was standing there.

He had marked his ten-dollar bill that he got into the game with. He knowed the serial number on it. And then he asked her for the dollar he bought two beers with.

□   □   □

Do you believe there is a Supreme Being? Do you believe that it is possible that you can live so close to God that anything that you want to *know, anything* that you want to know, if you lay down in your bed tonight and you go to sleep, you will see it?

I have lived so close to Him that if there was anything that I wanted to know, I lay down in my bed at night and I would have just like a dream. Like you sleep in a dream. And I would see it.

Exactly the way it was going to happen and everything. I would know it before it would happen. For three years anything I asked the Supreme Being about, when I laid down to sleep, I saw it.

I know there is a Supreme. I can't explain what it is or where it come from. I'm not too close to Him now because for this simple reason I drink, I do more than just drink, I gamble. But still and all I know that there is a Supreme Being.

That's right. And I believe that he believes in me and that any time I call on Him, He'll answer me.

He gives you the opportunity to ask for forgiveness. See, I know what *you* think.

God is good. He's more than good. He's merciful, period.

Not from what somebody taught me. I'm talking about from self-experience. Now you can believe any way you want, that's your business, but I know what I know.

What you believe, that you is. Your inner thoughts, that's the thing that matters, right? And I know. My inner thoughts tell me that there is someone above me. I don't know whether his name is God or what it is, but there is a Supreme Being. There is something.

I don't believe in no Heaven and Hell. The Bible tell you, Hell is the grave.

Do you believe that what they say Hell is? No, how can that be?

Common sense will tell you, look: I wouldn't throw nary one of my *kids* in no fiery pit. And He love you so well.

But you can believe that He can throw you in fire that will burn you up? That them that do wrong will be throwed in the pit, will go to Hell and be in a fiery furnace, burn all up and all that? If He loved you that well, He wouldn't put you in there. He merciful. He don't do that. That's the reason why I don't believe in Hell. God don't do that.

Maybe I'm wrong. I don't know. They say, you makes your Hell. In regards to how miserable you make it, it's just like they say. When you drink: you drink so much, you get hangover, you be so sick. That's your punishment right there. You pays for your punishment as you get along. If you's a mind to put up with, let's say, living here in this neighborhood: if you put up with that, that's your Hell.

That's right. I got common sense. I got common sense, and so you don't tell me about no Heaven. When you die, your soul be at rest. I believe that. Your soul be at rest. That's your Heaven. Because you're resting. You ain't got to be worrying about running around, and meeting this, that, and the other. That's Heaven. That's the way I feel about it, now. I don't know nothing about nobody else.

If you been a bad person, like Merrick, that man that stayed with Laurie? Merrick done bad. Lay you in the grave, heap that dirt on you. You been a bad person: you in Hell. Captive. In the grave. Take the last breath from you; lay you in the grave: you through.

That's Hell. You're laying down there in the grave. You're captive. You're through. Your mind cannot wander or do nothing when you're down in all that dirt on you. Six feet deep, and they put you down in that ground, put that dirt on you. You through.

I believe that.

□ □ □

You want to know, what does it mean living here? How it is living here? Well, you could have had that in three or four words. All you have to do is ask one person. I'll tell you: it's an MF living here. Really.

It's an MF. Living in this kind of neighborhood, living in this environment. I can tell you. People don't want to live like this, but there ain't nothing else they can do. They ain't making no money. So what are you going to do?

You don't have no choice. You take me. My husband works every day. I accept the living that my husband is able to provide for us. I accept that. 'Cause that's the best he can do for me, and I go along with it. He works. At the present time ain't nothing else he can do. So why try to be so, you know, high and mighty? Ain't going to change nothing no how.

People can try to make life easier, sure. If they have the opportunity.

Lots of times you have the desire to want to do this, you can't just jump out there and say I want to do something like that. You got to have the opportunity to do it.

I have the desire to do all kinds of things, but I got to have the opportunity to do them. I can't just jump out there and say, I'm going to do it. Because there's somebody out there to stop me. There's always hindrance; regardless what you started there's a hindrance. Because if I could jump right out there and say I'm going to do this and that, I wouldn't be living in this neighborhood. Just like I told you once before. I say, people don't live in this neighborhood because they want to. They can't do no better. That's the reason why they live around here.

These higher persons, if they had any mercy, we wouldn't be here in this neighborhood. See what I'm talking about?

Me. I live here. Why do I live in this neighborhood? Jacqueline Rahlins? *Because I have to.* I don't want to. But, the mercy is limited.

Far as my husband is concerned . . . I've got mercy towards him. I've got mercy towards him. Do you know why? Because he provides a living for me. I got mercy towards him because I know he can't do no better, and I got mercy for him. I'll go along with him. Not necessarily do I have to, but I do. So that's that, you know. I don't necessarily have to go along with it, but I do. That's my husband. I love my husband. You said you believe in love. I do too. I love my husband. This is the kind of life that he is able to provide for me, I'll go along with it, because I love him. Now, I'm not living here because I want to; if I could do better, don't you think I'd be living somewhere else? You accept life, you know. That's one thing that's mostly wrong with people anyway. They don't learn to accept life. I have learned to accept life, darling. I accept life.

I accept life. I know one thing I'm not going to do: I'm not going to be rude towards nobody and nobody be rude toward me. So I accept life. This is my life. And you might as well make the best of it, right?

And hope that with the four kids that I got, to make it better for them. Don't brood back on what you have gone through. Think about your kids that you got, to go on forward. That's what I think about it anyway. There's not a day that I live, even today, that I don't hope to provide a future for my kids, hoping I'll be able to do better for them. If I thought that my kids would live in a neighborhood like this, then I'd be through.

My kids is my push, you know what I mean? They should live in a better neighborhood, have their own things, get educated and get as high as they can. And I'll work my butt to try and see to that.

And looking forward to my kids getting an education and making something out of themselves, and getting themselves something— that's my life. That's all I live for.

That's all I live for. If I see one, just one, make something out of themselves, to get an education—I'm through, that's what I live for, that's my life. The fact about it, that's my life.

So . . . the rest of it . . . I live in a slum. Now, this is the slums, I know that. What can you do about it? Look forward, try to help yourself better. That's right. You know you can't do anything about it. And I'm not by myself, I know there is a whole lot of us lives in the slum, you know. If they got the same desires I got, then we'll all get somewhere. But, the fact, that's life here.

See, he fill your glass there. Liquor. That will ruin a lot of people's life. But not mine, because I feel like I got control over it.

You are supposed to control it. You get to the place where you think it controls you, you supposed to leave it alone.

I got a sister, she been dead two years. She died, this coming February the eighth, she been dead three years. That took her to the grave: she drank whiskey, wine, gin. Everything. She died from cirrhosis of the liver.

She died when she was thirty-three years old. That's too young. I feel like that's too young to give up life. Supposed to keep on pulling.

□ □ □

I have said, what was life to me. Everybody don't have to feel this way; I do. Therefore, each day is a whole thing. You don't just sit. . . . You can't get nothing by just sitting. You got to get out and make a effort. Don't get nothing by just sitting around and drinking, sitting around and drinking.

I stay in my house, for six days out of seven. During that time that I am in the house, I got something to do. Each hour that I'm in the house I'm doing something. This is taking care of home. You got this to do, then that. Then you stop and take out time for the kids. Well, you don't mind this.

When you get up in the morning, when your eyes are open, the first instant you wake up, you jump up with: "I got to do this," you know. That's what wakes you up. You know what wakes me up in the morning now? Getting the kids off to school. I wake up with that on my mind. Jump right up.

I get up and fix their breakfast. Give them their cereal like they usually eats, and get them off to school. The instant they out the door, they kiss me on the cheek and say, "Bye, Mother, see you after school." Then, it's played up. Each minute of your day, it runs like a schedule, you know. So that's it. And you don't look back at nothing.

That's what wakes me up in the morning. Getting up to get the kids off. Because just like I say, that's my life. I want to see them make something out of themselves. I didn't, but I want to see them do it. And I think now, that the reason why I didn't make something out of myself is stupidity.

Stupidity is the reason why I didn't make nothing out of myself. Exactly. You met Phillip, my oldest child. He was born when I was sixteen years old. He's just like all these kids, he's careless. Any time I try and tell him, "Honey, you don't know what you are going through here, you don't know nothing about life. You know, you ought to try and make something out of yourself." I'm just grinding my bones. That's all. 'Cause he was born when I was sixteen years old. From them on . . . of course, not that I didn't have no . . . I could have gone back to school, but . . . I chose to see about my kids, you know. It's just one of those things. But then, they don't know. They going out, they ain't only but sixteen and seventeen and like that, and they don't even want to go to school. They had better go on and try to get something out of it. I wish I had the opportunity they got. Now I see, but at that time I was like them, I didn't see it.

They really got a good thing. Just like my son, he don't want to go to school. You can't compel nobody to go. You can't make nobody go.

He was supposed to go to Tuskeegee, you know. I told you. And he got on the bus and got off. The man punched the ticket and then that's that money lost. His auntie sent him a ticket from Alabama, and it's laying up there on the refrigerator. It's dead. He didn't ride a mile. He just simply don't want to go. Why, I don't know, and I don't question him about it. I said, "You make out of yourself what you want to make out of yourself," you know.

He says, "Do you want me to go?" I said, "I really do"; I said, "If it was me, I wish I had the opportunity that you got." He said, "I'm going in January." I said, "Well, then we'll see when January comes," that's all I said. I'm not going to argue and fuss with him about it because that ain't going to do no good. No, no.

I'm not going to compel him. I'm not going to try to make him go. If he wants to go, I want him to go. Like I told him. But if he don't want to go, what use is it to me for him to be going because I want him to go? What is he going to make out of it? What's that going to do? Do you see what I'm talking about?

You can only make a person what they want to be. All this business about I've made you this and that and the other—you is what you want to be and nobody made you nothing. If you wanted to do that, you did it. Otherwise, if you didn't want to do it, you wouldn't.

And I wouldn't compel him to do nothing! He got the opportunity to go up until January. If he don't go in January I'm not going to fuss at him.

He'll get him a job, like I told him. He'll get him a job or go to Uncle Sam's Army, 'cause when you're eighteen you know darn well you're going in. After you get eighteen they register you, and if you're not going to school, they quick to catch you. That's his choice. What I got to do around it? That's his life. This is two different lives. This is the way I see it.

I want him to make up his own mind. But I give him my opinion about it. I gave him my opinion. He asked me. I told him, "I would really like for you to go, you know, but you make up your own mind." And truthfully speaking, I really yet today don't see why he don't want to go. He said, he going later, but still and all. . . . If it was me. . . . It's not me, it's two different worlds, it ain't me.

He had won a scholarship. But I know that you can't push someone, you can't make no person do what you want them to do, they got to do what they want to do. I know that, so that's the reason why I won't push him.

But I'll let him make up his own mind. He's seventeen years old. He's old enough. He the one that got to do the studying. I won't make him do it. I can't whip him, I can only talk to him. He live his own life. He got his life, I got mine. That's the way I feel about it.

We sit down and talk a lot of times.

He said, "Mother, you want me to go to school?" Well, that would mean being away from me, and his sisters, but I say, "I do really want you to go to school." He said, "Well, then I'm going." And got on the bus, and the man punched the ticket. I took him to the bus station, he got on the bus, and . . . then . . . got off and got back.

He said, one mind told him, just don't go. Got off the bus and came back. Got a cab and come back home. This is his home, you know. Wherever I am, I'm his mother, that's his home.

But that hurt me, you know, I mean, to know that he wouldn't go on back and go to school. I wanted to have him educated so he could graduate from the college. But if he don't want to go, I can't force him. Do you see what I'm talking about?

He say, "One mind told me not to go, mother, so I come back." I said, "Okay. You at home. You stay long as you want to stay," I said, "but when you make up your mind, well, I do would wish you'd go." And I do. But I can't force him to go, I can't make him. That's my child, I'm going to tell him, "You get out of here? You got to go to school, you got to do this"? I'm not going to do that.

Come January, if he don't go then, I still won't argue and fuss. But it hurts, you know. But I won't argue 'cause I love him, that's my child, you know.

You see, if somebody . . . you can say what you want to say. And do what you want to do. Be rude to them, this, that, and the other. Fight them, and all that. You still can't make them be no more than what they want to be. See, this is what he wants to be—exactly what he being is what he wants to be. This is his life. I can't live his life for him.

[*How did your husband feel about it?*]

He said he wished he'd go. He told him. But let me remind you that's not his son, that's my son. I had him when I married. But he talked to him like a daddy would. He treats him like a daddy would, you know, he talk to him, so proud of him.

He still is doing just what he wants to be. So if a person will be what they want to be, why you going to try to change it?

That's all. You can talk. And you can talk till your tongue hang out your mouth, they want to be what they are going to be, they are going to still be that.

I asked him that. I said, "I don't know why it is you don't want to go to school." He said, "I just don't want to go." This is the way he turned me off.

But you know what really got him, really? It's gambling going around.

He took his graduation ring and pawned it, for four dollar. I bought him a little watch, guess what he did with that. Where is that now? In pawn. For five dollars to gamble with. And the man talking about if he don't soon get it back, he going to keep the watch.

I said to him, "What I should do, I should call the police and tell him that this man took the watch in pawn from a minor, for five dollars to gamble with. That's what I should do," I said, "but I'm just being nice." I said, "I'll give him the five dollars to get the watch back. And don't never do that no more, you hear?" Got his graduation ring and all that.

It's the environment that's in his own case. I believe that's what it is. 'Cause he's always been a good child. He's always been good. I never had no trouble out of him, period. But this last time since he . . . got to be seventeen. Naturally, you know, when you're seventeen, you go through a change.

Playing poker. Shooting dice. . . . He didn't lie about it, that's one thing about him, he not going to lie. He told me. But, see, that's wrong. That's what's wrong with the world today, is grown-ups enticing the kids.

Maybe I didn't take that much time with him that I should, you know, or something like that. But truthfully speaking, I don't know which way I would get around to doing any more than what I've been doing.

We talk. Whenever I sit down and talk to him, he don't seem to want to sit down in conversation with me. He soon will be grown, and he is bigger than I, you know. The only thing I can do to him now besides talk is shoot him. (*She laughs.*) Really, this is the truth.

[*Well, does it seem like he's . . . particularly enjoying being able to be out on the street? To be with the guys?*]

He's overjoyed about it! And he told me, though, that he was going in January. And like I say, wait 'til January comes.

But he is . . . he is enjoying himself. He don't want to do no more than just what he doing, is the way I see it. Maybe I'm wrong.

He lived down there in Alabama in my old town from thirteen to this year. It's a really small place, I can count the stores. One, two, three, four (*she laughs*), or something like that, you know. And they got this . . . factory that makes cloth, you know. I used to work there. Worked there five years. They call it the cotton mill. They make cotton fabrics, you know. It's got three grocery stores, one drugstore, and two service stations, gasoline stations.

He graduated from high school there. And it's beautiful. It was first wood. Then they rebuilt it in brick, and remodeled it beautiful.

The principal there, she had taught three generations at this same school. This the way it go down south, you know. She had taught my mother, me, and my son. That's three generations. She was great big, she was over six feet tall. And great big, you know. She dead now. And when she died they had to have a casket made for her. But she taught there from my mother until my son. And she was the one that really built the school up to where it is. About two years ago she died. She was a great woman. Never married or nothing! She was a career woman, you know, she didn't want to marry.

That's the way Phillip's auntie is, that he stayed with in Alabama. She was a schoolteacher, too.

And everything he asks her for, she give it to him. She ain't got no kids. That's his daddy's sister. That really may be a whole lot of his problem. Anything he ask her for, she give it to him. She has sent two tickets since he been up here. She buy a ticket down, and put money in it. That's what got him spoiled.

He told me, laying up there the other night, "If I tell Auntie, anything, she going to send it to me." But that's wrong. And she's a schoolteacher, but she don't know no better than to give him everything he ask for. See what I mean?

She give him everything he ask for. She's the one who's paying for his college education. He don't want to go. He called her on the phone, and she talked to him and cried on the phone, you know. "All I want you to do is come on back," and this, that, and the other. But that's wrong. Don't do that. And, I'm going down in January. I'll tell her so to her face, that's wrong, you don't do things like that. And she's a schoolteacher, she teach tenth and eleventh grade in high school. But still and all, she want her nephew to have his way.

Yes, she'd send him everything he'd write to her right now and ask her for. All he's got to do is tell her, "I'm coming back," you know. She don't have any kids, she ain't married. She'll send Phillip anything. And he bets on that, he brags on that. And I told him, I said, "You act just like a hoodlum." That's the way it seem to me.

I said, "You just like a old hoodlum out there in the street." Which I'm telling him exactly what is right. And she making him be that. She's making him be just what he is. Now he know that regardless to when he come back, if it's next year, she's going to still send him to school. He know this. So he don't care. While the pressure's on me. It's a burden on me, 'cause I hate to see him get out there in the street and act like one of these old bums, hoodlum things out there.

[*You think he's going in January?*]

I hope so, but I don't know. He isn't making any effort toward it. Doesn't seem like he making no sign toward going. And I'll tell you, this guy that was teaching down at the school that he graduated from, he the one that helped to get the scholarship. And he felt mighty bad about it, he wrote me a letter, you know. He felt mighty bad about it.

eva miller

Left by her mother, raised by her grandmother, living in the South, in Illinois, and in Detroit, Eva is intense and outgoing. She moves from thing to thing—as she says, "My sign is the wind."

The following interview took place at a hard time. Eva was lonely and afraid. Her lover was in jail, awaiting trial, and she had recently fallen back into a former involvement with heroin.

Eva Miller

I was born in Mississippi, in Hunter. That's a small town; there are five hundred people or maybe a thousand. And they mostly work at a textile place that's near. My grandmother raised me. My father was in the Army at the time, and . . . my mother was here, in Detroit.

I went to Catholic school down there, and then when I turned fifteen I went to Joliet, Illinois, to live with my father. And there I started going to Douglas High School. And I started hanging out with this pretty rugged bunch. And I started skipping school and everything. And in order to be with the in-crowd, I had to start messing with boys.

And . . . I got pregnant. And my grandmother thought it would be better for me to be with her. So I went back down south, and I was going to school down there while I was pregnant.

Then my mother decided it would be better for me to come here to Detroit, 'cause they have better doctors and everything, so I came here and had my baby.

And I started to hanging around with another bunch after I had my baby. And I started smoking pot. And drinking wine.

☐ ☐ ☐

And . . . let's see . . . we did a lot of different things. I was going with this guy, and he . . . introduced me to reefer. And . . . then nothing really exciting happened, just we smoked reefers.

That's when I started smoking pot, and drinking, and I used to hang around with a boy named Junior and a girl named Connie. And we used to go to this guy's house and get high all the time. And, then, you know how you start switching boyfriends. And you start doing different things, like, oh, they want you to prostitute and everything. So then my grandmother died when I was twenty, and I went back down south, and when I came back, my boyfriend and my girlfriend had started being boyfriend and girlfriend.

So, on my twenty-first birthday, I was over to this man's house named Jackson, and this man I was telling you about came over and he . . . he introduced me to heroin.

And we went to this other guy's house named Ralph, who was selling the stuff, and he shot me with it. So then he tried to get me, this guy Ralph, he tried to get me to prostitute, but it . . . wasn't my shot.

I mean, when I say it wasn't my shot, it wasn't my thing. I couldn't do it. But I tried, and I stood on the same corner all night—and didn't make a quarter!

And then, this got into this dope thing. You start shooting dope, it's a hell of a experience. And then you start doing different things, like petty things, like stealing. Little petty things, just to get the stuff. And, like, I knew these two fellows who I used to go by and visit, and to get money from. In order to buy the stuff.

And I messed around, and he used to give it to me free at first. Then after he found out I needed the stuff, he stopped giving it to me, and told me I had to pay for it after that.

And . . . and . . . I messed around with the stuff about four months. And then I stopped.

☐ ☐ ☐

And then I started back smoking reefers and drinking whiskey instead of wine. I never did start back drinking wine again.

And then I started riding motorcycles!! (She laughs.)

[*Is that right?*]

Yeah. And then, this was just a whiskey thing. I would smoke pot, but didn't nobody else hardly smoke it. Because they felt like it was a waste to smoke the stuff and ride a motorcycle, because the wind usually blow it away.

And we started going different places on motorcycles. To different towns, out of the state and everything. And it was sort of wild and silly, the things you do on motorcycles.

Like they would go into bars. White bars? And if the bartender wouldn't serve us or nothing, we would tear up the bar. And, oh, we used to go to motorcycle races. And at a motorcycle race with motorcycle riders, there's no such thing as segregation. The white people treat you just like you white and the colored people treat the white people just like they're colored. Motorcycle rider don't think about prejudice.

And we just had some real blasts. Like we used to have beer busters. Throw each other in the river and stuff like that. And it was just a real wild party.

And then, I stopped riding motorcycles, and I started coming around this corner.

□   □   □

And over here ain't nothing, just but a drink. That's all they do around here is drink, drink, drink, drink. But you run into some wild things around here, with alcohol. Like, when China-Girl and them, they killed Arthur.

And that was a hell of a thing. Just *killed* him. And . . . people get beat up and stabbed and shot and everything around here.

It's not like any other places I ever lived in.

□   □   □

Nobody wants to get ahead on this corner. All the people I went to school with, you know, they all trying to get over now; they're all trying to get ahead or trying to be something. But with these people, all they want is a drink. A drink today, a drink tomorrow, and the next day. They just live for a drink. They just—they trifling! They just want to sit around, wait for their check, and, and . . . drink! Wine, whiskey, beer, anything.

Wherein as, in other groups, like the groups I been hanging around with for the last three months, well, they are bean droppers, and they're LSD users and scag users, and reefer smokers, and they *always* trying to figure out a way to make a buck.

They got apartments. They have wall-to-wall carpeting and wall-to-wall record players. And nice clothes and everything. I mean, they *want* something. Where these people on the Corner want to drink, and they don't care how their houses look.

The people I've been hanging around with, they all work. They work *and* they hustle. It's just a whole different idea.

This particular guy I know, he work at Chrysler, in the morning. And he get off work at two-thirty. And he's a homosexual. And in the afternoons when he get off work and come home, he sells scag. So, okay, let's say, he make thirty-two dollars at work that day; he come home that afternoon and he sell eighty pills for a dollar, he make eighty dollars.

Scag is heroin. In a form, but it's a waste from heroin; it's not as strong as heroin, but it'll get you high like heroin.

And he sell these pills, and they're a dollar each. Well, okay, he make eighty dollars. He make thirty-two dollars that morning and eighty dollars that night. And then at night he'll prostitute, he dress up like a woman and he prostitutes. Maybe he make from thirty to forty dollars or fifty dollars a night. And, then he gets up the next morning and go to work. This guy's *getting over*! I mean, he making money. He banking money *every day*.

He is! He *is* a dope addict, therefore he is using some of it. On his habit. But he ain't spending it all. Plus he got a fabulous apartment. I mean, he got everything that a man could want. Also, a *man*. He got himself his own man. You know, how could a man have a man?

□ □ □

And this *other* guy I know, now, he can talk people into *giving* him money. He cons people.

And this is his daily thing. And he got a flunky who sells dope for him while he out making money conning. Well, that's getting over, too. The guy selling the stuff for him may sell three hundred pills, in six hours. And *he* might could con a man out of eight hundred dollars in thirty minutes. So *he's* making money, too.

[*How could he get eight hundred dollars?*]

Well, he could get a ring. He could go downtown to a jeweler's, he could have them to make him up a ring of zircon. And they could have it *so* close to looking like a diamond, he could convince a man, with his line, he could show this man where this "diamond" was worth something close to two or three hundred dollars. And he "had a bagful of 'em." And "he just robbed this jewelry store in Chicago" or something, and "they gotta get rid of this hot ice."

He could run it on a square, who think he's hip to it and is not really hip to it at all. And sell him "a thousand dollars' worth" of zircons.

But then he got to try to watch out for this man, 'cause the man is going to try to find him, the minute he find out he's been got.

But the guy knows how to do it. What he do, he put larceny in the *other* man's heart. The other man, the square, think he beating *him*, think he making a fool out of *him*, so, therefore, he'll go on and buy it, and laugh at him. And all the time the square getting beat hisself.

I don't know too much about it. I've just heard him sit around one day and say how he run this thing on this man, and beat him out of his money. And the square laugh at *him*, and he was laughing to hisself at the *square*. And, oh, he'd make about a thousand dollars a day.

And then there's this other guy, he got five girls prostituting for him. I don't know what kind of story he told them to make them do this. *And* he sells scag. *And* he got a flunky also selling scag for him. *And* he a hustler, a gambler, anything. Racetrack . . . anything gambling. And he win a lot. And *plus* he had these five girls, and each one of them, they call girls. They get calls, and they usually make a hundred dollars a day each. So, *he* getting over, too. I mean *all* of 'em is getting over.

Now with them, this is all they do. Their daily thing is making money. They don't think of nothing but making money. Where *these* people back *here*, they'll sit around and put thirty cents, fifteen cents, a quarter and stuff like that, to get a bottle of wine. The guys over *there* maybe shoot fifty dollars in their arm at one time, three times a day, and spend a hundred fifty dollars, where these people *here* only spend fifteen dollars. It's a different world. It's two different worlds. And they're way apart. Far, far apart.

□ □ □

And, like with me, I don't know the *real* game, you know, but I could . . . convince people that I have different intentions from my intentions and beat them out of money, too. But I got a split personality. I can really convince myself that I mean this, and I know all the time that I don't.

It's really hard to explain. If I could sit down and think about it, I could really run it to you, just from the beginning, the way I learned it. From other people. You sit around and you look at people and you listen at people. And they tell you, don't do this and don't do that, don't do *nothing* unless you can get a buck.

Like with these guys around here. They all broke all the time. You could see a different one of them and they tell you they want to go out with you. And you tell them, "Okay, well, I'll go out with you, but I have got to go get this thing first," and get money from them. Like, all of them is really, deep down in their hearts, tricks.

Like you could just say, "I want to get a new suit. It's in the layaway. And it costs thirty dollars to get it out. But I will do this with you. And even if I don't get a chance to do it today, I *will* do it. And you know I'm gonna see you everyday and I wouldn't make you a promise if I wasn't going to do it."

And they'll go on and do it, thinking you're going to do it. Then all you have to do is have a story for them every time you see them. This is how I owe everybody around here. See? And you don't have to do it. And then you can always come up with another story and get some more money from the same person.

[*Yeah. But it seems like that wouldn't work very long.*]

Well, it does. You have to believe these stories yourself, that you run the people, in order to be convincing. When I drink, I'll be more convincing than ever. 'Cause when you're sober, you sort of feel it's kind of corny your own self. I don't know. It's just knowing how to do it.

□   □   □

[*Which do you enjoy more, of those two sets of people? Which would you rather be around?*]

The one that makes the money! But I'm scared of drugs, so I'm not qualified for getting the type of money that you have to have to be with these people. I mean, I can get enough money to go away every day and get high and like that, but you have to be in their category, you know.

Like all of them's like . . . now these LSD users, they tell corny jokes, jokes that I wouldn't understand. A dope addict could never really hold a deep conversation with a person that used LSD, because a person that used LSD's mind is much farther out. A junky couldn't talk to a LSD user. We'd sit down and try to talk to him; I've been with junkies that tried to talk to them, and they're pretty far out. And these Dexedrine users, they are pretty close to in the category with the LSD user, but a LSD user is farther out than anyone.

[*Even when he's not on?*]

Yes. He's always on a trip, you know. He never comes back, really. They be back, they seem normal, but they really be still on a trip. They be halfway back to reality, and they'll be halfway on their trip again.

□   □   □

I never experienced LSD myself. I'm scared of it because . . . I think I have . . . suicidal tendencies. And I could have a bad trip and kill myself. And this is why I won't mess with it. I could be wrong. But I'm afraid of it.

And, with scag—it don't scare me really, 'cause it only—it makes you *lazy*! For about a hour. And then after that it puts *larceny* in your heart. It makes you want to make money. All you can think of is how to get a buck.

I was like this three months. All I could think of was getting money. And it had me doing things that I could go to jail for.

[*Which had you doing these?*]

Dope. Scag.

To get some more money. And we went to these little, you would call them cities, around Chicago, you know and then it was . . . well. . . .

You know, like robbing places. I did . . . Bonnie and Clyde thing for a minute. . . .

[*Did that scare you, when you did that?*]

To death! Your throat would be dry and your hands would be wet. . . .

[*Yeah, I was just trying to think of that the other day.*]

It really did. Your throat be dry and your hands would be wet, and you be a nervous wreck. Because, you know, you might get killed. Or, you think, you might got to kill somebody, but you don't know if you can do it or not, because you never had to do it.

And this is what you be so afraid of. Like, this man, like this one time we ripped. This man pulled a thirty-eight. And I had a gun in my hand. And I couldn't do nothing to him but scream, "Drop it!" And I guess he lost his nerve before me. But really I had already lost mine when I seen his gun.

[*He didn't know that.*]

But I just kept screaming, "Drop it!" And then, then I jumped over the counter like I was going to do something to him, and then he dropped his. But I don't think I would have did anything but grabbed his hand. And probably make him shoot me because he was about as scared as I was.

But it was too much for him, and he dropped his, and fell on the floor, and started saying he was going to pass out. And everything. But he don't know it, I was scared. We'd have fell on each other.

[*It's just a miracle that one or the other of you didn't accidentally kill the other one, you know.*]

He would have killed me before I did him.

[*Well, either one of you, you know . . . what with the guy so scared. . . .*]

But I couldn't have shot him. Because I was looking . . . when you look somebody in their face . . . it's hard to look a person in their face and take their life. That's the only thing.

And I kept noticing, you know; going through my mind was pictures of the expression on his face. And if I would have shot him, I don't know what kind of expression he would have had, and I think I never could have forgotten how he looked at the time.

If you could have seen the scared expression on that man's face. . . .

But I must've had one on my face that was more frightening than his because he gave in before I did.

□ □ □

And then maybe . . . well, the reason why he probably *really* gave in was because the guy who he had pointed the gun at was pointing the gun at him, and *he* wasn't scared. So he could have been watching him more than me.

See? I don't know. Because the other guy don't show no emotion. This other fella who I was with, have no emotion.

He don't show nothing. He's just got this *cold* expression.

I never seen him show any emotion. Never.

He never. . . . See, he a Scorpio person, and he can be friendly this minute, but he still have some kind of look and expression that he always looking *through* you.

He never relax. He don't trust nobody. We ripped with him, and he never trust *us*. And he never really relaxed with us. We never knew his secrets. He didn't confide in us.

And we all skeptical of him. I mean, this is the way it was.

[*Yeah. I wonder what he was feeling.*]

Nobody never know.

Like, he said, "Well," he said, "you all can do what you want to. We ever get caught, do what you want to. So if you give yourself up, you're on your own. If I get caught, they ain't going to take me in alive. They're going to have to kill me because I'm not going to jail."

I mean, this the way the guy thought. He just couldn't jail. He'd rather be dead than be in jail. And they was going to have to kill him if they ever caught him. So if they ever catch him, I guess they'll have to kill him.

[*He never did do time?*]

He never been arrested.

Never got caught.

And he feels as though he just couldn't be locked up. And he said he'll kill or be killed before he'll be locked up and I think he means it.

[*Do you think he feels any happiness?*]

No. He don't like women, you know. He got this girlfriend, but the only time he go over and pick her up is when he wants sex. He don't like to sit around and laugh. He don't sit around, laugh and talk and coax and hug and kiss the girl. It's just sex, and then he take her home. No feeling.

I mean, I don't see how she can be bothered with the guy. And he only want her to prostitute, that's all he can think of, a way to get her to make money to give him. But no love and affection.

[*That is one thing I really don't understand. Why do girls do it for a guy?*]

Oh, she dig him. Or maybe she like him because he cold-hearted. You know? A lot of people, weak people, like strong people.

And the other guy who ripped with us, he was the pretend-to-be-mean type. He was mean on the outside, but he was all heart.

He *also* was a Scorpio. Two different types of Scorpios. He had a expression on *his* face that looked like he was mad all the time. But, his conversation showed that he had . . . he had a soul. Like this first guy I was telling you about, the one that had this mad expression, this way-out look? He didn't have no soul.

I mean, if he had a soul, it never showed. I don't think the guy had a heart. I mean, really. I mean it. You would have to see him and know him to understand it. He would come over, and he would sit down, two hours, and wouldn't say nothing to nobody in the room. And then he'd get up and say, "Well, I'll see you later."

That's the kind of guy he was. Or he would discuss ripping something off. This is all he talked about. The guy didn't care for people. He never sit down and had a simple game of cards, he didn't believe in playing cards. Not even for money. He wasn't a gambler. And he didn't use dope.

[*Did he drink?*]

He didn't drink. He didn't smoke reefer, and he didn't use dope. The guy was just . . . *cold*. He didn't do *nothing* to get high. Never. I never seen him high.

[*Or with any kind of kicks?*]

No . . . Pepsi-colas and potato chips! And then . . . but he liked money. I wonder what he spent it on? I never seen what he spent it on. Clothes, he loved clothes. And he like real high-priced clothes.

Like the second guy, the same time when we ripped, and this man pulled a thirty-eight? He had a pistol, too. But he didn't even take it out of his pocket. This one who *wanted* to be mean? He didn't even go in his pocket. He was just standing there in the middle, looking at the man with the gun and looking at this first guy with the gun.

And I pulled the gun out and told the man to drop the gun.

And he didn't do nothing. He was just dumbfounded. Just standing there.

And the first guy told him later, he said, "You could have got me killed." He said, "I should shoot you."

"Man, what you mean, you should shoot me?"

"I should kill you, I could have got killed just 'cause you didn't know what to do." And he said, "We'll never rip together again." And like that.

And then he told me that it was cool what I did, and everything. [*Did you really jump over the counter? While he. . . .*]

And took the gun from him. Out of his hand. I wouldn't shoot him. See, I couldn't shoot him. I knew I couldn't shoot. So I jumped over the counter and grabbed the gun, and snatched it out of his hand. That was all I could do, you know.

And I mean he threw it on the floor. No, he fell on the floor, with the gun in his hand. And I took the gun out of his hand. It had six bullets in it. Thirty-eight special snub-nose. And. . . . And that was the end of that.

What else you want to know? . . . You'd have to do these things to really feel them. Maybe another time, maybe I could just tell you, describe it to you better. 'Cause it's . . . you *feel* that stuff, you know. You *feel* everything that happen to you.

Like this . . . like . . . with drugs for instance. I started using drugs because me and my *mother* had this real deep thing, you know. This is why we don't get along.

We . . . we have a . . . what you could call a slight *hate* for each other, you know.

Because she . . . did several things to me . . . in my life, you know, like some things she did . . . Professor, that left a slight mental thing with me, you know.

I mean, like, I've never seen a woman drunk, in my life, until I came to Detroit. I never seen a woman . . . *sloppy drunk*, you know, and I stayed here two days. I call my grandmother and told her, "This woman is drunk and I don't like her," you know. And I was nine.

(*Her voice gets more and more hurt.*) And . . . I left . . . here then, and . . . she just sit and she drink corn whiskey and wine.

And . . . she had different boyfriends every other day, and . . . I just—I didn't have no respect for her. And I started acting like it, you know, and then . . . and then I got pregnant.

Then she met this man, and she used to go with his best friend. And he knew about it, and I couldn't understand why he'd never say nothing. He just used to always act real friendly to the man. He never said anything. I couldn't understand it. And then one day he just left. He just got tired of it and left.

And when I got my baby, I got on the ADC and everything. She quit working. And she just laid around all the time and stayed drunk for two years.

She was drunk two years. I mean, she was just sober long enough to get a bottle of beer and then go get drunk.

Two solid years! I don't see how you could just stay drunk for two years. And . . . she became a *bum*. I mean, she had a place to stay and food to eat and changing clothes and stuff like that. She'd clean herself up and go get drunk. And get nasty and filthy and come back and just . . . lay out in the middle of the floor, you know. And my friends come in.

And stuff like that. . . . I went to the drugstore, you know, and . . . a bunch of fellas standing on the corner by the drugstore drinking wine. Say: "Where your mamma at? I wanna do it to her." Stuff like this. And it . . . I don't know, it just . . . me and her, we're not real close now.

And I don't like for her to try to chastise me, because I never been like she have been. She ain't had to come get *me* out of the alley asleep, drunk, and . . . and I don't know what them people did to her, you know.

Then she asked me could she keep my baby. She was living with this man.

She asked me could she keep my baby, for the weekend. They was doing pretty good, you know, both of them was alcoholics. . . . (*She laughs*.)

Kenneth was three, he was born when I was seventeen. I was twenty. And she asked me, could she keep him for the weekend, her and Chris. So I said, yeah, 'cause I had got my own place and everything. And I was glad for them to keep the baby for the weekend, so I could go out.

And I went over there that Monday, after Kenneth, and she said, "Well, we enjoyed him so much for the weekend, let me keep him the rest of the week." So I said, "Okay."

So I went over there the following Monday to get Kenneth and she had moved. So I asked Chris, I said, "Where is she, Chris?" And he said, "I don't know. She left. And I think she over to Tim's house." This is his brother.

So I goes over to Tim's house. And she comes to the door and cracked the door and telling me, "Don't come back over here no more! 'Cause me and Kenneth is on the welfare and I told the welfare people that you brought him over here and left him, and I didn't know where you was. And you younger than me, you can make it. And just let me keep him long enough to stay on the welfare long enough just to get over, and then you can get him back."

You know, and she . . . run this con on me, and I fell for it.

[*You believed that?*]

Yeah. I said okay, and you know, I say, "Well, when you get yourself together"—see, she said she was going to get a job, and she was going to quit drinking and get herself together and everything. . . .

[*And she said that and you thought it was true? As long as you had known her?*]

Well, I mean, it was my mother. You know, and I felt like if this would help her get herself together, well, that was the least I could do. I mean because who wants to see their mother be a drunk?

[*How long did you talk about that? With her?*]

We sit and we talked about . . . two or three hours. And I said "Okay." And . . . then this police lady came and talked to me, you know, and I had to go downtown to court. And she went down and pressed file against me for a unfit mother! (*She laughs a moment.*)

[*Your mother did?*]

Yeah. And this—she got legal guardian . . . of my baby and everything.

[*Really?*]

And I hates her! I mean, this is . . . we . . . this is why we don't get along.

And now, she wants to make it up to me, but she can't make that up to me. For the rest of my life I'll still be branded. And she says we can just go down there and clear it up, but you just can't go down there and clear something like that up.

And she told the people I used dope. And a bunch of different stuff. And, this man she was messing around with, Mr. Lander, she got him to sign some papers saying for a witness. And then he come telling me he didn't know what he was signing. He knew what he was signing. He say he thought he was just signing legal guardian over to her. He didn't know he was signing for me to be an unfit mother and all this crap. But he knew. He had to know. Because the man explained it to him before he signed the paper, even if he couldn't read.

And this is why we . . . got a hell of a feeling for each other.

[*Why would she use you like that?*]

Because she wanted what she wanted, and the only way she could get it. . . .

And then, when she first did it, and moved in the project, I was working in Bonus Cleaners. And I lost my job. And I asked her, could I stay with her, 'til I get another job. She said, "Well, you can't stay with me, cause ADC people might come and catch you here." But a man was living with her. And I said, "Well, don't you think they'll cut you off ADC quicker for him living with you than they would for me?" "Well, they don't know he here." I said, "Well, they won't know I'm here." "Well, naw, you just can't stay here." You know, like that. And that was that.

I mean, *she is a vicious broad!* And I don't like her very much. Maybe you can't understand it.

[*Can't understand why you wouldn't like her?*]

Yeah.

[*I can understand why you wouldn't like her.*]

She *vicious.*

[*Why did she . . . give you to your grandmother, anyway?*]

She said she didn't want nothing that hurt her that bad. She gave me to my grandmother when I was one day old.

[*How old was she?*]

She was twenty-one when I was born. The first time I ever seen her I was nine. Second time I seen her I was fourteen. Next time I seen her I was sixteen.

□   □   □

[*When you were a little girl, did you know anything about her?*]

No, I never—no. . . .

[*You knew you had a mamma somewhere.*]

Mamma? My grandmamma.

[*Did you think she was your real mother?*]

No. She always taught me that that lady was my mamma, but I always told her that she was wrong.

No. And my mother never gave me nothing. Up until now, and I'm twenty-eight. This watch, she gave it to me last Christmas. It's the only thing she gave me out of twenty-eight years.

[*Wait—I'm curious, now. Like when you were a little girl, your grand-mother told you, I am your grandmother, I'm not your mother?*]

Yeah. I knew she was my grandmamma, far back as I can remember. But I always called her Mamma.

[*What were your thoughts about your mother?*]

I always asked her, where was she? You know, what she look like? And she told me she looked like me, and she said, "She your mamma," you know, and "Always respect her" and this, that, and the other. And it went in one ear and out the other, 'cause . . . then I *wanted* to like her. . . .

[*Yeah.*]

. . . and then when I was nine she asked Mamma could I come here for summer vacation out of school. She was sloppy drunk! And I stayed two days, and I went back.

[*I bet you were happy, though, when she first invited you, weren't you?*]

Yeah, I was anxious to see her and everything, until—she was drunk! And I had to put—get in the cab, and take the address, you know, and give it to the cab driver, and I didn't know nothing about Detroit, or where I was or nothing and he had to take us, and he had to . . . *drag* her out the cab and take her in the apartment then.

And I called long distance back to my grandmamma. And she told me don't unpack my clothes, just change clothes, and she was wiring me train fare back. And I went and put my ownself in the Traveler's Aid, and went back down south.

And then I stayed till I was fourteen, and I came back again for summer vacation. But I didn't want to come that time. Mamma made me come. Because she said it was my mamma, she was entitled to me staying for the summer. And she forced me to come back. And I stayed two weeks. And that's when I seen her in bed with a man.

And then she sent for me again, because, see, I didn't see nothing like that, you know. I never seen my grandmamma drunk. And I don't know . . . I just didn't dig the lady. I mean, I just couldn't see nothing in that lady. I still don't.

□   □   □

[*Did your grandmamma . . . have a husband?*]

Yeah. She was married twice. To my mother's father, and then she married again.

[*When you were growing up down there, who was it?*]

My grandfather? My grandfather was her first husband. And then she married another man. Then she had this boyfriend, after he left. She had this boyfriend but he never spent the night. He never went to bed or nothing. I don't know how they did that, but I didn't ever see them in the bed. And I seen her drink beer at night, but I've never seen her drunk. I couldn't understand why she never showed any effect from alcohol. She probably was high, but she just didn't let me know it. I don't know how she did it. That woman was the greatest.

[*Tell me about her.*]

She was the greatest! (*Eva's voice is happy now.*)

[*Describe her some.*]

She was short, and she was half a Indian. And she had real long hair, and she was a good-looking woman. And she was a mean woman! I mean, everybody was scared of her. And (*she laughs*) she went with a big man of the town, he was a white man. And she was considered as white trash; but she had everything any white woman had, there, and I used to have to pay kids to play with me, 'cause their parents didn't want them to play with me, 'cause I had everything that I ever wanted, up until I was sixteen.

And maybe this is why I changed so. Because Mamma died. The whole thing just was snatched out from under me. I didn't have nobody no more.

My daddy, I never seen him until I was sixteen. And I don't know nothing about him. And he had this woman living with him, and I didn't like her. And . . . I didn't like him.

I mean, I ain't never had a mamma and daddy, you know? My grandmamma was both of them.

And she just was the greatest. And somebody killed her.

Somebody killed her for a thousand dollars. With poison. She used to keep money in the freeze-box on the back porch. She had a garden, and she would put peas, and butterbeans, and string beans, and tomatoes in there. She would pre-cook tomatoes and freeze them in the freeze-box. And she put her money in there. It had a lock on it. A Yale lock, one of them locks that slide up the thing.

And she had a thousand dollars in there, and she had five hundred dollars in her purse. She always kept five hundred dollars in her pocket, I don't know why.

And she was going with this guy. I was here then. Kenneth was three years old. She only seen Kenneth once before she died. And this guy was younger than Mamma, and he had a girlfriend who was about my age. And they got together and gave her some rat poison, the kind that won't kill you 'til you drink water. I don't know what kind it was. Anyway, it make you thirsty, and she drink some water, and she laid across the bed with a stomach ache, that was . . . she just . . . went to sleep and died. Just like that.

And the man that did it . . . this white man said that he was a "good nigger" and . . . . "wasn't nobody gonna bother his nigger," you know. He went to her funeral. . . .

Just like that.

She left me her home, and insurance, and everything. She left my mother one dollar.

One dollar! I thought that was awful dirty of Mamma, but the lawyer said that she had to leave as much as one dollar or my mother could take everything she had. That's what Mamma left her, as much as she had.

She had to leave her one dollar.

[*So it would be clear that it wasn't an oversight.*]

Yeah. Yeah. (*She laughs.*) I don't know why she'd do something like that. My grandmamma was mean, like I say, and she . . . didn't have no great love for my mother, 'cause my mama was drunk down there.

That's why she left there, you know. Everybody . . . she was the talk of the town. In a small town like that, you can easily be the talk of the town. Just corn whiskey you had, in Mississippi.

[*Did . . . did you say they considered your grandmother black trash?*]

White trash. Because, this white man was taking care of her. . . . But she lived good. She lived better than any colored woman there.

[*Well, was she considered Black or white?*]

She was . . . she looked like a Mexican. You ever seen a dark Mexican? That's what she looked like. I got a picture of Mamma. But, that was in her older age.

But I have a picture. She was short, and heavy, she had a neat look. All these people next door here, Roberta, Catherine, Lorraine, all of them, they know my grandmother well. She used to go with their brother. And they could tell you how mean she was.

[*Is she from the same town?*]

Yes, we all are. And they could tell you how she chased him one night with a straight razor. She had him jumping up and down! (*She laughs.*) Ran down the street swinging at him with a straight razor! She was real mean. But she was all heart. You know? And if you did something to her, then all this Indian in her came out.

But she was all heart.

[*Were her other men white, or were they Black?*]

She had a colored boyfriend, but . . . you know, this white one was a under the cover thing, but everybody knew about it. Her husbands, they were all colored, but real light. She was prejudiced. What was wrong with her, she was color struck; she didn't want nothing blacker than her. That's the way she was. But she was my mamma.

Now, I'm glad I'm not color struck. I like dark men. That's the difference in me and her.

[*She treated you well?*]

I never wished for nothing! And I never ate nothing I didn't like. And she never forced me to accept nothing I didn't want. Anything I wanted, I got it. And she'll fuss about ten minutes, and then she'll give it to me.

Like one time I remember, when I was about ten, and these Cinderella dolls came out. And they was about three feet tall. And you could hold their hand and make them walk. And she took me to the city, and I seen one of these dolls. And I wanted Santa Claus to bring me one. So she said, "Them dolls cost fifty dollars. Santa Claus can't bring you one of them." So I *fell out* in the store! Just fell out, and just started screaming, and kicking, and pulling my hair, and screaming and kicking. She said, "Get your butt up! He gonna bring you one, but you better have never do that to me again," and she whupped me good when she got me home. But

I got the doll. That was all that counted. I wanted the doll, and I got it. But I was a spoiled brat. That's what was happening with me, I was a spoiled brat.

[*In what ways are you like your grandma, and in what ways are you different?*]

Like Mamma? She like money; I like money. And, oh, I got a lot of my grandma's ways.

[*I was thinking so, when you were talking.*]

She was real clean. And she had a open mind. And I'm like that. And she also said what was on her mind, and I'm like that. And . . . I don't know. I don't believe in having Tom, Dick, and Harry, you know. I flirt, I'm a big flirt, but I don't go to—all the way, you know, regular. I have to want to, and this is the way she was. I mean, I guess. I never really known her to have a man. But she had boyfriends, so I feel like, now that I'm older, they was doing something besides laughing and talking.

[*Hey, tell me about this southern town. Living in this little town.*]

Oh well, it was just a regular town. Just a ordinary little southern town, one out of them Tennessee-Williams-story towns. You know. I mean, everything was a scandal. Even the least little thing was a scandal. And everybody knew everybody, and everybody knew everybody's business.

It was a modern little town, though. And everybody was trying to keep up with the Joneses. Mamma was the Joneses in this little town. And our cousin across the street was running head-up competition. Her husband worked for the railroad, and he made pretty good money. So when Mamma bought a nineteen fifty-five Chevrolet convertible Bel Air, they bought a nineteen fifty-five Buick convertible. And when Mamma had her house remodeled into a ranch-style home, they had their house remodeled into a ranch-style home.

[*You know, that . . . you know, I grew up in Texas in a little town 'til I was twelve.*]

Well, you know what it was like.

[*Well, it was different from what you describe though. Maybe because it was so long ago. I left there in nineteen forty-four. And . . . Negroes in my town . . . there wasn't remodeling any house, there wasn't any money. There wasn't any money. You know those little cabins?*]

Well, nobody in that town lived in a cabin.

[*Those little unpainted one-room things? That was all there was.*]

Well, that's maybe because all of them mostly, in the town I lived, they worked in Shirley in this place where they made textile stuff for the Army. And I think they made about fifty dollars a week, and that's a lot of money. That was a lot of money in the forties. And this was in the forties.

[*That's what I'm talking about. No one in my town had seen money like that. They were chopping cotton.*]

No. Didn't nobody chop cotton. There was no such thing as this.

I mean, there was trucks that came there to try to get cotton pickers and cotton choppers. But nobody did. The younger people like my age would do it, you know, but for three dollars a day, wouldn't nobody do it. Because, like I said, they all worked at this mill, all the older people, and when they got seventeen, then they went to start work down there, you know. They would hire anybody. And it was a large place. It was a textile mill, and I don't know if that place is still there now, or not.

[*That's another thing, too, though. I've been assuming people had farming backgrounds.*]

But it's different; it's different now. Where I came from kids went to school, and they had jobs after school, like working in a gas station, stuff like that. When they came from school, they just went straight to the gas station. And this is where their money came from. And John Rahlins, across the street, where he came from in Alabama, it's a factory where they turn cotton into material. And everybody in his town worked in this cotton thing. In the mill, or something, they called it. His wife worked there, too. And her mother been working there for twenty-five years. So, see, it's like they started putting plants and stuff all over the South, and this took the people, the Negroes, away from the cotton fields. And I guess, that's the way it is all over the South now.

[*Well, it sounds like it put a little bit of money in people's pockets.*]

And in that town John Rahlins come from, there is this colored man, he's a brother-in-law of Jesse here, and he's a mason. He is a brick mason. And this man make two and three hundred dollars. Mere colored man, you know? And he is the best in this county. And he go all over Alabama laying bricks. So therefore his sister has a brick home. Complete ranch-style brick home.

And see, like we never had a outside bathroom. Since I was born. And we had telephone, TV, radio, everything that they got now. We didn't have to go outside for the toilet.

[*You would have laughed if you had seen my town.*]

Well, my mamma now, they had a outside toilet when my mother was coming up. But when I was six, I remember sleeping in the bathroom. In the bathtub. They built the rest of the part of the house around the bathroom. And we stayed in the bathroom until the rest of the house was built.

And in about ten years we got a telephone.

□   □   □

[*Well . . . would you live in the South?*]
Now? No.
I can never go back to Mississippi.

When I went down there for grandma's funeral, we went rabbit hunting. And we found a whiskey still. And there was about five of us or something. And we had about two gallons of whiskey apiece.

And I was drinking mine. (*She laughs.*) And they sent me to the store to get some bacon. I think it was four pounds of bacon, four dozen eggs, four loaves of bread, two box of grits—one box of grits. And, the lady short-changed me. Out of a twenty-dollar bill. And I called her some dirty names, some dirty white names. And I called the man in the store some dirty white names. I was drunk off corn whiskey. And I went back home and forgot about it. I mean, it just didn't . . . I didn't think about it any more. And I was making a long-distance call and I called the operator some dirty white names. (*She laughs.*)

And . . . that night, the high sheriff—the high sheriff is the marshal from the county seat. I never knew what the county seat meant, but it was the head place in the county.

And him, the high sheriff, the town sheriff, and there was a state trooper, they had a state trooper stationed there then. So it was three policemens and four higher citizens. All white men.

And they came and they asked my cousin, could I come out on the porch, they wanted to talk to me. And so Bob and them told them, said, well, they could come in, you know, and we was having Mamma's wake. It was the night of her wake. And told them that they could come in and talk to me, because anything they had to say to me, the whole family could hear it.

And they came in, and they said, "Is this Wilamina's granddaughter?" And then Bob said, "Yeah," and everything.

He said, "Well, you have her out of here on the next thing leaving after Wilamina's funeral. And she better not *never* come back to Mississippi! If she do, you'll read about her."

And that was the end of that. I haven't been back.

I took all my clothes to the funeral. My luggage. And the first thing leaving was a bus, and they was all at the bus station. They knew what

was the first thing leaving, and they was there to see me on the bus. I
thought they was gonna take me off the bus and kill me. But they didn't.
    [*Well, what . . . when the police said that, what did people say?*]
    They just said, alright, we'll—she'll be gone.
    [*Yes. And what did they say after the police went out the door?*]
    Nothing but just, we better get her away from here or they'll kill her.
And that was just that, because . . . they would have killed me.
    [*How did you feel?*]
    (*She laughs.*) Scared to death! Because you know how they kill people
in Mississippi. They kill colored people real fast in Mississippi.
    But I guess because Mamma was such a well-known Negro, and she
was well-loved by the white people . . . I don't know why, though. I never
could understand why they liked her. But all the white people liked her,
for some reason. Anyway, the white men did. I mean, that's just the way
it is. I think they all shot at her, you know, tried to mess around with
her.

    My great-grandmother, my grandmother's mother, was lynched. And
my great-grandfather.
    They lynched them. And they put champagne . . . you know, those
things you screw in the champagne bottle? They screwed them in them
and snatched the flesh out. All over. And then they hanged them. They
tormented them, then cut off their fingers and kept joints as souvenirs.
And then they hanged them. My great-grandfather and my great-
grandmother.
    But he looked just like his friend, Lyman, they were practically
identical. And Lyman shot a white man with a shotgun. And they killed
Grandmamma's mamma and daddy for Lyman.
    And my grandmamma and Lyman's daughter quit speaking for six-
teen years. They actually looked practically like sisters. Their daddies
looked so much alike. They were the same size and everything. And they
killed the wrong one.
    Maybe, too, that's why a lot of things Mamma did and got away with.
The white people there, you know, tried to make up to her. Because they
killed her daddy for Lyman.
    And Lyman left and went to Chicago. And when he died, they sent
him back. And they started back speaking when he died.
    [*Why did Lyman shoot the man?*]
    The white man raped his wife. And he shot him.
    [*So then they—?*]

They was chasing Lyman, and he run to Mamma's daddy's house. And Mamma's daddy run outside to see what was the matter. And they took him right on away, 'cause he looked just like the one that ran in.

[*They figured he was supposed to say thank you when his wife got raped?*]

Well, you know how that is. That was a long time ago. I mean that was in the twenties, probably nineteen twenty, you know, and then, nineteen-twenty negroes had it nothing like they got it now. Because I mean, they was still—ignorant animals.

[*Who was?*]

Negroes. In nineteen twenty.

[*I don't know why you say a thing like that.*]

Because, didn't you read about it? Didn't you read about . . . what's this guy's name . . . the one that led the first slave revolt? Nat Turner. Well, look how they thought he was a dumb animal. This is the way the South was then. All these books tell you like the South really was. And a Negro was a . . . was a animal, that walked upright. His brain was supposed to be smaller than a white man's.

[*Are you talking about what the white man thought or what the man was?*]

The white man wrote the books I read. They was describing how their forerunners thought, you know.

So I mean, that's the way it is. It's sad and sorry, but this is the way.

Now they know different. They thought our blood was black at one time, but now they know different. We're all equal as far as physically. But . . . it's a lot of mental things that . . . that is different in white people than in colored people, because . . . we have been oppressed.

And this makes our mental thing stronger, too, in a sense. In a sense, it's weaker.

I mean, like—in your instance of a white person, there's a strong and weaker, you know. Everybody has a fault. Everybody, I don't give a damn what color he is, there's something there. But we really all is human, and we all think alike.

Like this Muslim shit, "Let's get a country"? What we going to do? We still got to come back to the white man for everything we need. So what the hell, we might as well live with each other and love it. I'm like the hippies. I believe in the hippies. I mean, they believe in love.

What the hell? You should love. What else can you do? We all got to be together. So we might as well love each other. That's the way it is. This militant shit ain't going to last but a minute.

[*You think?*]

I know it. And if they start a war, they can't win it. So what the hell they going to do?

Go to school, get a education, and try to be equal. That's all you can do. That's the only way you can prove yourself. You can't prove yourself with violence. You got to try to get over. That's what Martin Luther King was trying to teach. That's why he a great man. Because he believed in non-violence.

Because violence gets you nowhere. It shows your ignorance. The animal instincts in you. What they want to go back to, throwing spears and being native sons? Shit.

What they want, to make a jungle of America? Or we going to be Indians again? And chase deers, and there ain't no more. What we going to do, starve?

[*Well, do you think Negroes are going to make it, if they get education?*]

Yeah, they could. This is the only way. They could only prove how intelligent they are by trying to be intelligent. But dropping out of school, and shooting dope, and robbing banks, they'll never make it like that; they only show that they don't deserve to be equal. Who wants to be around somebody next door that might throw a bomb in their house in the middle of the night?

[*What do you think will happen to the children on this corner?*]

This is their world. They don't know what's happening outside it. The younger ones do. They're trying to get out of this.

[*This corner here, is this an odd place? When you were living a few blocks away with Jesse, is that a thing like this, too? Or in the projects, is that like here? I don't know how you would describe life here on the Corner.*]

Just one hideous bottle, that's all. Day in, day out.

[*Well, was it the same over there with Jess, or . . . ?*]

No, the people over there are working people, trying-to-get-ahead people. And, they drink on the weekends. When they drink on the weekend, they're just like these people here. Friday, Saturday, Sunday. But Monday, it starts all over. They go back to normal.

[*What about the project?*]

It's a everyday thing over there. It's a lot of dope and stuff in the projects. It's a lot of drugs over there, it's a lot of vices. All the time.

[*There's very little drugs here, isn't there?*]

Ain't no drugs on this corner.

[*None? Really?*]

There is *none*. There is nothing but alcohol and some wine here. On this corner. Now, you go to the projects, and then you find a lot of drugs. You can't miss it. It's on every floor. Damn near every floor, maybe every other floor.

[*I just happened to have started this work right on this corner. Suppose I had started in the projects?*]

Would have got a whole different lookout on it. It would have been all white hate. That's what it would have been. And nobody probably wouldn't have even talked to you. Unless you was a white junky.

Professor, how am I going to keep on with you at this rate? We been talking an hour.

[*I've been meaning to talk to you for a year, so an hour don't mean nothing. Besides, you're going to be a star in this book.*]

I'm going to be scared of it. I bet you! I'm going to be a fool. (*She laughs.*)

[*I don't think so.*]

I've lived a foolish life.

Now come on and tell me what else to talk about.

[*Okay. I'm still puzzled about . . . this corner. . . .*]

It's just a place that everybody knows everybody. This is a little town. Come on. Think of something else.

[*So, there'll be more white hate in the projects. And there's hardly any here?*]

No, there's not any on this corner.

[*Well, what about the ripping crowd you were with? How'd they feel? They prejudiced?*]

It wasn't *no* prejudice there. 'Cause as long as you was game, you was a real fella. One of the fellas. It was hip. As long as you wasn't scared. That was all that mattered, being afraid.

And you find some real hip whiteys, believe it or not, in that dope thing. Whitey's rip; they just like me. And most white girls are prostitutes. They more or less don't want to take no gun in hand. But they will sell their body. That's weakness. I mean, who wants to have Tom, Dick, and Harry? They'd rather do that than really try to do anything.

I wish I could just sit down and just tell you this story. Maybe one of these days I can just sit down and tell you. From the beginning up 'til now. But it would be a long, dragged-out story, and it would be a lot of little incidents in it.

I could just tell you my story and it probably would make more sense to you, that way. We could just take a day and just sit over there and I'll tell you this story from the beginning to the end. 'Til now. Because I'm just giving you little incidents in it now.

□   □   □

But it's been a hell of a thing. A real thing. And with me, it's never been any white hate. 'Cause all the white people I know always been nice, to me. Even down south. They was nice to me down there. And that's why I don't have any hate. Not real hate, you know.

[*Are you happy?*]

No. I'm miserable. Can't you tell? I'm not satisfied. At all. How could you be happy living like I live? You know, just . . . different . . . a different thing every day with me.

I mean, like . . . like now, I shoot drugs just to get away from it all. You know. But I made up my mind I wasn't going to shoot no drugs every day. So I haven't shot any drugs for four days.

And it's miserable!

And really, every hour on the hour I think about going and doing it. But I just try to do something else to keep my mind off it. Like, when I get through talking to you, I'll probably go shoot some.

[*You better not. I'll tell you what. If you won't do that, we can take a break now and go get you a Jumbo, right?*]

(*She laughs.*) Okay.

[*I'll get you a Jumbo, and we'll talk for another hour, instead of you doing that, all right?*]

Yeah, well . . . okay.

[*I don't want you to shoot that.*]

That probably won't keep me from doing it, but I ain't going to. More than likely, I ain't going to anyway.

[*Well . . . I don't know.*]

I ain't going to do that anyway. That's for shit. It's a waste!

[*Is it good, when you do it?*]

It's different! It's different. That's what it is.

[*What do you. . . . Describe it, that's something, what. . . .*]

The high? How you feel?

[*Yeah. Like when . . . does it begin quick? Does it begin to change quick when you put it in?*]

Instantly.

[*Really.*]

The minute it hits your bloodstream! You be excited at first. When you stick the needle in your arm and you shoot it in, you get real excited. And then, when you finish running it in . . . you get real relaxed. You be real cool. You don't care. Just . . . things are just revolving around you, you don't be there.

Like, we could be sitting here, and everybody could be drinking, and alcohol is poison to a person that use it. And, to look at a person drunk, you would think they were the ignorantest thing in the world. And you don't want to be around people that drink, so you go back around dope addicts. A person that drink alcohol wouldn't understand what you'll be

going through. Your mind function faster than theirs. I mean, they . . .
in a stupid bag.

I sound crazy trying to explain it to you, but I don't know how. I mean,
like a weed smoker. . . . A person that run dope don't like to be around a
weed smoker, 'cause they'll blow their high, they talk too much. When
you smoke weed you'll be jolly happy. And when you smoke. . . .

Dope actually depresses you, that's what it does. (*She laughs.*)

It depresses you. But it's a state . . . it's a state of mind. I mean, you'll
be depressed to the extent where you enjoy being depressed. But you
think you're smarter than other people, you know. I mean, you feel
everybody a fool but you, and you the biggest fool there.

It's just a false build-up of some kind. I don't know the proper word for
it. But you're fooling yourself. Really. And killing yourself, too.

When you high, you just be . . . out of it. That's the way you be. Out of
it. You don't care nothing about nobody else, you don't like to talk to
people neither. All you want to do is nod and scratch. (*She laughs.*)

And *dream*. They're dreamers! Dope addicts are dreamers. That's all
they are. They're not doers. You know, reefer smokers are doers. Reefer
smoker explain something to you, he can run it to you in a way where it
might seem as though it would be the most boss thing to do at the time.

Where with a junky, a dope addict, wouldn't listen to a weed head.
And a weed head, any form of drugs, think alcoholics are stupid. You
know.

But then, they're all stupid. I mean, *weed make you think. Dope make
you dream. LSD make you trip.* (*She laughs.*) So actually, *none* of them
do nothing for you.

Alcohol make you stupid. So, actually, neither one of them, either
vice, is just as bad as the other. You just be in a different bag.

[*So what's good*?]

Nothing.

I mean, actually, you're supposed to be able to concentrate to an
extent where you could get high off of just being happy. But nobody has
that strong a mind. Like, with you, you don't have to indulge in nothing
to be happy. Whereas I indulge in all of them. Maybe that's why I don't
never get strung out on one thing, 'cause I do all of them. That way, you
don't just depend on one thing. Like I have smoked boo, drunk whiskey,
and shot dope, and I was going through all three bags at once.

[*At the same time*?]

Yeah, and this was a hell of a thing!

[*Is that safe*?]

It won't hurt you, I don't guess it hurts you. Alcohol don't mix with
dope, but the reefer wouldn't hurt you. But I was being stupid, being
happy, and nodding, and scratching, all at once. And . . .

[*How come you're unhappy?*]
Hm?
[*How come you're not happy?*]
I don't know. So many unhappy things have happened to me. (*She sighs.*) I don't know. I mean, don't nothing happen like I want it to happen. Everything I do turn to shit. Believe it or not.

Well, I was happy before Thomas went to jail, though. 'Cause it was ... I don't know, we had a ... understanding, yeah. We didn't have to keep secrets from each other, and we didn't have to lie to each other about nothing, more or less. And then, he understood me and I understood him, 'cause we was going through an astrology thing. And it was pretty deep, but it was helping us understand people around us and each other.

See, he got a strong mind. Not like the average man around here. Scorpio people like to learn, they like to go forward.

But this is what we was going through. And I was happy. And then this got snatched out from under me. And turned back into the same old misery.

[*Hey, by the way, is he, has he been charged?*]
With armed robbery.
[*They're holding him?*]
Yeah. Over there, next to Chicago. And he goes to court on Friday. And then I guess they'll set a trial day. This is just a hearing.

He was working at Ford, too. See, that's what I was trying to explain to you. Two hustles, you know. He was getting over. I mean, he wasn't never broke.

Since he been in jail, I've been back over there where he used to go and get high at and everything, and the fellas over there, they say he had me spoiled, and no other man could never do nothing with me. He'd do something like, say, he got me five pills and I'd do them. And I'll sit there and I'll tell him I want five more. And he'd buy them. Okay, and then everybody'd say, "Man, why you let her tell you what to do?" And he said, "Well, hell, it's as much her money as it is mine. She helped get it, you know."

And they say he spoiled me. Everything I said I wanted, he would— he was like my grandma, he treated me like my grandmamma treated me. And this was what I had been looking for, the same kind of affection that I got from Mamma.

And I could get that from him. I could get the same kind of treatment from him. He was the only somebody I ever known in twenty-eight years that treated me like she did. And maybe this is why I was so attached to him.

With Jesse, I never could have my way. With Thomas I could have my way, but then, he would only go so far, and then he would stop, and this is the way Mamma would do.

[*How long were you with him? Thomas?*]

Eight months. That's all, but, that was living . . . I mean. . . .

[*Good all the way, huh?*]

Yeah. Other than when, you know, like, if we'd hit something wrong. You know, it was spooky for a minute afterwards. We'd sit down and forget about it, get high—and it was over.

But he was just another Mamma. To me. And a daddy. And a man. He was all three.

And he understood me. If I get these hang-ups, he'd tell me, "Just sit down, tell me what the hang-up is." And I sit down and try to explain the best I could to him, and then he'd sit down, he'd try to explain it back to me in the way he felt it. And then we'd get together on it. And sooner or later we'd come over the hang-up. And it wasn't no hang-up no more.

And I never had nobody that I could sit down and talk to, you know. And feel real close to. And this is what it was with him.

□   □   □

Then he wasn't but twenty-one years old, and I don't see how he could have such a mind. He a high school graduate and everything. Like I say, he was deep in his astrology thing. And he don't believe in the Muslims, or nothing, he a *realist*. He like you, he don't believe in God.

That's bad, but he don't. Like he'd be talking to you, and he say, "Yeah, just like you and your God." He'd never say just "God"; he always say "*your* God." 'Cause he say a man is his own God. That's the way he feels about it; to him, he's his God. And he say, "I couldn't get on my knees and pray to nobody to give me nothing, I have to get out in the street and get it. That's the only way your prayers are answered. When you help yourself."

And this is the way he think. I wish you could talk to him. This is where you could get a conversation, and it would be a deep one. He can explain things. If he can get out of jail, I want you to meet him. And talk to him, and he can run his thing on you, this oppression thing and everything.

You should hear him talk. I used to listen at him talk and think he was crazy. And then I started thinking about some of the things he said; and they made a lot of sense. And . . . the guy was nuts! Really, that's what's wrong with him. 'Cause he make jokes about God. Really!

You know, like we have this album Bill Cosby made, about Noah's ark or something. Say, "God, me and you!" And this knocks him out, these kind of jokes. And I say, "That's not funny." I mean, really, it's not. Then he say, "Well, what's your God give you that I ain't gave you?" Things like this. "God gave me life," I told him. And he said, "You're a damn liar, your mamma and daddy gave you life." I mean, he say there's probably some kind of Supreme Being, but he wouldn't name it God.

I don't know what's wrong with this man, maybe that's why he have so much bad luck. Because he don't believe. God can have ways of punishing. And making him believe in Him, you know.

He don't believe in the Muslim, 'cause he say the Muslims is about as bad as any other religion there is. Because everything you make, they want you to will them everything you have. He say, "Shit, what the hell am I gonna take care of Muhammad for? Whoever the hell he is?" He don't believe in this. He don't believe in nothing but hisself. He had *start* to believing in men . . . and then he went to jail.

And I believe in him. 'Cause he *think*, you know. It's nice to be around somebody that think. Like Jesse is . . . a fruit, he got a flaky mind, and his mind is scattered into a million pieces, and he don't think. You have to think a little bit. Sometime, anyway. But Jesse never thinks. Never. He just a fruit. A vegetable. Just exist, that all. He don't want nothing, he don't look forward to nothing. Like you notice, they never wear decent clothes, they all dress in work clothes. All the time. But Thomas, he wore his clothes to work and put on his uniform *at* work.

[*How much was he making at Ford?*]

Different amounts of money, sometime a hundred and sixty-seven dollars a week. Different amounts. But, that wasn't take-home actually, cause he put fifty dollars a week for the credit union. And then he took a bond out, too.

Wonder why he was trying to save so much money? It took all of it to get him a lawyer. Five hundred dollars, he had just got in the credit union. And all them bonds. But they got the lawyer with the money.

[*You think there's any chance he'll beat it?*]

The lawyer said he would. I don't know. I don't know.

□　□　□

[*Hey, this corner's crazy, people come and go. What became of those two used to be around in the summer?*]

Veda? Veda? Her sister now, her sister's a dope addict. And, which other one? Madeline, yeah.

I don't know where Madeline is. They was both mad. In a way. I mean, Madeline was crazy. She was confused. She thought the world owed her something. And *Veda's* just dumb, she just can't help it. She don't think. She not a thinker, she's a doer. And she do things, and she know that she might get killed, but she do them.

It doesn't make her any difference. She don't want to live. They took her kids away from her. And ever since that, she been a wine head.

[*They took her kids away?*]

Yeah, they took her kids away for a unfit mother. The state did. 'Cause she was running an afterhour place, and she had kids. And they took the kids from her.

[*If they took the kids from everyone that had an afterhours place, there wouldn't be any kids left.*]

See, she was running a afterhour place, and her kids was living there, in this place, and they took the kids away from her, 'cause they felt she was a unfit mother to raise her kids in this kind of environment. An environment of a bunch of drunks laying around, stuff like that. So the state took them. And they're in homes now. Her other son is in a training school. He stabbed a little girl with a fork, 'cause she wouldn't talk to him.

Veda just turned to an alcoholic. This is what's bothering her. She don't care if she live or die. Because of her kids. And with Madeline, she just a nut. You know.

I mean, that's where the whole thing is. *All* of them crazy anyway, and *I* am, too, in a sense. All of us nuts, I guess that's what you could say.

[*How would you like to live if you could?*]

In a nicer neighborhood, in a nicer place, like maybe Conant Gardens. And maybe go to night school and then take a trade of some kind. That's the way I would like to live. With Thomas there with me.

This is what I would like. But this is wishful thinking.

Conant Gardens or someplace like that. A nicer neighborhood. And go to night school or something and try to get a trade. And Thomas'd be out of jail and working like he was.

[*Have you ever picked up something that you could work at?*]

A variety of things. I tried nurse's aide. I didn't like it. I don't like the idea of cleaning up bed sores. It's a nasty job. I cut that loose, I did it three months and it wasn't for me. And I didn't like working in the cleaners, counter girl; I don't like boxing shirts. Messing with them old nasty clothes. I done tried a number of different kinds of work. I worked in a paper company. I didn't like that. Glue don't never come off you. And I worked at Chrysler's, and I didn't like that *at all*! It was nerve-wracking, just *noise*.

And . . . I don't know what I want to do. I wish I could go to school and be a practical nurse, they don't have such nasty jobs. I don't know what

the heck I could do, you know, that . . . would keep my. . . . See, I'm the
type of person, I like to learn things, but once I get the hang of it, I lose
interest in it. It have to be something exciting to keep me interested all
the time. Maybe something like a stewardess or something like that.
Probably would never get bored with it.

□   □   □

But I'm easy to bore, you know. Maybe that's why I do such a variety
of things, because I stay bored all the time. I don't know, maybe it's
because I'm a Gemini. My zodiac is Gemini, and I got a split personality,
I was born under the sign of the twins.

And you should read about them people, they're crazy, but they have
the best zodiac there is. I can understand any kind of person. And I catch
on fast, and my sign is the wind. I mean, emotions is like the wind. Like,
you know, the wind shifts?

Well, that's the way I switch around, and. . . . I never stay interested
in nothing long.

[*You've got that understanding, I'll get you to become a psychiatrist.*]

I'm that crazy. I'm crazy enough to be a psychiatrist, but I don't worry
about other people's problems. . . . But I can always see other people's
problems and I can't see mine. And that's nutty. I mean, in a sense. But,
that's just the way it is.

Everybody, you know, have crazy . . . notions, and I do, too. And mine
is mad. In a sense, I could say they was mad, because I don't never—I
ain't never finished—I never finish nothing. I always start something
and I never finish it. I lose interest in it.

. . . That's my biggest problem, I'm confused. And bored. And dis-
gusted. And unhappy. And, it's a drag. You know.

Then I don't have no family understanding, with no kind of a family.
. . . I don't know.

[*Yeah, you're kind of alone, aren't you?*]

Yeah. I mean . . . my mother isn't a mother. You know. And . . . like I
say, Thomas was my whole family.

His family, they're worrying about me right now, because I ain't been
home since Friday, so I called them yesterday.

They asked me when I was coming home. I told them I was coming
home tonight. I ain't going. Because it's a drag, being around them. I
mean, what, you going to sit there and look at TV all day? That's a drag.

[*Is that what they do?*]

All day. I mean, Loretta, she work. But then Ann be walking around
. . . twiddling, doing her hands, twisting her hands, wringing her hands!
And holding a drink! She a alcoholic, and she be needing a drink. I watch

her wringing her hands, and I have to leave there. Or just go mad sitting
there watching her.

No, no. I don't like to be there. . . . Just . . . alone, just like you say. . . .
Just the whole thing is a drag.

[*You still have a capacity though, you know.*]

Hmm?

[*You. You've got a lot of . . . talent, a lot of capacity.*]

And I don't use any of it to better myself, you see. So it don't make
sense to have it. I mean, that's kind of crazy, too. I mean, knowing it, you
know what I mean?

[*You know it?*]

Yeah, see, I could get out of this, you know, and stay out of it, but . . . .
Whereas I'll go and stay out of it for a little while, and then, I mean, I'll
come back, you know. And mess around again, and then leave again,
and like that, you know. I never stay in it but a minute, you know. I
never just get swept behind it.

Mmm. . . . Well, Professor, I'm going to let—you have got to turn me
loose for a minute now. Shit, you been having me too long. You can still
find me that job, though.

will and rebecca stone

What follows are four of the interviews I had with the Stone family, three with Rebecca and one with Will. The first took place during the first year of our acquaintance. I was talking about child-rearing with Rebecca and another woman, in the Stones' flat, on a spring afternoon. The other woman left shortly after we began recording.

A year later, when the second interview took place, life on the Corner had become more difficult for Rebecca and she was outspoken in her anxiety. She did not grow up expecting to live in a world like this.

Several days later, I had a brief but spirited discussion with Will, who had come storming into the family's apartment, fuming from the frustrations of a day's search for new housing and for credit.

The final conversation, with Rebecca, came months later. The apartment was still standing and the need for new quarters was a little less urgent. That was fortunate, since Will's plant was going through a temporary contraction and had laid off some of its workers for a while. Will was one of them. Rebecca dealt with the layoff as calmly as she had dealt with previous crises. She continued to take care of the family—but note how the description of the meals has changed. The Stones had no choice but to hope that the children would be good sports.

Rebecca Stone (I)

Me, I have five kids. And I would like to see all of them grow up to be someone that I would be proud of, nothing I would be ashamed of that I had gave birth to them. Which we cannot predict, you know. Regardless what you try to do to raise them right, we can't predict what they're going to be when they grow up.

But I will be proud of all five of them. I know the neighborhood that we is living in now, it's not the best of neighborhoods. But it's the best that I could do for them at the time. And I tries to teach them, things that they see other kids doing that I don't approve of them doing, they shouldn't do it. And they all are interested in school. They want to go to school, get an education, and I'm proud of that because today if you don't have an education, you just nowhere.

And I also try to teach them there's no difference in one color from the other. They should be proud of their color, that they are Negroes. And I tell them, through life you will meet people that talk certain ways; it hasn't just started, it's been going on for centuries. And maybe when they get grown things will be different, maybe they will be all equal.

I am thirty-two years old. My baby will be a year old this Sunday. My son, he's eleven, and I have a daughter seven, then I have another daughter be five in June, and this little girl, she will be four in August.

My kids are raised different from me in some ways. When I was a child coming up, my parents was very strict on me. I let my kids get away with some things I didn't get away with, little old misdemeanor things. Like if I did something wrong and I was told not to do it, I got a whipping about it, a spanking. Well, I warn mines. I say, "I told you not to do that. Now if you do it again, after I tell you not to do it, I'll spank you. When I tell you not to do something, it be for your best." Because, I make a parable; I say, for example, like, "If I tell you not to cross the street, and you go across the street, now you may cross the street and get hit by a car. See, you'd be disobeying me, and when you disobey me, something bad will happen to you." So I have them, you know, pretty well under control.

The small ones may do it again, but the large ones won't. Kids are kids, regardless, you know. I can't say, because if they get out from my presence, I don't know what they do. Because I can't notice, or follow them, every minute. But the two oldest ones, they're very reliable.

I have tried to give my kids the things that they need. The most important things. These are. . . . Clothing. A happy home. And understanding. And Love. I think that's the most important thing there is.

It's a lot of kids today, that if they have understanding of love, and know that their parents care for them, that they would be better. And the average teenager there today, if they had someone to really understand them, they would be better. Mostly everything that the teenagers today want to do, the adults are against it. And that confuses them, and they start rebelling. Of course, that's only one person's opinion about it; that's what I see.

For instance, now, the kids down here, if they want to go swimming, they have to go way across the expressway. On the walkway up above the street. Which is dangerous because someone may push them, anything may happen. They need swimming pools at the school. At each school.

I think it would be nice, too, if the Traffic Bureau would cooperate and put a light up here at the corner by the school. Because there's so many kids every year get hit by cars, and on the next corner, the same thing happens.

If there was a swimming pool, at the school, the school that's close in the neighborhood, it would give the kids something to do during the summer when school is out, other than that they be going to summer school. They won't be in the streets breaking glass and picking fights and things.

These kids get bottles and break them. And then you see the kids get cut bad, and you have got to call the police, carry them down to the hospital so they can get aid for their wounds. I think parents should spend more time with their kids and try to understand them. And to know mostly what the kids are doing.

And some, they don't do that, they don't have time for them. Most of the parents today, really truthfully speaking, they don't have time for their kids. They send their kids off, send them off on a neighbor or something, send them one way and they go another. The only thing they is out after is a good time. And you go and you confront them with what their kids has done, they say, "Oh, no, my child haven't did that. Why do you come to me first, how you know that was my child?"

You get a kid telling people to kiss his foot and all that. A woman's little boy told me that last year. I went and told her about it; she say, "My son didn't say that." I said, "I don't make a habit of lying on kids. I have kids myself. He *did* definitely tell me this."

I've lived here eleven years, and when I first moved over here it was very nice. But it is dropping down and down. Each year it gets worse. People come over; they don't live here; they come and drink. They leave their containers, with beer and all, they come by and they disrespect your kids. And it's bad.

As soon as I can get enough money saved, I will try to move to a nicer neighborhood, to raise my kids, because these people that come around here, they don't have any respect for the kids. Or the adults.

I tries to tell my children there are things they see people doing, that it's not nice. I says, "I don't want you to grow up to be like that. I want you to be respectable and intelligent. Intelligent people do not do things like that."

I tell them it takes all types to make a world. But I hope they choose to be something nice. Not nothing I would be ashamed of and they would be ashamed of.

And some of the womens around here are just as bad as the males. You know, you just be standing back and observing some of the things that go on, you wonder, what makes them do that? Why they do those things?

They got to know better. They may be sick to a certain extent. But everybody's supposed to have *some* pride and dignity.

☐   ☐   ☐

[*Do you think your kids will find money easier to earn than your generation?*]

I think so, yes. If they have the proper education and everything, I think it'll be much easier for them.

It's easier for us today than it was for our parents. Or our grandparents. My mother, she was a housewife. And my father used to work at the steel mill in Alabama.

I was born in Alabama. And I came to Detroit when I was eighteen. I got married to Will when I was seventeen. And we came here to better our condition. He heard if you come here you could get a better job than you had down there. At the time he was doing construction work.

In some ways we bettered our condition. I don't regret it. Of course, I still feel there is still a chance to progress.

[*Would people in the neighborhood find it easier to make money in Detroit if they were white?*]

According to what kind of education they had. Now, some jobs are prejudiced. There is some that will give a white man a job. If there's a Negro looking for one, he will give it to the white man before he give it to the Negro.

I know. I know cases where this have happened. I know one time since we been here we had to apply for welfare. We didn't have but one child. And my husband was walking on the street trying to get a job. And they was taking applications. And, the way they did, they would call all the white first. And what they had left, they would call the Negroes.

Rebecca Stone (II)

This neighborhood, it's a place that I really wouldn't like to raise my kids.

This winter, it would be a education, in a way, for a child that was old enough to understand and see. Everything is going on in the neighborhood.

Like I told you before, I been trying hard to find a better place to move to raise my kids. I have been successful some in trying to save something. I hope we can move before this summer. Unless there's something come up again and I won't be able to move. Because there is people that live around this vicinity that use dope. Not only smoke it, they take these LSD pills. Plus there is the people that are taking these shots. There is also pushers around here. Really. You name it, it's out there.

You name it, it's mostly out there, I tell you that. People that wasn't even involved with it last year—now this year they is on it. People that you know and I know, too.

The guy that was out there barbecuing the other day. When you looked out the window? Well, he use it.

They steal, they hold up people. Do whatever they can to supply heroin to themselves and push what they have. To me, now, that's a waste of life. Because undoubtedly, I think, a person that commit theirself to that kind of life, they would have to need help. They really would.

You haven't been out here on the weekend, you mostly come by during the week. The kids don't have any place to play out there. Everybody come from far and near to this corner, get to drinking and arguing. And the kids don't have no place to play unless I carry them to the park. Most of the time I be so busy trying to get through with my work it be too late to carry them to the park, and then come back and fix Will's lunch on time so he can take it to work, and fix their dinner.

[*What park?*]

There's a little park, a small one, about fifteen blocks from here.

[*Can you let your kids out, just outside here, to play?*]

Sometimes I do. Most of the time I be out with them when I let them out. Because each year it gets worse and worse.

You take last summer. I don't know whether you heard about the shooting out there. It was real hot. The kids were up late; I always let them stay up late on weekends. I have a large window fan, but it was too hot, so I had them sitting out there with me in the front, sitting with me on the porch steps. And I almost wound up getting shot.

One of these people, her and her man, they come out there, and they had a loaded shotgun, and they was having words. And I was sitting out there in front with my kids. And so when they started to arguing I started getting my kids together to get in the house. And the gun went off, and it was pointed at the sidewalk, and dirt and powder burns hit me in the face.

It's easy to get shot. Nobody was really hurt, but I had my baby in my arm at the time. Freak accidents like that, it could cost a life.

Now we wasn't bothering anybody, just out minding our own business. I remember eleven years ago, this place was much nicer than it is. It now seems everything drifting in. The landlords, I guess they get to the place where they don't care, they rent to anybody.

You know, the house across from Selena's burned up, half of it, and I thought the people would be moving away. But so far they still here and hasn't left yet.

[It seems, though, like there are fewer people than there were in the summer.]

But you know why? Because it's cold out there and they're not able to gang up. See, the main thing about it, if these people around here didn't associate with these riley people, they would stop coming. But, there's always somebody going to associate with them, because they figure there's somebody going to buy something to drink. Then there's a crowd and then they start drinking. And then arguing.

Hey, some of these people just come here and just *use* the Corner. The couple you were just talking to, they don't live around here, they live far west out there. But they came out here. They fixed themselves up a place to barbecue! And that's the way the rest of them is. They come and help themselves to what they want. And then they disrespect your kids.

And it really can create a problem. You know Cleveland, the tall fellow with the raincoat? And you know that he got killed, he got stabbed out there during the summer. That tall fellow who used to live next door one time. And he died after he got in the operating room, when they got him to the hospital.

And then for instance last year, I was giving Will a birthday party. And China and her man came, and her husband was there. He had a knife. And they acted like they were just drunk. But, you know, that ended in death.

I wasn't raised like this. I don't approve of my kids being raised like this.

I am used to being around nice, intelligent people. Now, you've heard these people saying that the worst place is Alabama. Well, my grandfather lived in Alabama. He was the one who partially raised me. And the white people that was around him, they always treated us nice, because he had been knowing them for quite some time. Most of them knew him when they was kids. And they respected him. And he respected them. Not up until I married and moved away did I experience the words of "nigger." The white people that lived down there, when we lived down there, they didn't use those kinds of words. But since I married and came here. . . .

Now, I will say, in my home town where I was born there was a lady. And some white mens came one day, one afternoon about sundown, and took her away. And the people found her the next morning in a small shallow stream. Her body was nude and she was dead, face down. But this has been since I moved away from there and I can't say exactly what is going on now because I wouldn't know.

But in the earlier years, it was nice there. The only thing that really happened that I was old enough to know about was when Emmet Till— Do you remember him, this little boy from Chicago that got killed? I wasn't there then either; I was living in the north end of Detroit at the time. And then, that was in Mississippi.

Now, my nephew, he lives in Alabama, still. And he was in a freedom march once, where brutality was. And he was injured; he was beaten with sticks by the policemen and some white people attacked him. But me, I never have been hit by no white person. And I never have hit a white person. I am the type that I figure if you are nice you can get along with anybody. As long as you treat them right. As long as you have a person that want to be nice.

A person that is violent, I understand there's no getting along. I look at it kind of like they are some kind of freak, the only way they can feel big and be seen is by the way they act. Like people say, it's an act of stupidity. That's what I think it is, too.

I know there are people who have been taught against the Negroes. And there are some Negroes have been taught fear against the white man. To me, way I see it, I see no difference. The only difference is his skin is lighter than mine. Because, underneath the skin, we both bleed blood, we have veins, we were made, we was created equal. And the same with a colored man and a white man. The only difference is just the skin. We give birth the same way and everything. Some of us have the same religion.

[*Did it seem strange when you moved to Detroit?*]

Yeah. There was a difference. For instance, the place was larger. This was the first time I had been out of Alabama and this was the largest city I had been to. And another difference was the way people talked. And the way they react.

I came with my husband so he could find a better job. They would pay more here than they would in the South.

[*Did that work out?*]

Yes. We've had out little ups and downs. Still and yet, there's something always happening. You make a plan, there's setbacks. You just can't let it get you down. You plan to do something, then you always wind up having to use the money for something else. Something else always comes up.

But there is a difference. I say there is a difference because in Alabama, at the time, white and coloreds wasn't going to school together. Well, here, at some schools, they do. And that was one difference. And here you could eat at the restaurants with the white people. In Alabama you couldn't.

But, I was fixing to say, as far as discrimination goes, well, that's here, too. Because there's people here which, you know, they hate Negroes. And they say their place supposed to be in Africa. Well, I was born in the United States. I don't know where my ancestors before me came from. But I was born in the United States and I figure this is where I should stay.

And I've heard people say that some places they went they call Negroes animals. They wasn't humans, they were animals. I think I read a book about slavery and hanging? I forget the name of the book, I bought it for a friend of mine. Where they hang this guy, I think it was in New York. And before they kill him, they cut out his . . . parts and put it in his mouth. And made him chew it. And then they hanged him, afterwards. And I read about hangings that happened in Alabama. Well, that was before my time. Because all this I'm speaking about now was before my time.

□   □   □

I'm thirty-three. I look older than I am because you know, I'm overweight and then, too, I'm having my teeth extracted. Since I started having my teeth extracted, to me I look about twenty years older than I did beforehand.

I started last summer. I thought I would have them all pulled by now but I wasn't that lucky. As I say, when you plan something, something always stop it. I plan to have the rest of them extracted, replaced, this summer.

[*What do you do for fun? Everytime I see you, you have all your children around.*]

Well, that's most of the time. I spend a lot of time with my kids. Very seldom do I go out. Oh, I go out in the summer sometime. You know, I be out front then, talking with my friends and sometime they may come on in.

Very seldom I go out to parties. Don't go out to clubs or anything because. . . . Actually I don't have the money to spare for baby-sitters. And most of the time when I go I carry my kids with me. But I play cards. I like to go play cards. And sometimes we play dominoes.

[*Yes . . . now, are you going to have more children?*]

No! No, I have enough. I did want two sons. But now? I have four girls in a row. I give up. Nooo.

[*You got something to keep you from having them?*]

Oh, yes. From the Planned Parenthood. I have birth control pills. That way as long as I take them, I know nothing will happen.

[*Did you just start that after the baby?*]

I was on once before and I gained a lot of weight and I got off. And I was off two years before I got pregnant. And I got pregnant again. So this time—weight or no weight, that's it! Better to have the weight than having other kids when you're not able to do for them. I think every kid deserves a good life.

[*I tell you what let's do. This wouldn't have interested me 'till I had to start cooking for my kids. Tell me this, what do you feed the children, breakfast, lunch, dinner?*]

What do I feed my children for breakfast? Mostly grits, bacon and eggs, toast or either biscuit, and milk or juice, one. And for lunch they would probably have fried chicken and rice. Some type of vegetable.

Every meal we have meat. And I like to feed my kids green vegetables.

[*Do they eat them?*]

Yeah. Way I fix them. Spinach with turnips and mustard—and they are good. At first they wouldn't eat it 'cause I used to just fix it, the spinach, boiled.

Sometime I take the spinach and wash them and take these green onions and chop them up real good and I put in about two tablespoons of butter. And let the onions simmer. About ten minutes. Then I add the spinach to them. And they're good.

They're actually not too funny; the kids mostly eat everything. But they don't care too much about dried beans and nothing like that. The only dried beans that they'll eat are pinto beans. Sometimes I fix them with tomato. They like it with something like a chili with tomato sauce. And sometimes I fix them neck bones. They eat those. Ham hocks. Then cut an onion up in it, then add a can of tomato paste. Let it cook good. They like corn bread, too.

Tonight for supper I haven't planned. I don't know whether we're going to have pork chops and mashed potatoes or what. Something quick, because I didn't put anything on to boil today.

Will Stone

Why do I live here? Because I can't do no goddamn better. That good enough? But I sure ain't going to live here long. For damn sure I have got to move.

They are going to condemn this place. and it ain't going to take them too long. There's rats here, man. There's a rat hole up in the kitchen ceiling, there's one in the bathroom floor, and there's one right behind the couch.

They are going to condemn this place. And it ain't going to take them too long. There's rats here, man. There's a rat hole up in the kitchen ceiling, there's one in the bathroom floor, and there's one right behind the couch.

I just came back right now from looking for a house. And I'm fixing to go again. We looked through real estate, finance, every damn thing. You name it, I'm trying it.

[*Will, how old are you?*]

Forty-three. Forty-three last Friday.

[*Happy birthday. How long you been out here?*]

At the job I am at now? Five years; going on five years, at Rawson-Monroe. A janitor. At least I was a janitor up until last week. Now I'm working in stock, and I make a little bit more. Janitor wages is at a hundred and seven dollars a week. Now I'm driving the Hi-Lows. When I was janitoring, I was sweep, mop, do anything that go in the janitor line.

Now I got to get money for a down payment somehow. Some way I have got to get about three hundred and fifty dollars. Bit by bit try to save it up, find somewhere to save it up, that's all.

[*Is there any saved now?*]

Eight dollars, I think. I'm paying on the TV, that's forty a month or fifty. I'm not paying on anything else, I don't have a car, never could afford one. I mean I could afford one, I just didn't. . . . The money goes. Insurance, rent, groceries, you know, with five kids. And I usually take two or three days off a month.

The only thing I can see is start saving about fifty dollars a week. At least twenty-five.

[*Could you make more money at another job?*]

Yeah. Oh yeah, I could make more money. But I mean, when I got five years at Rawson's why should I throw my seniority away up there and get another job?

[*What good does seniority do you?*]

A lot. Like I mean, as long as there is a plant there, I can work. But I can get out here and get me a job today, and they take and lay off, I'd be the first man laid off tomorrow. Understand what I mean? I be lost *that* job *and* this one here.

I like the job. I like everything about it. Janitoring is one of the best jobs in the world. I near about have my own way, I'm my own boss. I'm working four o'clock to twelve-thirty. . . . But you know, I'm a worried bastard right now.

[*Will, what do you do for pleasure in your life?*]

Nothing. Don't have no pleasure.

Don't have no pleasure. Get drunk, that's about the only pleasure I can have. One day just like another, all of them the same.

Get up, go to work. That's about the size of it. Plain old day routine. Get up, go out, bullshit with the fellows, get a couple of drinks, come on back, and get ready and go to work. That's about the size of it. Come home at night, go to bed, get up 'bout nine-thirty, ten o'clock, same thing all over again.

I got a whole lot of things I hope for. But—hoping and getting is different. But right now, I'm trying to look for another place to stay. The biggest question right now is that. Right there. After then, I may be looking for a whole lot different. But right now—

I can make the monthly, if I can get the down payment. I know I can save it. But the idea is having somewhere to stay until I *can* save it. I ain't got the notice, but—it's going to be condemned. That's what the landlord say. The landlord, Houston, he's colored, he own this building and the one across the street. They got so damn many violations against it, they going to have to—you know, he ain't able to keep them up. So they're just going to condemn it. The Health Department been here two or three times.

The only thing I can do is go on and save me twenty-five dollars a week 'til I can . . . I mean, I . . . Hell, by the first of June, I get a vacation pay anyhow, about three hundred and seven dollars. This here the end of March. So if I could just stay somewhere until then. Understand what I mean?

[*Could you stay with relatives?*]

Yeah. There are relatives. I can always find somewhere to stay. But I mean, still, me and my wife and kids, I want something that's— *Damn* the relatives and anybody else, just go on after myself! You understand my point of view? I ain't *never* been a man that believe in staying on somebody and don't pay my own damn way! That's all.

You can *find* plenty of houses, what the hell. Hell, you just moving out of one dump into another. At least you should better yourself one degree or the other.

I wish to hell I'd have been in your shape when I went out there to see that little fellow at the finance company. I've owed a goddamn bill ever since nineteen fifty-six. Something like ninety dollars, on account of a radio and TV. That's the only thing kept me from getting the money.

I say the hell with it. I don't care too much about dealing with finance noways. You never will get the interest paid. Take you from now on to pay the interest. Never will get the principal paid. Three hundred and fifty dollars? Damn, you *never* would get it up.

Well, I'm going to try to find me somewhere to go, man. I mean, I can't buy right now, no. But I got to find somewhere to move 'til I can save more. A place to rent. It's necessary. We got to. I ain't got enough to buy right now. But he told me he's gonna condemn them.

The landlord, he say, there's so many violations, he has got to nail it up. He don't know when. He say it needs more money than he getting out of the place. He ain't made no money off the deal. You're in the hole on these places. People come in and move out owing him a whole lot of money. Hell, he can't make money on places like this.

Well, let me go now. Let me go. I'm going out to look for a place. Somewhere.

Goddamn if I know. Look every damn where, I think. Only thing I can say is, where the hell the money to get me one?

But, well . . . you rent a place, it ain't going to cost you but sixty-five dollars a month. That's with light and gas. If you can *find* one with kids. You understand what I'm talking about? *If* you can find one with kids.

Rebecca Stone (III)

Some years you progress and there's some, regardless what you do to try to get ahead, it's always something come up that will pull you right back to where you started. I have experienced these things up from nineteen fifty-eight up until now, off and on.

Everything is running smooth and all of a sudden something happens, either your husband get laid off or something, that puts you in a rut, makes you fall right down it. Then again, it could be one of the kids up and gets sick. That's a lot of worry and unhappiness. There's a lot of things that can happen make you unhappy.

Then, there's the other times. When everything is running smooth.

The kids happy and healthy and well. Your husband, he happy, and you happy, and he's trying to progress. And, you know, I couldn't think of anything that would make anybody happier. You know, have your health and everything. It would mean a lot.

That's the way life is. Changes. God didn't promise that every day would be fine. You have to put up with, you have to accept, the bad with the good. People say, life is what you make out of it. No. Maybe to some people it is. But a lot of things in life you have to accept it as it comes.

I remember a time in nineteen fifty-eight in November. My husband, he was laid off. He was working at Connor Bakery on the Avenue, and the place went out of business. And he drew his compensation out. He got his last check, and we went to apply to welfare for him. And we didn't have nothing in the refrigerator but one cabbage. And Raymond, he was a baby then, he was about a year and a half.

And we had about one can of milk and about two jars of food. So we went to the Welfare and asked for help. Then they told us, before they could help us out, they gave him a list of the things that they wanted him to bring. So I had to call my auntie long distance to get a copy of our marriage certificate, because when we were staying on the North End it got misplaced.

Anyway, we got it. But the main thing, we had two more weeks to go, that's when they gave him an appointment to bring these things back in; we were waiting on the certificate and we didn't have anything. And he went to the Veterans' Administration. Well, they wanted proof that he'd been married. So he turned around, he told them, "Well, I'm not married, sir, I am single." So he got forty dollars from them. So that's the way we was able to get enough food, some money for food to carry us until we was able to apply for welfare.

There have been some tight squeezes for us, but mostly we've managed to get along until we can do better. Then I maybe could add that that is one thing that might help to keep a family together sometime. If they stick together and don't pull apart from each other. It helps, you know, if both be understanding.

I guess, in a way, when things are bad, it is more pressure on my husband than it is on myself, because he are the provider, the one that provides for us. And sometimes I get depressed and I start complaining to him about the things that I don't think that he's doing, necessarily, that could help some. Then again a woman must show when they is worried more than a man would. I know when he got laid off here and he told me that it would be four weeks before he got a compensation, I was wondering. Because he didn't have but one check to pick up when he came back. How in the world we was going to make it? With these five kids to feed and everything. But, so far, we did pretty good. We have came this far and nothing happen.

[*How* did *you make it?*]

Well, I managed to skimp. Where I was cooking two or three items for one meal, I would cut down on it. And on the breakfast meats, where I was giving them meats, well, I cut down on that. Where I would give them grits and eggs. Now, for instance, when I had them for breakfast yesterday morning the only thing they had before they went to school was just some grits. Which I thought they was going to complain about it. But they didn't complain. They ate them and went on to school.

And I had to cut the milk, you know, and their juice. And all those things that in general they be getting. I can't afford them now. And so far, they've been pretty understanding about it. They haven't complained too much. Because they know their daddy's laid off from work and everything. Most of the time, when they get out of school, they generally be looking for money to spend; they may complain a little then. But about the food, they haven't been complaining too much.

[*Did you have some cash saved up?*]

No. The only thing I had saved up was seven dollars in the bank.

On this last check that he got, he gave me ninety dollars. And I owed a girlfriend of mine ten dollars that I had borrowed from her. So at home I just managed to skimp, and save, and do the best I could.

So I was telling myself, by the time I be wanting something special, a steak or a roast or something, I just say, "Awww, so what the heck! It's only food." I say to myself, "If I can get *beans*, I can get myself to be just as *full* as if I have a steak."

Well, we made it so far. We made it this far. We got to make it the rest of the way. My husband has to pick up a compensation check Tuesday. There is a possibility that he will be called into work sometime next week.

Last year, we thought we'd be all right, but he got his foot broke. The workman's compensation, they sent him one check. Then the guy came out and said he wasn't eligible for it, that he had to get it straightened out with the other insurance.

Anyway, there we were then. We didn't have any food. The day the check was supposed to come, we borrowed ten dollars from the guy downstairs, thinking the check would be here. And it didn't come the next day, and we had to go and apply to Welfare for help. Then he had to go and get papers making a statement that his foot was broke and everything and what had happened. This other insurance company hadn't ever paid out. So we stayed on welfare until he was able to go back to work.

That was in July. We had to wait six weeks, it was about the twenty-first day of September when he started back to work. And so that time we was getting food orders from the welfare and they was paying our rent. He got called back to work then.

But that was quite some time, you know. There was Christmas coming up and everything. It was quite some time before we could manage to try to get back on our feet where we were before he got hurt. And during that time, too, my baby she was in the hospital, she had three spinal taps. She stayed in there a week.

They said they never did find out what was wrong. There was nothing wrong with her spine, she wasn't a victim of epilepsy or nothing like that. And after that they had me to bring her back for EKG and so they took that and it came out negative. . . . And I really had my share of ups and downs.

☐ ☐ ☐

And my oldest girl, when she was fourteen months old, she had chicken pox plus she had bronchitis and she was in the hospital. When she was in the hospital the bronchitis turned into pneumonia and she stayed in there fourteen days. Out at Pasteur Medical in the contagious building.

She was sick when I carried her to the doctor. I didn't know. I carried her to Lister Main. And they told me to carry her to Pasteur Medical. Said, what did I want to do, start an epidemic of the chicken pox? I didn't know, because I hadn't experienced that before. And I didn't know where to carry her to. So that's what they told me at the admitting desk at Lister. And they told me how to get out to Pasteur, so I carried her out there. And the doctor told me that she was very sick at the time. She got okay, but she was out there for fourteen days.

And my second little girl, she had two major operations, plus, she got bit by a rat when she was three weeks old. When she was five weeks old, she had her first operation. She was born with her ovary wrong. Then when she was two and a half, she had her second operation, because on the other side her ovary came down and they operated. Then she was anemic once. They gave her blood from Friday until Tuesday. Plus, plasma too.

But, my son, I never had no trouble. Except he fell and hurt hisself one time. That was last summer, too.

[*These operations and things like that—who pays for the hospital?*]

Well, the first one she had, we was on welfare. And the second one, he had the insurance and that covered it. Up here where my husband worked, they covered that. When she was anemic she stayed in the hospital a long time, I think about three weeks. Her hospital bill, it was eleven hundred and forty-seven dollars, and the insurance paid it all except fifty-eight dollars, and we paid that. They did a bone marrow test, I don't know what that consist of, but anyway one test was fifty-eight dollars, with the lab and everything, and we had to pay for that because when they turned it in, they didn't say whether she was in the hospital as a patient or whether she was a out patient. And so the insurance didn't pay for that. We had to pay for that.

I have had my share of ups and downs. It's all through life. And you still have them. I have found there is more bad days than there is good days.

□   □   □

Now, I do not have relatives around here. My husband, he have a brother that lives nearby, and he have a cousin. That's all the people he has here.

We came here in nineteen fifty-five. Will came here in July, I came in August. We was married about a year and a half before he come here to get work.

When I came up from Alabama, I was eighteen. I would not like to go back there and live. If I had to, I could. But what would I want to go back down there for?

The South is different. Especially when it come to work. Plus, there was segregation everywhere. And they always gave the worst thing to the Negroes. They wouldn't allow the Negro to go in the diner and eat. If they served you, they'd have a back window that you went to. They would serve you from there, but other than that they didn't allow you in the establishment. In a lot of ways, there's a difference in the Southern life.

Now, as far as violence with any white people or anything like that, no. The ones that I knew, I respected them and they respected me.

[*When you were little, did you pay attention to segregation? Did it matter to you?*]

No, I was raised there, you know, and brought up. And I knew, of course, there was a difference. See, my mother and father was separated when we was very young, and our grandparents raised us. And the place we was raised was in the country. And the white people, they was nice to us. On Christmas, there was a couple that didn't have any kids, and their last name was Farmer, and we used to call them Mr. and Mrs. Farmer. Well, they would give us gifts every Christmas. They came out there. And every time, my grandfather probably would give them some beef or pork, because he raised all that himself.

And there in Wheeler County, there wasn't any difference. But after I moved from Wheeler County and started going to school in Hershey, that's in Henderson County, where my mother had remarried and was living, I noticed a big difference. The white people that I knew in Tysonville, which is in Wheeler County, they was more friendly than the ones that was in Hershey. But my mother, she had quite a few white friends in Hershey. Later she was very sick, and they came to see us, sent get-well cards and flowers, and some gave her money.

But everywhere you go there is some nice white people and there is some. . . . But, that goes for the Negro race, too. There is some nice colored people and there is some that's not . . . so nice.

But speaking about working, you'll make more here than you would if you was in the South. Because there's a lot of places down there that don't have any unions, and if you inquire about the unions, they will fire you.

Then, too, you have your equal rights about voting here and everything, but you don't have that in the South. And that means a lot.

For instance, if we had a candidate running like President Kennedy. And he was for the poor people, and the Negroes. And the colored people down there wasn't allowed to vote for him. Well, here I was allowed to vote. And things like that mean a *lot*.

Now, housing up here is hard. It definitely is. The Negroes have to pay more rent here than the whites. If a white moved out of a building, where they may be paying about thirty or forty dollars a month, they redecorate the building and everything and rent it out to a Negro. If they was charging the whites forty dollars a month, they will charge the Negro eighty dollars a month. That's right.

Then, too, I have read about where they have let Negroes buy in these nice places. Negroes that had enough money to. Well, some of the whites will put their places up for sale and move out. There is some that will adjust, and there is some that never will. There is some that go on hating the Negroes for the balance of their life.

[. . . *Do your kids run into discrimination?*]

No. The school that they go to, they don't have any problem. They are treated equal. The same lesson that they give to the white kids, they'll give it to the colored.

Now the school that I attended, the elementary school that I attended in Tysonville, you should have seen it. It wasn't nothing but no more than a vacant four-room house. That's all it was. And it didn't have electrical wiring in it. That is for real. And they would not fix the road so that the school bus could get from the main road over to the schoolhouse. So I would fall into the mud, walking from the schoolhouse onto the school bus.

Then after I got out of elementary school and started going to high school, well, the whites had more convenient things. They had opportunities to have better books and everything. For instance, like the books that they had used, some of them they would give to the colored. But if not, most of the time we would have to *buy* our books where the whites got theirs free. And that made a difference.

[*Did you think anything about it at the time?*]

Yes. I thought that they had it easier than we did. A lot of times, we would have to work for the money to get our books in order to go to school. And there was a tuition fee that we had to pay. My three sisters and myself, we had to pay twenty-two dollars and fifty cents in tuition fees. That was once a year. But I was thinking all the time that the public schools supposed to be free, but we had to pay that. And if you weren't able to pay it all at once you had to pay for it so much longer 'til you got it paid. Or else you wouldn't be able to get your report card.

The schools here, most of them teach Afro-American history. When I was going to school, they didn't teach me anything about that. Where you'd only read about something in the history what some white person did, you have a chance now to read in the history about something that a Negro have did. And that means a lot. Because to me, the way I see it, that we are being recognized now as much as a white person, in some ways. The colored person, he wasn't otherwise anything that was important then, because didn't nobody care enough to try to write anything about us. And now today, they have an Afro-American museum, they working on that, and the art, they have that. When I was coming along, you didn't know anything about that.

[*Do you think your kids will grow up with more pride?*]

I think so. And I think that it will give them courage. Because they will see there's not just white persons that's went and gone ahead; there is Negroes, too, that have got ahead. That can give them more real confidence and determination to go on and try to select and to be what they want to be. After all, if someone was successful before them—

[*Well, what about good times; what do people do to have a good time?*]

Well, for good times we may go fishing. First, you know, we may have a picnic, or either we would fish and then later we may go to the picnic tables and have dinner. Jackie Rahlins and her husband John and his kids and Will, myself, and our kids. And quite often we go to ballgames. And we go to a few shows together, card parties, different things like that. I likes to play poker, but it's been quite some time; it's been over a year. And sometimes, as I said, I drink occasionally. Not every day, but just to be sociable.

You remember the time that they raided that party over here, and they took everyone to jail? Well, I always am saying to Will, "Oh, every time the party starts getting good, you always force me to leave." So, he had made me leave that party before the police came. And the next morning after it was all over, I said, "I really am grateful that you *did* keep on getting me to leave."

And they used to have a softball team. I used to watch them play ball. They used to play back of the schoolhouse; we used to go there on Sunday afternoon. And then sometime Will and Mr. Wainwright, they get the kids together and go swimming. And that gives me some relaxation because I have a chance to be free to relax without being bothered with the kids. He don't do that too often, and when he do, I really appreciate it.

The kids get to bed, mostly through the week, about nine-thirty. After I get them to bed, I generally wash dishes and clean the kitchen, and then come in here and sit down. Look at a story or a couple of stories until Will get off from work. Because, when he's working, very seldom I go to bed before he gets in. I always stay up. He come home and then we sit up and generally watch *The Texan* together on Channel Seven. I think they come on about one o'clock.

And I like to play Monopoly and different games. I never have shot dice, but I certainly have played cards.

nathan coolidge

Nathan, former Golden Gloves boxer, former Marine, truck driver, and warehouse worker, grew up in Detroit. He enjoys confrontation; I once saw him face down a man with a knife. He has had five children.

The first of the following two discussions took place over a long, hot, June afternoon. I had picked Nathan up at his frame house some miles north of the Corner. We drove to the Corner and sat in the car, watching the day and chatting. Then we drove through the city, passing through scenes of Nathan's childhood neighborhood. Eventually we picked up his uncle and talked at the uncle's house.

The second interview took place in the spring several years later. I had become suspicious of my interviewing strategy. I had determined to ask respondents to be more responsible about deciding what material should be presented to the white reading public.

Nathan Coolidge (I)

I can give you a story. My life. Starting when I was a little kid, going on about three or four years old. I was living in the area around Hastings. Hastings was the worst street in Detroit. They still got prostitutes over there now, in the old condemned houses. I used to go down Hastings, them prostitutes used to get kids, nine, ten years old, they'd get them to go down to the five-and-ten-cent-store, and have them to stealing perfume and lipstick, little cheap perfume, go down and steal a batch, they'd give us a quarter for it. 'Til my father found out I skipped school stealing it. That was the last time.

We can talk. I ain't doing nothing today, just sitting around. That's all we'll be doing all day. Sitting around, seeing the guys, having a drink. I don't go to work 'til six.

[*You never have got much concerned with liquor, have you?*]

Oh, no, no. I just drink on the weekend. During the week I drink a beer or a shot or something.

I never have drank to any extent. I remember when I was seventeen years old, couple of older guys messing around with a little dope. And that started getting me in trouble. I couldn't work, I couldn't get the money to take care of that habit.

I kicked that. I never was a big drinker. I smoke a pack of cigarettes in about two and a half days. My wife, she has sometimes two packs every day. She can't understand I can have a pack of cigarettes for three days. I never had no habit. When I drink a beer or something, I want a cigarette.

[*This corner . . . would you bring a kid up on this corner?*]

No! Houses condemned. Rats in the walls, dying between the walls, smelling.

We just saving and saving. My wife had been married once before, and I had been married once before. This is both of our second marriages. She had three kids of her own. And since we been together we got twins about a year old now. Twin boys.

And I had two kids by my first wife. I'm trying to get them now. I'm in court. They want to live with me. They don't want to live with my first wife. They want to live with me.

I've been having a whole lot of trouble in courts. She had me locked up three weeks ago. The wife I got now, she come down and put up four hundred dollars and got me out. Back child support, you know. Like I told her, I'm not going to pay no more money, therefore, I'm going to wind up right back in jail.

If she'll give me my kids, I'll continue to pay her the money. And I'll keep the kids. And I told her, I'll pay her the money. If she give me my kids. But she won't. So I told her I ain't going to pay her nothing, 'cause they don't want to live with her. I feel as though a child's not going to be happy, he's not going to be raised properly, if he's some place he don't want to be. You know what I'm talking about?

My oldest boy, he ran away again night before last. His stepfather had slapped him.

He hits them. He kicks them around. He took his foot and stomped the youngest one. He's eleven. He had his back turned to the oldest when he was stomping the youngest one, and the oldest one hit him in the head with a bottle. Then the man turned around and starting beating the oldest one.

And both of them, sooner or later, they'll kill him. And I tried to tell the people down at juvenile court. "Only thing I can see, the best thing I can see, is you to give them to me. To save you people from trouble in later years, and save me some trouble, and to save my son, you know, from ruining his life."

[*What kind of man is this, the second husband?*]

I don't know the guy. I went to try to talk to him about three weeks ago. That's when they put me on this peace bond. I went over there, knocked on the door, just to talk, you understand, to find out what's going on. He want to tell me a bunch of stuff, and jumped and tried to pull my pistol. I had to pull my pistol and make him get himself together. Then after I let him go—I didn't want to shoot him—when I let him go, him and her went to the office to go get a peace bond on me. I went over there too, I went over to the police officers, I told it to the police officers. I had my pistol with me, I brought it over there this morning, I don't carry it around the Corner.

I went over there to talk with him. He works for the city. He's a little short fat guy. But I never did get to talk to him, he never did let me get to talk to him. I might would have had to shoot him if it don't be for my first wife. She told him, she said, "Bill, he's got a gun! He's got a gun!" Just like that. When she said that I pulled it out. And she jumped in between me and Bill. She was actually in between us, I didn't point it even, because I was fit to shoot him then. Right at that instant I would have shot him. I would have shot him. Because I came there with all intentions of talking to him like two grown men are supposed to talk and get an understanding. Without fisticuffs. Like I said, two intelligent people supposed to be able to sit down, get a problem solved without killing each other. You know what I mean. But this guy, he wouldn't accept it.

I only seen him three times. Me and my wife, we been separated since nineteen sixty-three. We divorced in nineteen sixty-six. All that time, up until last week, I don't think I saw her ten times. I just don't go around. I figure if I don't go around, there don't be no misunderstandings. I don't have no feelings for the woman. She don't want me, she probably have the same feelings toward me. So if you don't associate with each other you don't run into each other.

□ □ □

Now, when I came this morning, I brought my little pistol. Put it up this morning over at Wainwright's, bring it there and knock on the door. Because you never know. You know Haskell, he lives around here. Just like Haskell now. He's the kind of guy, he would have a pistol, he would take advantage of you. He tried to take advantage of me once over here. He tried to take advantage of me once. And ever since then, when I come, I bring my pistol and I carry it to Wainwright's house. Carry it right there, and give it to him or his wife. Then, when something like that happens, it don't take me but a minute to go get myself together.

I've been coming back and forth around this corner about eight years, maybe nine years. What brought me around here was one of my good friends was living around here. Used to live a block down. Well, me and him went to school . . . in fact we used to box together down at Brewster. We was on the same boxing team.

[*You went pretty far in boxing, didn't you?*]

Yeah, I boxed in the Marines. I was heavyweight champion one time, of the outfits where we were stationed. I fought Golden Gloves, too. I did good here in Detroit. That was in fifty-seven, fifty-eight. I left and went in the Marine Corps. When I came out, I was too old for Golden Gloves, I messed around down at different gyms. Every now and then I used to go down to King Solomon's, fight down there. One of the boys that started out with me, Bull Lemon, you probably heard of him. You see signs around about him. He is about the number four contender now. Bull Lemon. Only thing that messed him up, he got in some trouble and hurt a guy.

Me and him started in, started together, at Brewster Center. We used to walk up and down the street, feet on the ground, holes in our pants . . . Bull Lemon. With our noses snotty.

□ □ □

[*Yeah . . . what kind of home did you come out of, Nathan?*]

Well, my home that I come from, my family, was alright. My father, he worked all the time two jobs. He been now working for the City of Detroit about thirty-one years. He's head mechanic at Fourteenth, the garage there. He's the head mechanic. And he always did work two jobs up until about a year ago he got kind of down. He worked two jobs about thirty-five years. He got down, his stomach, with ulcers in it. So, he stop working the two jobs. Because he was a truck driver in the daytime and work mechanic for the city at night.

We lived in the projects. We lived in the project from around forty-five until fifty-five. My father bought a home on the East Side, and we moved out of the projects. That's the only place we lived, those two places, until I was grown. My father and mother still live there. Got two little sisters there now, so actually I've got four sisters and a brother.

My brother, he comes around here every now and then. He's younger than I am. My brother is about twenty-four, about twenty-five, he got a wife and six kids and one on the way.

He can't seem to keep a job. He got fired at Chrysler, he got fired at Ford's. I don't even know whether he's working now.

[*Well, you like that job you've got now.*]

At FoodMaster? At the warehouse? It's a good job. I like that.

[*How much do you make an hour?*]

I make right around three eighty, three ninety because I'm on afternoons; I get the afternoon premium and everything. For forty hours I get home with about a hundred fifteen, a hundred twenty dollars, after everything is taken out. Of course, I don't claim any of my kids. I don't claim no dependents. I wait 'til the end of the year and I always get a big income-tax check back. That way, I don't owe the government, they always owe me.

It's about the best job that I've had in my life besides a truck driver. I used to drive a semi, drive a semi for Boheyn Manufacturers. I didn't like that because it kept me away from home too much.

[*But when you say it's a good job at FoodMaster, what makes it good?*]

What I find makes a job good is the hours that I have to work and the people that I work with. In the whole warehouse where I'm at, there's only two Negroes there. There's one on afternoons and one on days. And, usually, in a place like that, you'd normally have a rough time, you'd always wind up with the worst jobs, and things like that. But as a matter of fact, it's just like, you got a job to do, and another guy is working, he gets finished with his job, he comes over and give you a hand, and it's just a nice atmosphere.

It's a nice atmosphere. Everybody treats you just like they want to be treated. Nobody tries to be better than you or more than you, or anything like that, you know what I'm driving at. . . .

[*You have worked at the plant also, right?*]

Yeah, I used to work at Ford. I got a lawsuit against Ford's now. I'm suing Ford. I got ran over out there with a high-low. I had nine years' seniority at Ford. Haven't been out there now in about eighteen months. Fact, I'm looking for my workmen's compensation.

[*On the accident?*]

For my workmen's compensation the whole time I was off. They got to pay me for that, I didn't draw any money on it.

[*Even though you were working there at the warehouse?*]

Well, I just got this job at FoodMaster about a month ago.

[*Were you out of work in between?*]

I was out of work all the time in between there. I worked a couple of odds and ends in another name, another name and another social security number. I haven't been back in no other plant no more. 'Cause I can't do no extreme lifting.

They want to operate on my back now. I got three ruptured discs in my back. They want to operate on it, but just like I say, that back ain't bothering me and I'm not going to bother it. They just saw that on X-ray. But until it hurts me, then I'm not gonna bother it. . . .

[*Were you laying off because you wanted to?*]

Laying off from work? No. I would line up work for two or three factory relief jobs, and they kept turning me down. The doctors would turn me down. They wouldn't let me pass that physical. So I messed around and messed around, and I . . . just gave it up.

And accidentally I was down into the whiskey store right down there on Kotlus, across the freeway bridge. I was down there, I went in the store and got a pint of whiskey. There was a guy sitting in the car, just like you're sitting, two of them was set in the car, they kept looking, and I was looking at them. And I had my pistol in my pocket, and the guy say, "Hey! Come here!" Just like that. I walk around by the side of my car, say, "Yeah, what you want?" "Come here a minute." Well, I thought they was police. And I say, "Well, come here for what?" They say, "Come here, I want to talk to you for a minute." Well, I thought they was police. I didn't want to go over there.

And I walked back around the other side of my car and I eased my pistol out of my pocket and dropped it in the grass. And I walked over there. He asked me, "Say, you got a job?" Me and my brother-in-law was together. And I said, "No, I don't have a job." Said, "You want a job?" Then I didn't know what to say, because I was trying to figure who he was. They looked like police, you know, two guys sitting up in suits, white shirts and everything, and clean-cut, and everything. I didn't know what to do, I didn't know whether to talk to them. I said, "Yeah, I want a job." He told me, he said, "Get in the car."

I said, "Look here, man, get in the car for what?" I said, "I ain't broke no law," I say, "What you want to do?" I thought they was just fucking around. And he told me who he was and everything, and I said, "Okay." So we got in the car, and they backed up and turned around, and went back down to the warehouse general offices, and give us a little IQ test. Fill out the application, they give us a little test. And they sent us over for a physical, and the doctor passed me. Gave me the job.

I wasn't even looking for a job. I had gave it up. And they don't know I started to run when they called me. Because I had that pistol.

[*Yeah. Well, what did you live on in between?*]

In between? Well, my wife works. See, my wife, she's RN. She worked, and then I hustled quite a bit. Me and a friend of mine had a little blind pig over there on John R. I could pick up about a hundred fifty, two hundred dollars on Friday, Saturday night.

And my brother, he was working. He would come by in between; my wife didn't get paid but every two weeks, so he'd come by in between and drop five dollars, ten dollars on me, I could buy my gas and cigarettes with. I could always go to my father and get a few dollars.

I had more money then, when I wasn't working, then I do when I'm working. I managed to keep money every day just about, in my pocket. When I'm working, I can't manage to keep nothing.

[*Yeah. You made more just on liquor than you're making working. And you weren't working but a couple of nights then.*]

That's right. Just Friday and Saturday night. . . . Biggest liquor sale right here on this corner, Mr. Wainwright over there, Sunday morning. He pick up fifty to a hundred dollars on Sunday morning. Can't buy in the store then. Get him a few cases of wine, few cases of whiskey. Ain't no problem making no money right around here. Stores not open, the guys don't want to go to Canada, you go to jail. I went over there and bought some and went to jail over there myself. Selena had to come and get me out.

[*Well, what do you think of the work in the plant? How's that strike you?*]

The plant? I don't like it. It's too fast and they expect too much. Production is set at one thing, and when you start making that, the next thing you know, they send a time study man down on you, and then they giving you some more.

They always fix it where you are steady doing this same movement. I left out at Ford Motor Company so tired, I left there so tired, I got to the parking lot out to the plant, set in my car, in the wintertime, and start it up, and doze off to sleep right there in the parking lot. Woke up, and the guys was coming out for lunch. That's how tired I've been at Ford's.

That Rouge plant, that Dearborn assembly . . . work you to death out there! I seen a guy sit on a box and died! Right on the assembly line, right on back on side of the line. Had a heart attack and died. And they didn't stop that line either. Put him off that box and laid him on the floor, covered him up with some paper. Kept that line running.

[*When you were working there what kind of money would you bring in during the year?*]

During the year? I would make around . . . the most I've ever made at Ford's was about nine thousand dollars. You got some guys, the repairmans and things like that, they get up in the bracket of around ten five, maybe eleven thousand. But the time they're doing . . . they're working seven days, and they working ten hours, eleven hours, sometimes twelve hours, stuff like that. . . . Actually, work straight forty hours a week, the best you get home with would be about . . . much as you'd make in a year would be around five thousand dollars.

Five, maybe six at most. If you do a lot of overtime. But actually, working right on the assembly line, there's not too much overtime you can do. Because after eight hours, you're beat. After eight hours, you dragging, you can't hardly stand up.

I tell you another strange guy, that was Haskell. Now, what he would do, Haskell would go somewhere and have a job and and work midnights. He wouldn't work days, and he wouldn't work afternoons. And he around the street, walking around the street, and nobody would think Haskell had a job. He been working out at Ford's about three years.

Me and him ran around the street together every day. Ran around the street and drank together, messed around together *every* day in the week, and I didn't know he had a job! His *mother* didn't even know he had a job. And then one day I happened to accidentally run into him out to the plant, you know. He's working over in the stamping plant, and he was going on midnights, and I happened, I happened . . . I was walking through the stamping plant to go see my brother, and I saw Haskell and he tried to duck, but it was too late. I saw him, you know. I figured he was the one that . . . Hell, Haskell walking around here, every time you see him he'd have a hundred fifty, two hundred dollars in his pocket, and . . . wasn't working, you know? But Haskell *was* working. *Every day.* And he let me in on the secret, you know.

[*Well, that's something that struck me, on the Corner, you know, that people can know each other very well, and then really not know where the other guy lived or what he did.*]

That's right. Actually they don't even ask questions. You don't even ask questions. You come on the Corner, they accept you.

[*You know, I got a lot of questions. . . . Like: are people happy? Take men, take women. Who's happy here? They really happy?*]

They happy.

[*How much sorrow is concealed behind that?*]

These people right here, let me tell you something about these people: long as the rent is paid, they got a couple pieces meat in the refrigerator, five dollars, at least about five dollars so they can buy a drink, pack of cigarettes . . . they're satisfied. They don't care nothing about no lot of money and Cadillacs and new homes and furniture and stuff like that. Don't care about that. Leave them alone, they'll leave you alone. That's right. They happy. They don't worry about nothing else.

Now, me, I always wanted to own my own property, you know, always wanted to *own* my own property. Now, when I was living over here I never did hardly hang around on the corner. Then I moved way uptown and I'm over here just about every day. . . . Hah! That's funny. . . .

[*Well, how come you want to do that and . . . what's different about you?*]

I don't know, I just always have wanted to have my own home. Even when I was a kid. I sat in one of them apartments. I didn't like projects. I just didn't like them. Growing up, I lived in the projects, I just always wanted my own back yard, my own front yard, my own basement, my own house!

[*Let's move this car. Get a beer.*]

□　□　□

. . . There's a whole lot of places we are going by down here that you ordinarily couldn't get in, that if you was with the right people you could get in. Like right down here, that place we just went by, I didn't use to know nothing about it myself, I used to go right next door to it. This is a dope house. This is where guys go that you see walking down the street that's got seventy-five dollars and eighty dollars a day dope habits.

[*How can it cost that much? Somebody was telling me about that the other day, how some money had gotten run out on them . . . eighty dollars a day!*]

You know Selena's boyfriend, Carl? That's what his cost him, seventy-five and eighty dollars a day. I used to take him every time he went over there. Every time he'd go over there, he'd buy ten pills. The pills were a dollar a capsule. He'd buy them, cook them, and shoot them. He'd go over there . . . I've took him over there as many as eight, nine times a day.

[*Is that heroin?*]

Yeah, heroin. I think its heroin. I know they cook it, then shoot it, anywhere in the vein they can find. With an eye dropper, you know. They they wind up with, sooner or later, just about every guy I know that do it winds up with hepatitis. Because the needles are dirty and it's filthy and they wind up sick. Actually killing theyselves. I know when I was about seventeen years old, eighteen, I didn't know what the hell I was doing fooling with myself. I come down with hepatitis and wind up with jaundice and everything. Doctor told me that hepatitis came direct from filth. And the only place I knew I could have got some filth was shooting one of them dirty needles.

[*Oh, I know another thing I wanted to tape-record the other day, it was when Mark started talking about how he hated white people.*]

Now, I'll tell you something about Mark . . . Mark is a very intelligent guy. Now Mark got about three and a half years of college. . . .

[*He works at the hospital, doesn't he?*]

He used to. He used to work at the hospital, he was a nurse. He's a registered nurse. And he dropped out. . . . That's his profession, and he dropped out because the money wasn't right. And he's some kind of inspector or something at Ford Motor Company.

[*With three years of college?*]

Yeah. I imagine it takes about three years to be an RN, don't it.

[*School to be a nurse must take a while.*]

Yeah. It's about three years.

[*You know, actually, you're a bright guy, too. . . . I don't know if you think of yourself that way. . . .*]

Naw, I never thought about it . . . I never thought of it that way. . . .

See that school right there? That's the first school I went to in my life, St. Catherine, school and church. It's not a school now. I think the Methodists or somebody got it now, for a rehabilitation center.

[*Did you finish high school?*]

Yeah. I finished high school. I started going to college and, then . . . I started . . . my father was going to send me, but I messed around, and my first wife, me and her messed around and she got pregnant. We got married, and I took off in the Marine Corps.

[*How long were you in the Marines?*]

Ah, about four years. Pretty close to about four years and four months. Got an honorable discharge. The only bad thing I had on my record was, I couldn't get back to the base on time. I always came back a day late or a day and a half late. . . . Wouldn't give no trouble about it too much. Commanding officer, me and him was pretty well together. When I was there, I did my job. But problem is, he had a hard time keeping me there. He wrote my mother a big long letter. That's the only thing. I do my job. Thing is, I got to get there. I have a hard time going to work. Once I get there I do my job.

[*Is it difficult to find work, or. . . .*]

It's difficult to find good work. You can find you jobs for a dollar, dollar and a half an hour, you know. Unless you go in the factory. It's not too hard to get a job in the factory.

□ □ □

See the brown house back through there? The next building over, I used to live there. Right where my grandmother lived. I used to go and live with her. When I was a kid, I used to ride my bicycle right around through there. Find these people's back yards with apples. . . .

[Look at the kids riding around! Graduation! Kids happy, riding all over town, honking their horns; last day of school.]

Best time in their life, getting out of school. Graduating. Now they got to face the mean world.

[Everybody I've talked to in Detroit has said, "The best time in my life was when I was in high school."]

The best time in mine was when I was in high school and in the Marine Corps. I had a good time in the Marine Corps. It's always the best time when you ain't got no responsibilities, you ain't got no worries.

When you ain't got no responsibilities, you always have a good time, you never worry about nothing.

I have a brother-in-law, one of my brother-in-laws, he sets back and sells marijuana. This is all he does, and he averages right around four, five hundred dollars a week. This is just selling a can, a half a can, and just like that.

[You really can make more hustling than working. . . .]

Oh yeah. It's always more money hustling than working. That's why most of the young guys you see now, they won't work. Some of them work. Some of them got education and skills and everything to do a job, and never will get a break. Then they get around and try to make a hustle, you see. Get more money off of it.

[So how come you work?]

Well, just like I say, I got to work because I don't want to take a chance on going to the penitentiary. First thing they do is send you to the penitentiary when they catch you. So you got to go to work to survive.

I make a little hustle every now and then. I mess around with checks and money orders and stuff like that and make a little money, but I never made it an everyday thing. I've went out with between eight and nine hundred dollars' worth of money orders, I either would cash them right there or if I don't cash them all within an hour or so, take the rest of them, give them away, sell them to somebody. "Hey, give me five dollars, and take some money orders," you know? They take them, and then they are going to do what they want to do.

Get what I want out, then I step out, I'm gone. Anything you do too long that's illegal, you're bound to get caught sooner or later.

[Where do you get your money from? Where do you get the money orders from?]

Get them off somebody that's got some, like Ernie. Big Ernie, big guy that come around here sometime. He's around there last week . . .

selling twenty-dollar bills for five dollars. Counterfeit twenties. Sell them for five dollars. You couldn't hardly tell them unless you knew it, couldn't tell them apart.

Guy might pull up on the corner and say, "Wanta buy some checks, blank company checks? Want to buy some hot money? See where you can make some money out of it, five for twenty, five for twenty." Yeah, I've got five for twenty. If it looks good. I go right up in the gas station and cash them. When I get it cashed, go to another one. Runner, carried one to the *bank*, cashed it, and got away. Runner, he went to the *bank* and cashed it. The teller didn't pay it no mind. He went down there, carried it right on in, and cashed it.

[*I think he likes to be where it's a little hot, he really does.*]

□   □   □

Where we're driving now, this here is the East Side. And most of my family lives right around in here. My cousins, my brother-in-laws, my sister.

[*What if I was doing my interviewing around here, would I be running into different lives than on the Corner?*]

You might. You might well be running into different lives. Mess around here, you run into a little danger, too. You don't know the people. You got a lot of cutthroats and thugs up here. This is where all that mugging's been going on up in here. Got a lot of prostitutes and all that right up in this area. I was raised right over in here; I've been around over here for years. I know damn near just about everybody you see walking on the street, maybe not by name, but I know them . . . all the blind pigs, all the . . . see them around this poolroom next to the Bar-B-Q there; I used to run by that poolroom all the time.

The one owns that Cadillac on the corner there, he used to barber in the style of my hair. Barbershop there. His partner, Little Maxey, he just died. Over shot. Over dose of dope. Right here about two months ago. And all the big pimps and dope pushers and everything was at his funeral. All the big pimps. All you saw was Eldorados, Fleetwoods, and diamond rings, diamond rings big as quarters.

Yeah. And after the funeral they had a big dinner, and had whiskey, dope, anything else you want. Little Maxey.

[*Nathan, why does a girl give her money to a pimp?*]

Most of them get strung out.

[*That it?*]

Yeah. What the guy do, he fool around get her on dope, and than she got to come to him in order to get the dope. Then some of them, he just get her and brainwash her. Then she don't get herself together. Had one of my best friends get killed, he was started pimping about two years ago. And a little girl named Maggie, he was pimping her. He didn't have his business together, because a friend of hers told her that she saw Harv going to the Rock of Gold Motel over there on the Boulevard with another girl. And, when she found out, she went over there. She knock on the door, he answered the door, and she shot him six times. Killed him. Killed him. He had just started to get hisself together; he bought him a new Cadillac, opened him up a little blind pig, and he was really getting ready to go for hisself.

[*What kind of life would you want for your kids?*]

I don't know. I intend for them to have it better than I did. At least while they home, I'm going to make sure they get education. As long as I got the control where I can make them get it, you dig? But after a certain age, then you can't *make* them do anything, you know.

Now, this here is my uncle's house. You come on in.

□   □   □

. . . And I told my uncle that what you're trying to do, Professor, is just what's going on, where you can write. You can write a book. Be sure you're going to give me a copy when you write it, I want me a copy of that book. Want to read it. It should be a hell of a book because you ain't writing it out of just from your mind, you're writing true facts, on what's going on.

You will have a hard time publishing it if you writes everything true in it. They ain't going to want it to go. It'll be the damn truth! Because you write true facts.

See, what they will do when you write the truth about *how* the Black man is living, it will always be a son of bitch up there somewhere that don't want the truth out there in no book! You dig what I mean? And this is what you're trying to do is put it out there and tell it with the truth in it, where they can't get around it.

[*Hey, Nathan?*]

Yeah?

[*Hey, why would anyone want to stop the book, actually?*]

Why is that? I'll tell you. Them big-shot white folks, they will stop that book for one thing. Let me tell you why. Because they don't want the real truth out about the breaks and the way that the Black man is treated. This is why they will stop it.

See, that book you write, you are going to have a hard time, once you get it all together and write it, you are going to have a hard time getting it out.

[*Yeah, but, look here now, you and I have been talking for two hours. You haven't said anything about how the Black man is treated.*]

Naw, because you haven't asked me nothing about it. You said you was going to ask the questions.

Just like I say, the white man, right now today, he don't want to let the Negro or the Black man, whatever you want to call him, be on the same level as he is. Do you understand what I'm talking about? He wants to always keep you a second-class citizen. This is what he wants to do. And all these people that you been talking to are mostly Black people. And the things that you are learning and you are putting on tape and you are writing it like you see them, they are not going to—you are not the first one to probably try to write a book like that. You are going to have a hard time publishing that book. They are going to try to stop that book. Because see, you don't do like the average guy do, only talk for a minute, you go and just about *live* with these people.

[*Alright, now, maybe I've asked the wrong questions, because I've let you run on some here. So you lay it out now.*]

Right now, right now what I think? Is wrong, is about the world? I think the world is this: I still say, you know they say that the Black man have every equal rights, the same as the white man. But he don't. He don't! The white man's doing . . . he won't never let you . . . he, he is always steady and driving and driving, doing everything he can do to knock you down. After you get up, he'll knock you back down again. Most of them will pat you on the back, grin and laugh in your face, and *stick* you in the back as soon as you're not watching. They'll do it. They'll do it.

And another thing, they say, "We're equal opportunity employers." You know what I'm talking about? The only equal opportunity employers they got in the city of Detroit that I know of is Ford Motor Company. It's the only one. Chrysler and General Motors, in order to get what is called the apprenticeship, in order to get an apprenticeship or something like that, if you not a white boy, you got to *know* somebody. At Ford Motor Company, if you're qualified for an apprenticeship, they'll give you a test and if you're qualified for it, they'll give it to you. They're the first one that had a Negro foreman. That was years ago, years ago!

But what I was telling you is this. See, you know what people tell you, say, "Well, yeah, since President Kennedy we got a whole lot. And since they had that riot we got a whole lot." They still ain't got nothing. Ain't got *nothing*. Ain't got *nothing*! Only thing we got is what the white man want you to have. Other than that, he won't give you nothing else!

[*You're talking out of the other side of your mouth now from what we were talking before, when I asked you the question whether these people were happy.*]

They're happy. You know *why* they're happy? Because this is the only thing that they . . . see, they've never *had* nothing.

[*They're not asking because they don't expect—?*]

They're not asking. They don't expect. Because if they ask for it, they don't get it anyway.

I tell you what you can do, you can go to any jail, any institution, any penitentiary. And you count. You count. For every *white* man that they have locked up, they got at least fifteen to twenty Black. Now, there's one thing to look at.

As far as I'm concerned, I'm not like the average Negro and the average white man. I see what I want and then this is something that I strive for. Can't nobody expect for somebody to just walk up and say, "Here take this." You understand? Now a Negro he's supposed to get right out and do the same thing. And just like, if you didn't go to school and study hard, and strive and drive for what you wanted, you wouldn't be a professor, would you? Nobody wouldn't have walked up to you and said, "You be a professor; we are going to make you a professor." You understand what I'm talking about? You sacrificed. But you have the same thing happening as far as the Negroes are. You have some of them, just like you saw over there on the Corner today, some of them over there are qualified for some of the damndest jobs that you want to see. Aren't they? You've talked to them and you know they are. All right. The reason most of them don't go and get those kinds of jobs is because, in the first place, when they go get them they carry them through so much red tape and through so many changes that they just say, "Well, I ain't going to get it anyway." You know what I'm talking about? "I ain't going to get it anyway."

Just like, I had a friend of mine the other day, Malcolm, he got this job, and I don't know *how* he got this job. This is at Hammond-Harper, where they make tractors and everything. Malcolm walked in there, and he dress neat, sharp, and he's an intelligent guy. He walked in, he asked them were they doing any hiring. And they asked him what was he applying for. Well, just like I say, Malcolm, he's intelligent, he reads specs and stuff like that, and he apply for the job. He got that job, and you know, he came home . . . he got the job and when he came home . . . the job pay him five dollars and some an hour, white collar and everything. He got the job and came to my house, he was so surprised he got that job, do you know that he was actually *shocked*. He was shocked.

Shocked because he got the job. See what I'm talking about? But he got it. And now, he come around and tell me the other day that he got the job and he finds out that he's the first Negro that's held a job like that in Hammond-Harper. They've been making tractors, and they made stuff for horse and buggy, that pulled them plows for horse and buggy. They been in business that long. And just now he's the first Negro that got a job like that. And you *know* all this time there's been Negroes that's been qualified for jobs like that. Been Negroes qualified for jobs like that for years, ain't it! So I say, you can't ask for nothing.

. . . But you know, it's all hard, I mean just regular living.

□   □   □

. . . Now, this is not really my uncle. This is my stepmother's brother. He, actually, he is no kin to me by blood. But as far as I'm concerned, I'd rather come to him; I will ask him a question before I go to my own father. You understand?

Because my father, he's weak-minded and he'll set down and let my stepmother tell him anything that she want to and boom! No sense talking to him then. But I can talk to my uncle and I can ask him something, and, I bet you, you can get on the telephone and call my daddy right now, he will say the last time he saw me has been better than two months ago. Sometime it be eight or nine months. I will pass right by his house and come to my uncle's house. And sit and talk and drink and do anything we want to, and boom, his business is his business and my business is my business.

And I'm a grown man. I'll be thirty the fourth of November. You see what I'm talking about? And me and my uncle are not actually blood kin, but I'd rather be with him or around him. . . . You want me to tell you the honest-to-God truth? I love my uncle. And, matter of fact, sometimes I wish he had of been my daddy instead of my own daddy.

And my daddy's a good man. But the only thing that's wrong with him is that he's weak as far as a woman—my stepmother can tell him anything, he believe anything. She was the cause of me to turn around and start up—I was seventeen years old and she was the cause of me to turn around, my daddy picked up a chair, and she was the cause of me to turn around and fight him.

He too good a man. I ain't going to turn around and say a lie, that he's not a good man, because he's a good man, but he's just not the type of man to get out and be around things and can analyze things. You understand? Because a person *tell* you something don't mean it's so.

He's a good man. The only thing that wrong with Daddy is he don't know people. He don't know people. I know he's a good daddy. And I love him. He the best daddy any child could have. My daddy's the best. The biggest greatest man in the world.

He sacrificed his whole life to do one thing. Just to raise kids. He worked hisself to death. He worked hisself to death. When I was born my daddy was twenty years old. I'm twenty-nine; that makes him forty-nine years old.

He's the best man in the world. I'm twenty-nine years old. I've never heard my daddy curse. I'm twenty-nine, my daddy's forty-nine, and I've never heard him curse. I'm talking about "damn," "son of a bitch," or something like that, I never heard him curse.

I'm going to tell you something else, my daddy don't have any education. Only education my daddy have is the education that my sisters and me gave him when we was going to school.

He got enough mother wit on him. He got a lot of mother wit. Because like I say, he's a good man. He's a good man and he don't know nothing about the streets, about getting out here, partying, fooling around with these girls, and drinking liquor, drinking liquor and all that. Only time he drink liquor is like when friends come around. Now my uncle will go over there and carry a pint of whiskey over there, and my uncle will sit there talking and make him take a drink. But other than that, as far as getting off work, cashing his check, buying a pint of whiskey—he won't do it. You know what he'll do? He'll get off work and cash his check . . . he might not cash it . . . he'll carry it home and sign it and my stepmother, she take it and cash it. You understand what I mean? He's a good man. That's one thing I can say. He raised me. I had every opportunity I wanted. Not only me. My stepbrothers and sisters. He would have worked hisself to death to give us an education. That was how it was. Me and my daddy. It was different.

Now, my mamma. You know, when I met my mamma I was twenty-one years old. I found out the one I took after. I don't take after my daddy, I took after my mamma. My mamma's wild. She's a wild sister! You understand? She'll buy a pint of liquor and she will tell you, "There! Get you a drink!" I'm serious. She is.

I fought my daddy. I was seventeen years old. She had told him what she want to. I came in the house and Daddy picked up the chair, the one with the arms on it, before he asked me what I did. Before he even asked me. He didn't ask me nothing. She had told him everything, and he was so mad about this he just picked up the chair when I come in.

She will tell Daddy every kind of thing when there ain't nobody around but my daddy. She is wrong. She tell Daddy things and brainwash him the way she want to and he'll listen to her. She don't be right.

And the reason I'm scared of him is because he will come at me and I can't kill him. I can't kill him, he is my daddy.

Nathan Coolidge (II)

[*Well, I tell you what, in terms to what to talk about. . . . I've been thinking about the stuff that's been going into this book. . . . I think it's important to take it seriously that . . . it's going to really be read. Like . . . like if I just wanted to serve my purpose then . . . then we could talk about all these things that have been going with you . . . and I would have a colorful book. You see, that'd be colorful, okay. But, see, that just . . . that's not right. The truth is, the damn thing's going to be read. Okay? And what it's mostly going to be read by will be white, middle-class kids . . . going to college. . . .*]

[*So I think . . . I've come to think this last year that I should quit trying to figure what people should be talking about. And if somebody's going to say, "Yeah, I'm going to do that recording," you ought to think about that. The truth is, to be thinking about . . . there's going to be somebody who you're never going to see. You're never going to see this reader, this reader's not going to really know who you are. Here he is, he's a white kid who lives in a suburb and he's bought this book for a course and he's trying to build up some kind of idea about what some white people or some Black people living inside the city are like. And you should think about, you know, if you had this person. . . .*]

[*Well, first of all, one real question, do you want to talk to him at all? Because maybe you don't want to. It's one thing to say, "Yeah." You know, "Yeah, Rafe's an alright guy, it's alright to talk with him." Well, that's alright. We can turn the tape recorder off and talk. You know. But think about, think about this, for real. Somebody's going to read this. You know, here he comes, and what do you want to tell this guy, if anything?*]

Really, I don't want to tell him nothing. I don't really want to tell him nothing. And he ain't doing nothing to help me, no kind of way. . . . Anything, try to keep me *down*, where he can stay up on top. Try to avoid him, stay away from around him, as much as possible.

[*He's trying to avoid staying around you, you're trying to avoid staying around him?*]

I try to avoid him, to stay away from around him. As much as possible.

[*Well, I think that kind of thing should be said.*]

I wouldn't really, wouldn't want to come in contact with him if I could help it, because that class will more or less try to . . . more or less will be trying to do things to try to push me back, you know what I mean? If I could stay away from around him, then I could reach, going *around* him, and try to reach the same level that he's at. But if he's around me, he's steady trying to push me down, where he can stay up. He'll try to put the hardest work on me and stuff like that. See? That's what he'd be wanting to do.

[*See, this, I was talking with . . . a couple of students last week about this. And two of them were Black students, Black graduate students. See, I put to them, this same proposition. Really, what should be in there? In a way they said what you said.*]

Yeah.

[*They said, "Really, you're kidding yourself, Rafe, if you think. . . ."* They said, "*Really, when you describe who's going to be reading that book, why should they know anything? About how people in the city live?"* They say, "I don't want to tell them anything, because if they find out something that's hurting us . . ."*]

They going to make it worse.

["* . . . then they are going to make it worse. If they find out some way we're making it, they'll say, 'We'll try . . . ' "*]

Try to stop them.

["* ' . . . to stop them there.' "*]

That's right, that's what they try to do. Exactly what they try to do. You see . . . you have . . . if you see a way that you making it, things easier for yourself, the next thing, you look up and they done set up a block, someplace. You got to try to find another way. See what I mean? They try to keep you down all the time, they want to keep you down and they hold you down with one hand while they're reaching up with the other hand, pulling theirself up and holding you down. And any kind of way that they see you making it, they are going to push you down. That's why I wouldn't want to tell them anything, any way I was living, you know . . . any kind of way I was living and having it, anything easy, I wouldn't, wouldn't want them to know, them to know about it. Because the next thing you know, you look up and that way is stopped. That way is stopped. Somebody'll find some way to put a block over there, got to find another way to make it.

Anywhere you'll go, they'll give . . . see, the white boy, he get a job better, faster, and easier than the colored boy will anyway. Because I went down here, the place I got hired at, down the street there?

[*Rawson-Monroe?*]

Yeah, Rawson-Monroe. I went down there Monday. And they told me to come back Tuesday. And two white boys that was there at the same time I was, they hired both of them. I came back Tuesday, and they told me to come back Wednesday. I came back Wednesday and I was the only one there at that time. And they needed some men then. I was the only one in the office. They gave me an application, I filled it out, and the guy asked me did I know anybody else need a job. Because they need two men right away, two more men right away. And I told them, yeah, and I got hired right away that day, starting the next morning. But if anybody else had of been in that office the same time. . . .

You go into that plant down there, the guys that's working in there, most of them live right around here, colored guys, but any other, most of the white guys live, that's working there, live way out in the suburbs. Live in the suburbs, and most of them are relatives. Cousins, nephews, and you know, stuff like that.

Some of them just came here from down—in fact, I was working right with a guy Friday. I was working with him, he's from Kentucky. He's only been here, I think he told me, he's been here about three or four weeks. He came here and started working the second day he was here. See? His uncle works down there, his uncle got the opening and sent down there and got him and they held the job 'til he got here for it. That's the way they do that. Most of that's relatives, you know, that thing there.

But you go up there and talk to them, I bet you can find at least twenty-five or thirty of them right now that haven't been here six months. And been working ever since the day or two after they got here, right down there. And people around here needing jobs, on the welfare. You know? It's enough people right around in the city. All they got to do is run an ad in the paper, or just tell one person that's working in there that they hiring. And they'll have—shoot—it'll be so crowded down there, they couldn't open, you couldn't get in the employment office.

You tell anybody down there they hiring, you think I'm telling a lie, you walk right up on the Corner, and tell four or five guys down there, say, "They're hiring down at Rawson-Monroe." Then tomorrow morning around eight o'clock, just ride by Rawson-Monroe, and you'll see guys from all over town standing up there in employment, in that line, trying to get in there. People on welfare. And I don't see why they should have to send away to Kentucky or Tennessee, someplace like that, to get somebody to work when there's men right here that need jobs. Men with families, you know? That's right. They need jobs and they'd work, if they could get a job. I know plenty of them.

I went up there this morning, to work, and passed the employment office. And I seen, about fifteen or twenty of them standing out there before they open up. This was at about quarter to seven this morning. About fifteen or twenty men, standing around the office door, there, this morning. It ain't open 'til eight o'clock. So, that's just it, this is just how fast the word will get out. Once they hire somebody, they'll come back and tell somebody that they hiring, they'll smooth down there.

They'll probably send all those guys away from there this morning. And then turn around, and somebody's relative will come there tomorrow. *Yeah.* Right from out of town, you know, they ain't been in the city twenty-four hours; come and get a job. Talking to a guy in the personnel office, he told me he drives thirty-five miles every day to work. Guy working in the office there, one of the guys, said he drives thirty-five miles every day to work.

But they can't change that. That's the way it's been, that's the way it's going to always be. . . . Guy go to school, go to high school, go to college, and come out and then wind up out to Ford's on the assembly line. Might luck out and get a foreman's job if he gets some seniority. Education don't mean nothing. Unless they go be a doctor or a lawyer or something like that, you know. But just, getting his high school diploma, and maybe two years of college, that don't give him nothing but a laborer's job.

I know when I got to high school, they told me, "Go get your high school diploma, you'll get a good job." My father told me that. I graduated, I came out and I went into the Marine Corps. And came out. And what kind of job I was able, was ever able . . . the only job, the only good job that paid any money I've ever been able to get over to was factory. In the factory. I had a couple good jobs driving trucks, semi-trailers. But as far as jobs, like *they* was talking about I could get, I ain't seen *no* jobs like that. *No* kind of job that's not doing no hard labor.

□   □   □

It's just a hell of a thing to think about it. I don't. . . . That's why I never . . . very seldom think about it. I just. . . .

[*Well, you wouldn't, you wouldn't have talked about that at all if I hadn't put it to you this way, would you?*]

No. I wouldn't even mention it.

Don't do any good to talk about it because it don't help none. The only thing it makes you liable to say the wrong thing and it'll wind up in the wrong ears and make it worse on you. See that, that's a weak point, then they start pressing right at that point, you know. Make it worse on you, you now.

It's like down there in the County Jail—when I was down there, they come through every now and then and look and see was you suffering, you know? And I don't care what would be wrong, I was *sick* down there and I wouldn't even tell them. 'Cause if they figured that I was sick, they'd say, "Well, you see the doctor about one-thirty." And you'd be looking for one-thirty to come and you see the doctor, and one-thirty come, and another deputy come through, the other dep had changed floors. And you say, "I was supposed to see the doctor at one-thirty." "And what do you think you're in, the Cadillac-Sheraton Hotel?" And that even make it worse when you figured you was going to see him, you know. And they know that.

I laid down there sick, I was sick as a dog. I wouldn't tell nobody. I just . . . laid in my bed for seven or eight days, wouldn't eat nothing, I couldn't drink nothing, or eat nothing during that, and I wouldn't tell them nothing. Whenever they come through, or look, I would get up and read the paper, get up and walk, just like it wasn't about nothing, you know. See, I was sick, though. I wouldn't let them know . . . that is was getting to me, you know. I just . . . when they looked at me, they figured, well, "He can take it, he's strong," you know.

[*Yeah.*]

Guy cracked up down there, two or three guys hung theirselves in there. Stuff like that, because they couldn't stand it. But I wouldn't . . . no way in the world I would hang myself down there. I wouldn't let them know that they weakened me that weak, you know? I wouldn't let them know.

That's all that is, really. I *believe* that's what they try to do, try to break them. Try to break you. That's what I believe it is. Most of those white guys is try to break you.

Then you got some Uncle Toms just go right along with them and get them a job and then they push them up to front for them. But I would shoot a colored policeman faster than I would shoot the white ones. Because he worse, you know?

[*Because he's running for the white man?*]

That's right. That kind is worse. They worse. They have them around here, sneaking in afterhour joints. Dressed plain clothes. Shit, they worse than the white man. You know, to do something like that. Now that's the job I wouldn't even take. I wouldn't take a job as a police. When I first come out of the Marine Corps, they tried to get me a job like that. I could've got a job on the police force.

I wouldn't even take a job like that. Come down in a poor neighborhood and they walk in, a guy going to the A & P, and steal a loaf of bread and a can of sardines, and they carry him downtown for simple larceny. And give him five years. That's simple larceny. But they charge him with larceny from a building. Simple larceny's not supposed to carry over ninety days. Because it's under a hundred dollars.

But, instead of giving him simple larceny, they give him larceny from a building. Larceny from a building carries five years. They give him that. It'll carry four years. They give him larceny from a building instead of simple larceny. That's the way they're doing it. And you get a *white* boy come in there, he done stole something for seventy-five dollars and they charge him with simple larceny. Because it's under a hundred dollars.

That's right. Now you can set right down there in court and see that happen every day. I left a friend of mine down there I grew up with, he got caught in Hudson's with a pair of silk underwear. He was a dope addict.

He got caught with a pair of silk underwear. Which costs, I don't know, about two or three dollars. And they had him, he had been there four months, waiting to go to court. For larceny from a building. Which is simple larceny.

And this time of the year? This time of the year? This is the easiest time of the year I know to get in the worse trouble there is, right now. Because they figure they might start another riot. They try to get all the young men off the street now. Lock them up fast as they can. Lock them up.

This is what they're trying to do. This is what they're trying to do. They can get the majority—what they want to do is get the majority of younger men off, figure from between seventeen to around twenty-five. Those are the ones they're trying to lock up now. They lock them all up down there in the County Jail and sent them out to the House of Corrections, send them up to Jackson to all them farms. And the County Jail. That's why those jails stay so full. You go in there and look in there. You can figure, for every one white boy you see in there, it's maybe forty, forty-five colored. You know what I'm talking about? And you check the ages on them. They want the younger ones off the street. They don't too much bother the old ones because they figure the older ones'll go down to the welfare and beg for that aid, you know, and stuff like that. They ain't going to go out and pick up a pistol and put it in their hand and walk up there and say, "Set it up." They ain't going to do that. You know what I mean. They figure, the younger ones'll say, "Shit. This ain't enough money." You know. "I got a family, I'm going to get me some money." Yeah, walk out there and walk in the bank with a shotgun and shoot four or five people and take it, you know.

This is what they're doing. I just watched it all last year. All last year when I was sitting down at that County Jail, I watched—you could tell when the guys come in, new men come in. You could tell which ones would be out within a week. And you tell which ones would be in there the whole summer. That's right. The ones come in there thirty, thirty-five on up, in that age? Within a week's time they'd be out back on the street. And they come in there twenty-five, twenty-six, on back down to around seventeen? Those go on up to Jackson, Ionia, and all the places like that. Most of them don't even make it to the House of Corrections. The House of Corrections mostly get the guys from twenty-five to thirty. And after thirty, they don't hardly even send them to Jackson, unless it's for murder, or capital crime or something.

But them young guys can do anything small like that. They can do any little small—that's why they have more or less, you got them laws switched around, like that larceny I was telling you about. Simple larceny? And larceny from a building. Or if you take something from a person, they'll say larceny from a person. That larceny from a person carry ten years. And if it's just a pack of cigarettes, you can get ten years for it. See what I mean? They have the laws hooked like that so they can put them on people the way they want to put them on. Like, if I was a young guy and they wanted to take me off, well they charge me with larceny from a person. If I an older guy or somebody they don't want to send me away, they just say simple larceny. That's the way they do it. They switch it around.

That's just the way the law is. I think the laws is just made more or less to control—it's more or less to control the Black man, that's what this law here in Detroit is made for. That's what it's made for. They should have—if they're going to make a law, a law should be made just one law to control everybody. You know? Shouldn't be one law for me and one for you. Shouldn't be like that, but that's the way it is. And I know it. Money's the only thing keep you out on the streets.

I've spent a whole lot of money. I'm thirty-one right now, and I've spent—if I had just the money I done spent trying to stay in the streets free? I'd have enough money to last me from now on. I spent a whole lot of money. I mean, I spent a lot of money. And every lawyer you talk to, he wants six hundred dollars, boom, right there, before even just . . . just touch your case, he wants six hundred dollars retainer's fee. If you got any kind of case on you, he'll want it.

Money will keep you out there and . . . being the right color. Colored man, he need a lot of money to stay out on these streets free. That's no lie.

A lot of guys around that's dealing, selling dope and everything, making big money, and the cops know they making big money. And they come in on them. I got a friend of mine right now making big money. Police come and rob him every now and then. During the Christmas holidays they come in once. Took five hundred dollars from him. Let him go on and stay in business. And they come up there, been about a month ago. They come in and took five hundred dollars from him, took his woman to jail, and then he had to go and pay a thousand dollars at the station to get her out back on the street.

[*When you say they took it off him, you mean they were searching around the place and take it off or. . . .*]

No, they come up there and ask him. And they told him, "You want to stay open up here, come up with some cash." That's right. Five hundred dollars.

Just like we had a place around the corner there and they come around and ask Luther for it. He wouldn't pay it. And they kicked all the windows out and tore up the whole place. Couldn't deal . . . we couldn't sell no more whiskey and that down there. Really, they thought we was making money, but we wasn't making that much money. Because there was too many of us partners in it. There was four of us in there as partners. Just really making enough money to survive off it, you know.

[*There's not that much money around here anyway.*]

There's a lot of money around here. If you go into the right thing, like you're selling dope. There's a lot of money around here in dope because the dope fiends around here, they are going to get money.

They get the money. When I first got out of jail, when I came out of jail I had spent every dime I had. They had made me sell my car, I had to sell my car, I didn't have, have a rag, a stitch, to put on my back. And Linda helped me get on my feet when I first got out of jail. She came down to see me while I was in jail and gave me a little change. When I come out, she gave me fifty dollars. I bought a quarter of mixed dope. I opened up around there on the next street. And I dealt around there eleven days. In eleven days' time, I had made enough money to get myself back together. So I stopped then. I had made enough money to where I would have enough to hold me over to where I could get a job.

It's just a hell of a thing. That's the only way to make any money now is get you a dope thing. And then you got to know who to get it from; you got to know who to get the pete from, the dope to deal; you got to get the right connections and everything and know them. If you don't have the connections to get it, you still in bad shape. You got a thousand dollars, you can't buy enough to deal. Because it would just give you that amount at a retail amount, you know. In order to get it wholesale where you can make money off it, you got to have the right connect.

Like I say, you can take fifty dollars and open up with dope and just don't use it, and just turn it, and shit, in a month's time you can make ten, fifteen thousand dollars in a month. Thirty days. Easy. Stay open twenty-four hours. Just get somebody to help you, you be there twelve hours and have somebody else there twelve hours. Twenty-four hours, seven days, you can make ten or fifteen thousand dollars easy. Because it turns around so fast, just keep turning, fifty dollars will bring you maybe a hundred fifty. Make about fifty dollars' worth bring you about a hundred forty-five, a hundred fifty dollars. Put that whole hundred fifty dollars back in it, you know, it keep. . . .

[*Just keeps building up. . . .*]

Like that, and then open you four or five other places, have four or five other people dealing for you. You can get a guy to deal for you for a hundred dollars a week. One hundred dollars a week and three do's a day. Give him a hundred dollars a week and three do's a day, he'll deal for you. You get you four or five places turning like that, good money come in fast. . . .

I mean right around here. You'd be surprised at the money that's right around here. You know Fish Eye, used to be around here, used to stay around the corner? He had a dope joint upstairs, around the corner there. He started dealing around there two years ago. And right now, they say Fish Eye worth maybe . . . I don't know, maybe a hundred fifty, two hundred thousand dollars. In cash money. And he still is dealing. He's still dealing. He got two fine new cars.

And he just started two years ago, didn't have nothing. Just come from the prison. Penitentiary two years ago. Came out here flat broke. Took fifty dollars. His woman was on ADC, gave him fifty dollars. He started dealing. She riding around in mink coats, Cadillacs, and stuff. It don't look like that much money is right around an area like that.

[*No, it doesn't.*]

But it's here. Because the guys that use it, they go downtown, they go all out in the suburbs. I know some guys who go out in the suburbs and just knock on the door and just move a whole house out. Color TV's and stuff like that. That's all they do. They got one of those little van trucks, this is their thing, they just ride.

□ □ □

[*Would you feel funny about . . . about dealing in dope?*]

Would I feel funny?

[*Yeah.*]

I never felt funny about it. I never did feel funny about it, because I was just surviving. But. . . .

[*No, I mean like if you stuck with that. If you were doing that steady.*]

If I had to do it steady?

[*No, now look. Look, you know, what I'm thinking about, let me be straight with you. So you're talking about this here . . . that dope's bad for the man who's using it, right?*]

Yeah. That's bad for the man who's using it. He can . . . he might OD anytime, he could OD anytime because he never know what quality it is; if it's a good quality, just a little bit'll kill him. You know. It's bad for the man who's using it. In the long run, it'll mess him up anyway. It's bad on his liver and his kidneys and his veins and if you snort it, it eats up your membranes. It's bad, period, on you.

[*Well, that's what I'm talking about. When I say, would you feel funny about it. I mean, suppose you were handling this. . . . Is that going to bother you that you're hurting the man who's buying off you?*]

It wouldn't bother me for the simple reason that if I . . . if I let it bother me and didn't sell it to him, he'd only just go someplace else and get it. He wants it, he'll go someplace else and get it anyway. (*Pause.*)

[*This thing wasn't so big a few years ago, was it?*]

No.

[*I mean, that's like a new thing, isn't it?*]

Yeah. It got big in sixty-seven. Right after the riot. Right after the riots . . . right after the riots came and the riots was over. Within a month after the riots was over, that's when all that dope come here. That dope came right in here after that. And what most of the people said, most of the big guys I know said that . . . they said that they came around here . . . that . . . the Mafia, most of the big white people, put it right in here. In the ghettos. Put it right in here. Going to kill off the younger set with it, you know. But they didn't intend for it to spread like it did. It got in here, there was so much of it in here that it spilled out and hit the suburbs, too, see. And then that's when they come up with all these programs. That's what happened.

But . . . it got in here and a lot of people got in good shape, man, selling dope. I know some guys that . . . shit . . . never seen a hundred-dollar bill, never seen a diamond ring. And then, right now rolling in money right now. Rolling in money. Rolling. That guy, Fish Eye, he in good shape. His brother, and his brother's in the penitentiary, still got six joints running. They caught him for CCW. Carrying a concealed weapon. And possession of narcotics. He bought the possession of narcotics case. He bought that case. But they sent him away on CCW for nine months. Because he was on parole for CCW, just got out from doing nine months. He was on parole, they sent him right back for nine more months. But he bought the possession case. The possession case carried twenty years. He bought that case. Anytime you got enough money to buy twenty years you got a lot of money. You got a lot of money.

[*How do you buy a case?*]

How do you buy a case? You buy a case through a lawyer. Go down and get a lawyer. Tell him what the deal is and what kind of case you got

or your partner got. He'll tell you how much it'll cost you. And then . . .
he'll take it from there. Who he deals with, I don't know.

He got to be dealing with the courts. All the judges is driving big
Cadillacs and stuff like that. This is all—if you got money, just like I say.
Just like my lawyer told me. . . . Well, my father, he works for the city.
And I was using a state-appointed attorney. And my father, he came
down and told me, said he was going to get me a lawyer. That would get
me on probation. He said the lawyer guaranteed me probation. But he
wanted twenty-five hundred dollars. So he went and got this man. All
right. I was supposed to go before one judge for my trial. They postponed
my trial on that date; after I got this lawyer, they postponed my trial
from him, they took me in front of a different judge. When I went before
him, he give me eighteen months probation. Now this was known before
I ever went to court. Four months before I went to court, my lawyer told
me I was going to get eighteen months to two years' probation. So when
my father gave him that money, he told my father what I would get. But
it took me so long to go to court because he had to maneuver it around in
front of the judge that he wanted to go to court.

That's why I say, you can do anything you want to for a little money.
He told me, you know, he said, anytime that you out here with a gun or
anything, he said, try not to shoot no police, you know. He said for fifteen
hundred dollars—he said to me, he told me, if I shoot anybody out here
in the street, he said, for fifteen hundred dollars he can keep me on the
street. That's right. Fifteen hundred dollars keep me on the street.
Make sure it's, it's, it's a nigger, you know, ain't no white man, fifteen
hundred dollars, I can stay out here on the street. He told me that.

□   □   □

[*Hey, Nathan?*]
Yeah?
[*With all this going on that you can see, how come you're friendly with
me? I'm white.*]
You not the only white guy I'm friendly with, I got a couple of real
good white friends. You know, that's regular, you know what I mean?
They ain't guys just . . . just out to try to make it all for theyself and keep
you pushed down. I can just about talk to a guy and tell when a guy just
wants what's due him and not what's due somebody else and his too, you
know? This is what I'm talking about.

I got a couple of white friends. In fact I got one I was raised up with.
Mike, he used to live over here nearby. He lives out on Six Mile out there
now. He comes around every now and then and in fact we go out, drink,

mess around together, go bowling sometime, you know. I got three or four real regular white friends, you know. Real regular . . . real regular.

[*Would you think any of this is ever going to change?*]

Naw. The only way to change is just like what's his name? Mohammed? Mohammed said, you know they want to integrate. But why integrate if they don't want to, the white don't want to integrate, why try to force them to integrate? You know what I mean? Just let them live the way they want to live and leave them alone and we live the way we want to live and leave us alone. You know? No sense in making somebody do something they don't want to do. Because when you try to force somebody to do something, then it's quite natural they'll retaliate. And I found out as long as you leave the white people alone and don't try to take nothing from them or try to do anything to hurt them, nine times out of ten, they'll walk around you and go about their business. They won't bother you. But if you bother them, they'll retaliate on you. The same way, if they bother us, we'll retaliate on them. That's about the only way to . . . try to just live and let live.

No sense try to make somebody do something they don't want to do. They don't want you to go to their schools, well, don't go. You know, you can't just make people do things they don't want to do. Even if the law says well, the law says well, colored can go to the school. All right, colored can go there, but what's going to happen? It ain't going to be nothing but a big conflict, or fighting in the halls and all and shooting and all. And what sense is that? People getting hurt for nothing. You know?

So I feel just, I can get around them and I can get along with them and get along without them. And I don't bother. As long as they don't bother me, I don't bother them.

I see guys get together, right after that Martin Luther King, he got killed, well . . . they get together and going up here on the street. "We goin' up there and jump on some whiteys." For what? They ain't did nothing to you, what you want to jump on them for? It didn't make sense to me. You go up there and jump on them, if they any kind of man, well, hell, they going to try to defend theyself, and if you hit them, they hit you, then it's gonna be something right there. You can get killed or they could get killed, and where'd it all come from? Because they was white and you Black, you go up there, you going to jump on them?

I got a friend of mine in the penitentiary right now. He killed a white boy. He went up there and tried to take some money from him and he . . . didn't give it up and he put up a scuffle. They gave him natural life in the penitentiary. He wasn't but about eighteen then, eighteen or nineteen years old. He doing natural life in the penitentiary for what? That don't make sense. He had never seen that boy before and the boy had never seen him before. It just something that he read in the paper or heard on the radio. "Between the races something going on." Then he go on out and "I'm gonna jump on the whitey." Now that don't make no sense. I walk up and down the street, mind my own business, and everybody else's business is their own, but if somebody bother me they got troubles. They think they got a black cat in the corner, because I'm going to try to take care of myself. I'm gonna try to do it. That's one of those things.

[*But what . . . like that work thing, take that.*]

That's all of it. Rubs off of that. Most of the guys, the average guy you see that . . . has got malice in his heart and mad and . . . dislike white people, that's for the simple reason is because he feels as though they're living better than he's living.

[*Well, they are.*]

Yeah, I know they are. They got better jobs. They got to live better. You got better jobs making more money, you got to live better. And this is what . . . what most of the guys have in their minds and heart against them, you know.

[*All right, so here. . . .*]

Hurting them and killing them don't give you no better job.

[*All right, but here's this little boy. And he's your son.*]

Yeah.

[*Two years old. What's going to be for him?*]

Probably . . . probably the same thing. It might just . . . just a little change might come in like it did for me, the difference between me and my father, a little change'll come. You know. And then the white'll give up, you know, will give that little change, you know. Will give that little change, you know, as time goes on. Things have got to change with time, because times is changing. And this is when they . . . they giving a little more as time goes, you know.

[*Well, what are you going to tell that boy about how to carry himself? What are you going to tell him, what waits for him, what are you going to tell him how to carry himself?*]

I'll treat it the same way as my father taught me, is that: I'm equal to any man. And don't let no man run over me, don't let no man . . . take my manhood from me, you know? Stand shoulder to shoulder, face to face, eye to eye, with any man, look him in his eye and talk to him. Because I'm equal to him, you know? And I'm going to try to do the same thing that my father did. My father tried to give me a good education. And I'm going to give him the best that I can afford. Because like I say, I went . . .

my father . . . I didn't go to public schools until I was in the . . . well, in about the eleventh grade. When I went to public school. My father paid for me to go to Catholic schools. All the way up through, see.

□   □   □

[*Well, what do you—look here. What are you going to be doing ten years from now?*]

Ten years from now?

[*Yeah.*]

Mm. I don't know.

[*What's your life. . . .*]

Let's see, I'm thirty-one—ten years from now I'll be forty-one. Ten years from now, I intend to have bought and paid for me a new home. I intend to do that and have some money in the bank. If I can't get it working, I might go back and sell dope again.

carl foreman

Carl, raised in Detroit, came to stay on the Corner with Selena Mason. She was a beautiful woman, some years older than he, who had a number of children. Carl kept his distance from me through the summer and autumn. I spent much of December trying to help Selena's eighteen-year-old son, Michael, free himself from an impulsive commitment he had made to serve in the Marine Corps. My work for Michael lessened Carl's distrust; he began to talk to me. I came by one January morning and found him baby-sitting and we had the first of the following conversations.

Not much later, Carl had to serve time in the state penitentiary on old forgery charges. We lost contact. After his release, he returned to Selena, but continually instigated trouble with her. Ultimately he was picked up after an incident that could have caused serious harm. After some months in the County Jail, he was sent to a nearby forensic facility for a psychiatric work-up. He had that facility contact me. I was glad to be back in touch, made a series of visits, and we collaborated on a strategy for his defense. Carl wanted to continue our recording, which he found diverting, and we spent some hours at the machine.

Carl Foreman (I)

Like I was saying, I don't think my life would be too interesting to talk about, I'm just another colored guy that's grown up, got in trouble like everybody else, and that's about it. That's about the whole thing right there, in a nutshell.

I have feelings, don't get me wrong. I don't walk around without emotions, everybody I think has emotions, but as far as . . . expressing them or telling somebody my feeling, I don't go around doing that, you know.

Now I did mean what I said to you yesterday: Michael was living here with his mamma, but now he is at the Marines, at boot camp—and that's another Black boy beginning to die. He's at an age when *white* kids are going out, going to go college, and *he's* just starting to get messed up.

And where young kids are concerned, there's a difference here, you know. A marked difference. After *one* gets a certain age, one's got to go to work. Or either join the service, and then come back and work. The other one, he'll probably continue on into college, and he'll probably be that one's boss one day, you know. So it's just a big cycle.

I mean, to anything, there's two sides to anything, you know. There's two sides to this race issue, or whatever you want to call it. I don't think Michael was being messed around whatsoever.

Don't get me wrong, I'm not no patriotic guy, neither, because I wouldn't go, period, to fight for the United States. Or even go in the service. But I think that Michael, like I told you, he had problems here. And his problem was trying to get away. And this was the onliest escape he could see. You know. Because you can see right now that he didn't want to go to the service. He's there and he wants out.

Instead of going and talking to someone that could probably help him, he was hard-headed and wouldn't listen to nobody. If I was here, I certainly would've talked to him. I don't know what I would've told him, but I think I could've talked him out of it. But then there's some kids like him, there's people like that, they got to learn themselves.

I don't see why he's got to serve. You know? I mean to come back to what? What kind of future does he have, actually?

He could probably finish school, he can go to college, but then, actually, what does he have then, actually, after that? Actually, just what is he going to have, after he finished college? Even? He going to have shit. He's just going to be another colored guy that finished college.

Oh, there's things opening up, of course. It's better now than it was in nineteen thirty, we know that. It was better in nineteen thirty, then it was in eighteen sixty-four. But yet and still, a guy can have the qualifications and he still can't go to the height or reach his goal. He can go a little ways into it, and he can't go all the way. And to me, this is more . . . annoying . . . than, ah, not even—I'd rather not even have it. They can go to a certain stage and that's it. So they get to the certain stage and that's it, they buy them a little home and then they go around and say, "Look, I make it." I don't think they made it, because they haven't reached their full potentiality. You know what I mean? And if I can't do what I really want to do, I'm not going to do it, period. You know? It doesn't make sense. Not to me.

Understand me, this is a small percentage, yeah, this is a small percentage here, that make some money. On the average, on the average, the average person makes—I mean, the average Negro, I'd say, make between five thousand and eighty-five hundred dollars a year. Then, if you work like a dog, and work overtime and double-shift it, then you'll make maybe, nine to ten five a year. If you're a foreman and you're lucky, then maybe you can go to about thirteen. Possibly. About twelve, you know. But the average one of us—yeah, *us*—we make about five thousand a year. That's it, you know.

□   □   □

The friends I grew up with . . . my best friend, he's dead, he got killed in a holdup. He was trying to get money. He didn't learn it just don't pay to hold up people.

It's not really funny, you know, it's pathetic. The guy was a smart guy, too, he wasn't a dummy neither. Maybe this was the reason why he pulled a holdup, because he was *too* smart, you know. But anyway, he got killed in a holdup.

And the majority of the others, the majority of the other ones, they've been in the penitentiary. If they haven't been there, they're . . . well, most—well, all of them have been in the penitentiary.

And some of them are out now. Some of them are living what society calls a useful life. Like, they've got a job now, and they've got wives, and they're working, and they're not wild no more, I guess you'd say. Kinda calmed down, that is, according to society.

But then I have some friends, too, about five or six of them that went on and did things. One that's a writer, another one that's an artist, two of them artists, another one studies rocks and fossils. He's in Africa now, studying. And I know a couple of girls who are teachers. But those are about the onliest ones out of all that I knew. Of course, you have to realize that the environment that I was raised in, you see, I wasn't raised in an environment where generally the kids make it. That way.

Now, if you ask me how many of them became successful pimps, successful hustlers, or successful prostitutes, or dope fiends, or whatever you want, you know, then I could name a great many of them. Really, I mean just last week I saw four guys come through that I had known and they're successful according to hustler life. They're known throughout from California to here as good hustlers and anybody will hustle with them. And they were driving the Cadillac. And had lots of clothes, you know.

□   □   □

And you ask, does hustling feel good? I mean, how can I explain it? When you're hustling, man, it's just like a job. You know you're going to make whatever you make a day. When you become good at hustling, and you know you're qualified, you don't worry about money. You know it's out there, and you know you're going to get it. Because it is out there, you know.

So you get up in the morning, just like any other guy, and you say, well, I'm gonna make me a hundred and twenty dollars, a hundred and twenty-five dollars today. And that's that, you know. And, you go out there, and you make it. Then you come on back.

Now, the thing about hustling, and a legitimate job is this: Where you can go and make your daily wages, and work for three years, then go and get some credit, can buy something, the hustler still can't do that, you see. Because nobody is going to trust a hustler because everybody knows it's ups and downs out there in those streets.

And then one day, if you hustle long enough, you're going to get busted. You gotta go to jail, you know. I mean, this is the price that you're going to pay for it.

The price *you're* going to pay for your job is you're going to die one of these day, you know. Just like the hustler, too.

□ □ □

I mean, put it like this: Although I'm working now, there's one time I thought I'd say, "Man, before I can make an eight-to-eight or five-to-eight or seven-to-four, I'd rather be dead. In my grave, you know." If I gotta join that kind of system and stand out there and listen to all that noise and look at all these sonofabitches that've been working for thirty years and still working.

I said, "I can't do that. Not when I qualify to make me two or three hundred dollars a day, it doesn't make sense. For what I've learned and what I've spent half my life trying to learn." And wound up doing it, though. Going, doing it.

But then still the fact still remains, man, I mean, you work all your life, man, and then you die, and that's it, you know. I mean, there is this little glamour thing to this hustling thing, where it's not with that working-man thing. The working man has the security and everything, he still works thirty-five or forty years, retires, for about five years he lives on, and then he . . . kicks off. Well, a hustler, he parties every day, you know. The money's easy, the broads are around, and, whatever he's doing, drinking or using, he has fun doing it.

To an extent. It's fun sometime. But then, you know, *everything stops being funny after awhile.* And it starts becoming a damn drag.

□ □ □

And this is what generally happens to a hustler. And what starts to change the guy. Starts him to say, "Well, you know, maybe, maybe this guy over here on this square side, it ain't too bad, and maybe I should try this thing, for a little bit."

Because it becomes a drag. Even with me, it became a drag. After awhile . . . I was making pretty nice money, not a whole lot of money, but enough for me to live comfortably on. Nice car, nice clothes, and things. But it was the same old thing every day. Get up, hustle, beat somebody [con somebody]. And you get tired of beating people. After awhile you start seeing people that you done beat, man. Or you keep looking over your shoulder. Or you jump at a knock on the door, or if the police come up to you to give you a ticket or something, man, you almost jump out of the car.

So you get tired of this after awhile. I mean this is what happened to me, man. And you try to find yourself something different, some other bag. And this is what happened to me and so I'm just trying to find something different.

And I don't know if this is going to work, because at times, man, I get tired out there at that factory. You know, I say, shit, it ain't even worth it, man, standing out here. And it's hard to stand out there when you know that you can go . . . you can make this and that.

I mean, understand me, this was the first thing that was opened up to the Negro, anyway, hustling was. As far as for him to make money. I mean, education wasn't opened up, you know. When the Negroes was starting to learn to hustle. When I say hustle, I mean conning, I mean pimping, and whatever you want to call it. I mean this was the first thing that was really opened up to him, so that he could get some money.

So every kid that comes up, he's got a dream of being something, you know. Where the white kid might idolize Babe Ruth or Mickey Mantle, or whoever, you know . . . right now it's different, the colored kids have idols now.

But when I was coming up, the most important man in my neighborhood was Joey Flood. And Joey Flood was a pimp. And Joey Flood had seven prostitutes, and he had a Cadillac, and he wore diamonds. And he was really important, you know. In my eyesight. And I idolized the guy.

Later on in the game, a guy named Tony B became my idol. Because Joey Flood to me wasn't shit, because he had to live off a broad, this wasn't too cool to me. But, Tony B didn't. He made it on his brain. He was a con man, he was swift. He played con.

So I came in contact with him myself. I got to know the guy . . . by being around and by being able to learn fast. I got to know him, and he took a liking to me, and by taking a liking to me, he took me under his wing. And the same thing you're doing now using a tape recorder, he used a tape recorder to learn me how to play. How to play con. He'd run the game down, and he'd be the vic [victim] and I'd play both parts. Until I learned it to perfection. Now this didn't come about in two weeks or three weeks, or a month; this come about in over a period of three years' time.

And I became pretty good. But actually, you know, I mean, maybe if I'd a had somebody . . . or seen somebody else . . . I mean, there was Joe Louis, but what the fuck, I didn't know Joe Louis. You know. And I don't want to be no fighter because I don't dig getting hit in my head. And I'm no baseball player, I'm no Jackie Robinson, you know. And I can't act worth a damn. So I mean, leaving all of them, this was the thing that I could do best.

So I did it, you know. And I paid the consequences for it because I went to jail three or four times, prison, that is. Couple time . . . all in all, it's not been easy, but it ain't been hard. I only been in jail something like eight months out of the last four years. Before that I was out eighteen months generally, eighteen months of partying. And then I went, and I did two years or something. And then I come back and partied again. 'Cause I was ready to party.

☐ ☐ ☐

But like I said, it gets to be a drag, too. This gets to be a drag, you know? I'm not condoning it; I'm not going against it. Because, I mean, it gave me a whole lot, man. You know, I ain't got nothing against the game because even now, if push comes to shove, I'll get back out there again and hustle. And I know that. And it won't take much for me to do it. I'm just like on the brink now, I'm teeter-tottering here, you know. I'm trying to see just what's in this shit, this work bit, man.

I'm just trying to see . . . you know, it's killing me. To be honest with you, yeah, it's killing me, man.

See, when you're raised up, like if I had a son, I'd start the kid around ten or around eight, I'd start learning him how to take out trash, and stuff. I'd give him a job and give him a sense of responsibility, then. "This is your thing, this is what you got to do, kid. Whether you like it or not, you got to do it. Why? Because I said so." You dig? Later on, when he got around thirteen or so, I'd make him get a paper route, to let him know, "I'm not gonna give you money all the time because when you grow up, I'm not gonna be able to give it to you. And why you got to work? Because the world says you got to work." So right from the start, he gets a sense of responsibility, and he forms a work habit.

☐ ☐ ☐

See, you got to have a work habit. Wow, I'm twenty-eight, man, I ain't never worked in my life. This is the first job.

Wow, every night I go out there. I look at the machine and I want to tell the foreman, you know, man, take that machine and ram it, 'cause I ain't going to do it.

But I did it and I'm hoping to eventually form a work habit. It's easier now than it was at the first, man. For about the first couple weeks, goddamn, I thought I was going to blow my mind. I said, "Wow, I just can't go out there no more."

Because the people out there, they talk different from what I talk . . . I mean, I can talk to them because of course, like I say, I can talk to them because of the fact that I learned to talk to squares. But to me, what they're talking about it, it doesn't even interest me. I mean, they're talking about going *deer hunting*. And I don't want to kill no deer! This is what they're talking about, deer hunting, or a guy's talking about what his wife cook. I don't care what his wife cook, or his baby's got the pneumonia. I don't care about this, because you see, I never had this before.

Now I talk to a couple guys around there, you know. They bug me, too, but I got to talk to somebody so I talk—I don't have to talk to nobody, but I talk to these two guys, you know. And they're hip squares, you know. These are the guys that run around, and they try to be real hip. And I listen to them, you know. And they're saying, "Man, this job here ain't shit." And they're saying this and they're saying that. They don't even know where they're at. And they're asking *me* for advice, and I know *I* don't know where I'm at.

But they're always telling me, "Yeah, man, I got this going for me and I got that going," and I egg them on, and I make them talk, you know, and tell me what they got going for them. 'Cause some day, who knows, I might be able to beat one of them. I mean, they're not my friends, anyway. They're associates. So, anyway, they're always telling me what they got going, but they're steadily working here beside me.

And I ask them questions. "Man, what do you really accomplish, what do you got?" One's got a car. That's a big deal, man. And, one's got a home. . . . Big deal. Fifty-four years old, he's got a home. With, I think, it's twenty-five years to pay for the home. Like I told him, "Man, you'll be dead, man, before that home ever gets paid for, more than likely."

He's living in it now. True. He's living in it about . . . well, they work double shifts, you see, they work sixteen hours. And then, when they come home, they sleep about six hours, so I'd say they're at home exactly two hours out of a day . . . when they're awake.

So what the hell is the use of, what good is a home to him? I mean, yeah, he'll give it to his kids. Cool. All that's good. But, fuck, if I got to work sixteen hours a day to give it to some *kids*? I ain't gonna do it!

They're working double shift. I worked a double one! I worked a double one last weekend, man; I worked a double shift! I worked from eleven o'clock Friday to seven o'clock Sunday morning. But after that, after working that way once, I told the foreman, "You got to be crazy, man, to ask me to even come back here, to do something like that. Don't ask me no more, don't even come around me with it."

See, I got a hostile attitude, man, against them jobs, I just don't like to work. Like right now, I mean, being honest, I really don't like to work. And I'm lazy, I know I'm lazy. The onliest thing that can hold my interest a long time is something like art, or reading, or something like that, man. Other than that, I don't dig it. Not too much.

It batters the mind. This is what gets me. This is what gets me. If I can go out there for eight hours, if I could lose consciousness, if I could go out there for eight hours, and stand there and just go *psht, psht*, you know, push buttons, that'd be all right. But I can't. I go out there and it seems as if, man, it's not all night, man, it's three nights.

And I see the same people, doing the same thing. But what really gets me, I guess you can understand what I'm saying, what really gets me is when I see guys that's been there all this time, man. Thirty years. And here's a guy sweeping the floor. Here's a guy walking around, an old man now, sweeping the floor, man, and I ask him something, "Hey, man, would you bring me a can of grease," or something. You know, he's supposed to do this. "Get it yourself, I been working here thirty years."

I mean I won't even argue with him. One night I asked the guy, I said, "Man, you've been here thirty years. So-in-the-fuck-what? And you got a *broom* with a pair of *yellow coveralls* on. That's *all* you got to show for thirty years."

"I got this, I got that."

"You ain't got shit, man. You know? Thirty years of your life is out here *for somebody else.*"

This is what I mean . . . I know even right now, while I'm talking to you, I ain't gonna make it. Cause I ain't gonna work no five years for them.

I'll probably work out the rest of this year. I'll probably work until I get finished with this court thing, and I get a good recommendation from there, and then that'll be good, and then I'll probably devise me some kind of means to get *me* something, you see.

Now the onliest difference is, after a while, after coming over here, I see something. I *can* work, but *I* got to have something, though, too, see? I've got to work for *myself*. That's the difference.

Carl Foreman (II)

I will be in the jail for eight or nine months most likely, before coming to trial. I would say that, as far as we're talking primarily about the County Jail, I would say that the system there is lousy. Everything about the jail stinks. That there . . . I can't really name anything good about it, say anything good about the place. Because it's just a rotten jail. It's ran all wrong. To me, and I been in all kinds of jails, from here all the way across the country. I've never seen a jail run like it is.

You can't get in touch with your lawyers when you want to. This is illegal. You can't see your people but like twice a month, and that's only for maybe half an hour. It's a lot of brutality down there, whereas police jumping on inmates and et cetera. The medical aid is terrible, it's just terrible. You got to be damn near dead in order to get some kind of medical attention. I seen a guy suffer a heart attack and they took him out and they brought him right back in. An old man, sixty-some years of age. There's rats there, in the jail—in fact, I killed one. And there's roaches. The food is terrible; it's always cold and its nasty. It's just a run-down place that's not really fit for a human being to live in.

And so this is why you have so many guys copping pleas there. Instead of staying there, at the jail, they'd rather just go ahead and spend maybe three or four years in the penitentiary at Jackson than to spend maybe seven or eight months down there, because of the fact that the conditions are so terrible. The way the justice is set up, I guess it's supposed to be you're not guilty until found guilty, you know. But like there, you're—it's like it's serving time in Hell, man! And it's just—it's just terrible! That is the onliest way I can describe it to you.

And the mental thing on a person is really bad because you don't have any mental outlet there. Not anything. They don't have any library. They have a little book wagon that comes by with obsolete books that really are no good. You can't get books in. Your people can't send you books in. So therefore, you have nothing. They don't even have chess on the wards, on some wards, so you can play chess. They got cards. You have got to buy everything off the wagon from the jail, which is up, the prices are up higher, a little higher than they are normally, so the jail's making a profit on you there. I don't think they're giving you your full rations of food per day because you never get enough to eat down there. You're always hungry.

You have to watch it down there all the time, continuously. Myself,

I'm scared to go back down there because like I told the police: "If you hit me, I'm gonna kill you. One way or the other. I don't want you to touch me." And I watch myself down there. I don't say nothing to the police down there. I don't converse with them, nor do I say anything derogatory to them, you know. Because I don't want one to touch me, period. And the way it's set up, it's all wrong.

It's over-crowded. Guys sleeping on the floor, guys spitting and puking; a guy's kicking the habit—he's shitting and he's throwing up on the floor. And you're *there*, man. It's filthy. Half the toilets in the joint don't flush. The block I was on, it didn't have any cold water. We had to get cold water in plastic bags. So this was a hassle. It leaked all over the floor so guys were sleeping in water. If you buy something off the wagon, like pies or stuff, you have got to put it up on the bunk or else the rats'll eat it up if it's on the floor. You know what I mean? And it's just a horrible set-up. I can't say nothing good about it.

[*What does it look like?*]

Well, they have two sides. Now, on the new side you have like a dorm. It's dormitory style. It's like ten or twelve bunks to one cell block. Like you're in there and you got one table or two. You got these bright flourescent lights that are on all day long until eleven-thirty at night. And sometimes if the guards just feel shitty he'll leave them on all night so you can't sleep in there. You got a radio that stays on constantly twenty-four hours a day so you can't hardly sleep.

[*You don't control them?*]

No, no, you don't control. They control it from upstairs. And in the new side, the onliest place you can exercise is in this little area where you're at. So it's maximum security, you would say. It's maximum security, it's not minimum security.

But at the maximum security actually it's better than that so-called minimum security they have there, because of the fact that you have a single cell by yourself and you're able to keep it clean. But they have a catwalk about three feet wide that they let you exercise on up there for about two hours a day. Then, you're back in the cells and you're locked up.

You got a radio and they play whatever they want. Any kind of old jive music they want to play, they blow it. Unless you got a dep on that will get some jazz on it. You got no books to read up there. So like, it's just like you just sit—sit around twiddling your thumbs, or you invent something to do while you're there. Or if you got somebody that'll write you, that's good, because you write letters, and you get some letters, whenever they want to let your mail in. Or if they have time to bring your mail up. Sometime, like I was there this time, they didn't bring our mail up for a week. They didn't have time. They said they were too busy.

But the old side, that's the side I'm talk about. It's so—it's just—just depressing. It's falling down. The plumbing is all messed up, like I said before. Ah, it stinks. It's filthy. Everything is wrong with it, man. There ain't nothing right with it.

And not only that, the deputies, I don't think these guys are even qualified to be over other men because a lot of them are just naturally brutal people. They have no compassion for other human beings at all. In other words, they don't look on you as a human being. They're looking on you more as—as a convict. But what I think they fail to realize is that we're not convicts yet, because we haven't been convicted when we're in the County Jail. We're awaiting trial. We are not really guilty of no crime. We're guilty of being too poor, not to get out on bond.

That's the thing we're guilty of. Because rich kids come in there, white kids come in there from Grosse Point and they go back to court out there in Grosse Point and the judge will not let them come back to the jail. He say "To hell with it. I'm not sending them to the Wayne County Jail. I'll put them on the street before I let them stay there."

But for the average black kid out of the inner-city ghetto, he's down there not because of the crime he committed, but because he's too poor to get out on bond. If he got out on bond, two times out of one he would beat the case. You see what I mean?

He stays in there for two or three months and finally the prosecutor comes over and tells him: "Look, kid, listen. We got a deal for you. We don't wanna keep you in here no more. I know you don't like your surroundings in here." "You're right, you're right, you're right." "So I'll tell you what we're gonna do. We're gonna take you over there; we're gonna give you two-to-five. We're gonna let you off easy this time. We're giving you a break now." And the kid says "OK, OK, when will I leave?" Right? He's that happy to leave there.

Then when he gets up in Jackson, he realizes what has happened. He could have beat this case. The guys, the jailhouse lawyers, tell him, "Man, what's wrong with you? Didn't nobody see you go in there. Didn't nobody see you come out. Why did you plead guilty?" He says, "Oh, man, I don't know, man." Well, the reason is because he was down in all that squalor, all that filth. He wanted to get away from it. So he took the first out he could.

And to me, if I had to do a year in Jackson or six months in the County Jail, I'd rather do a year in Jackson. I would. As much as I hate Jackson. I don't like Jackson either, but I'd much rather go to Jackson, because at least I could keep my mind occupied there. Whereas in the County Jail I can't keep my mind occupied. I can't. There's nothing to do except sleep and get up. And sleep. And maybe they got some old flunky cowboy books around there to read. And I don't read cowboy books because I don't like cowboys. And that's about it, you know. As far as that jail's concerned.

It's hard for me to describe the jail to you.

[*There's nothing to do?*]

Nothing.

You judge your average stay in the jail, from the time you're booked down there 'til the time you get out, you're going to stay there about nine months. You're never out on the outside. You never get outside to exercise or nothing.

[*Nothing?*]

No, you don't go outside for nothing in that jail.

The onliest time possible for you to go outside is if you had a case, out in the suburbs, like out in Inkster, or some place. Then you would go outside and get into a car and you'd be transported. But if you're going to Recorder's Court in Detroit, you never get outside to exercise. You never see the sun, because of the fact that when you go to court you go through tunnels down underneath the street to the new courthouse building. Then when you come up, you right in the courtroom. So you don't get a chance to go outside at all.

[*Your cell doesn't have any window onto the outside?*]

No. No. You have a set of bars, you got your cell bars. Then when they let you out, they let you out in the exercise thing, what they call the Rock. And the Rock is enclosed by bars, too. Now, about four to five feet from *those* bars, you have the windows.

And these windows, when I was there, they were open. But I understand since I left that they've closed all these windows because supposedly guys were getting dope up there. And they were throwing mail out the window and stuff. Quite naturally, they're gonna throw mail and stuff out the window because it's the onliest way you can get it out and know it's got out.

But other than that, as far as you getting any sunshine— No. You're not going to get no sunshine in there.

When it's hot outside, if it's ninety outside, well then you, you figure it's about a hundred and five in there. They got no air conditioning. They got nothing in there.

[*I'd go crazy in there. I have to be outside. I can't stand staying inside more than so long.*]

Sometime you feel like you going out of your *mind* in places like these, man, cause you just can't find nothing to do.

[*That's what gets me. They don't have any activities? You're not working?*]

Oh, no. You're not working. And everybody would want to work rather than sit around.

[*Well, how do you pass the day?*]

If you're lucky you got a deck of cards, so you play pinochle for a while. Or either you got guys on the block who got money, so you gamble all day. Or you get lucky and you get some dope up on the thing, and you drop some beans and you go to sleep. If not, you just sit around.

[*How big of a space are you in? If you're in the dorm in the new part, how big is that?*]

It's not too big, man. It's not enough for—well, see it's supposed to be for ten men. But they'll have about fifteen men in there. In other words five of them will be sleeping on the floors. And so you got fifteen men in a area really meant for ten men. And actually the area's not big enough for ten men. So you got guys throwing cigarette butts all down on guy's bedding that's on the floor. You got guys pissing where you got to sleep. The shitter's right out there where you have to sleep. And the guys are not flushing the toilets. And then you got guys yelling all night long.

[*Okay. If you're not in the dormitory, what kind of a space are you in?*]

Then you're over on the old side. You've got two-men cells. But generally there's three, and sometimes there's been four men in one cell. And a cell is just about as big as this room is. Not even as big as this room.

[*Like if I stood up and stretched out my arms I could just about touch the walls?*]

Yeah, that's how wide it is. But the cell's not that long. The cell would be about this long.

[*So it's about an arm's length plus maybe half an arm?*]

Yeah, and you got two bunks, and a sink, and a shitter.

[*In the daytime it doesn't seem like there's enough room, seems like if you're walking around you'll bump into each other.*]

Well, in the daytime, they let you out.

[*Well, during the daytime where are you?*]

You're out on the Rock. You're just walking around. Or laying down.

[*How big a space is that?*]

That's about as—oh, on a big Rock, it's just about as wide as this room. A little wider than this room. And, say from here out to that light out there.

[*That's about thirty yards.*]

Yeah, about thirty yards long. And you exercise in that. You walk in there. You walk around.

[*It's that narrow?*]

Yeah.

[*Like about three yards wide? That's like a* dog run *at a kennel!*]

Yeah. And in there you got one, two, three, four tables. And you've got like a picnic table in the end. And you've got a shower which they open once a day. When it's working. It's generally not working, so you don't shower for maybe a week or two weeks. Then when it's working, it's so hot you can't get in it. Or it's so cold that don't nobody want to take a shower.

[*How about clothes? Laundry?*]

You get clothes once a week. You have got to have your own underwear. You wash them out yourself. Guy ain't got none, just too bad, he don't wear none. They give you one sheet which doesn't cover up the dirty mattress, with piss stains on it and shit. If you lucky you can get two.

It's just rotten down there, man. I can't name, I can't say anything constructive about the place. There is nothing constructive about it. They treat you like dogs. They holler at you. Everything they got to say, they can never, I've had to ask officers time and time again, "Don't holler at me, you know? Because I'm highly emotional. And I get a shitty attitude if you holler at me." I guess I'm lucky because I'm big.

Because the average kid out there in that inner city, Black kid, he's not no criminal. I mean he might of took something; but he's not no hardened criminal. He took something, he stole something, he did wrong, he committed an offence, but he's not no criminal—yet. But— when you start putting him in a place like the Wayne County Jail, you turn out that rebellious side of him. And the first thing you know, you've *got* a hardened criminal. You've got a guy that's going to say: "Fuck you! Fuck authority. Look what they did to me down there. Fuck 'em!"

I've heard them, a lot of kids say, "Man, when I get out of here, I'm going on the wild, I'm going on the knot, and the first police come up to me, I'm going to blow his brains out. I wouldn't give a fuck." And they mean it.

They mean it. That's why so many police are getting killed now. You notice how many police are getting killed? And it's always the young guys that's offing them. The guys are twenty-one and twenty-two years old. Before, you heard of police get killed, it would be a hardened criminal, a three-time loser, maybe shot it out with the police, he don't want to go back. But now it's a guy who's never been in trouble before, maybe once before, he's been in trouble, he might of been down through that Wayne County Jail, say, "Well fuck it, before I have to go through that shit again, I'd rather die." And they'll shoot it out, and they'll kill a policeman. And now his whole life is screwed up. Where maybe you could of stopped it if you would of had some kind of decent facilities for him when he first got arrested, if you could of gave him some kind of help, what he needed, you know what I mean.

Half the guys—man, I say, over half the guys shouldn't even be in there. Should be out on bond. First offender, for breaking into a car trunk, twenty-five-hundred-dollar bond. What kind of shit is that? That don't even make sense.

That don't even make sense. I don't see how a judge could justify that. And then they're hollering about, "Our court dockets are so full." They don't care.

They don't give a damn about—they don't care about them kids, man. They don't care what's happening with them. Ah, it's pathetic. It really is.

I mean, I know *I* get bitter, and generally, I'm an easy-going guy. But when *I* get bitter, it's *got* to be bad. And I'm constantly on edge down at that place.

That's why it scares me. It's not so much what they are going to do to me, because I already have made up my mind if one of them touches me, I'm going to hurt him. As bad as I possibly can. That means if I could kill him, I'm gonna try that, too.

What scares me is that I might do this! And then I wind up for life—for what? For one of them motherfucker's lives down there. It ain't even worth it. Because to me, all of them, most of the guards, are perverted, sadistic bastards. And really, that's what they are.

But I know that system down at that Wayne County Jail, it's got to be changed. 'Cause if you don't. . . . For a while they've been containing it because they keep the guys separated, but eventually . . . I say in the next year, I'll predict this: In the next year all hell's gonna break loose down there in that Wayne County Jail. Because, you see, you got a understaffed, understand, you got sixty guards controlling a thousand-some-odd men, you see. And if those guys ever would really think, and get those keys away, and open up the jail, and let them guys out, imagine what would happen. You'd have a thousand felonies loose in your city. You know. That's what would happen, because they couldn't contain them. Oh yeah, a lot of them would get killed. No doubt in my mind. A lot of them would get killed. But there would be some that would get loose. There are some dangerous individuals down there! There are some dangerous individuals. Some individuals that were on Rocks with me who—I wasn't scared of them, but . . . I was leery of them. I didn't want them around me that much, because they were killers.

I mean, in a way you need prisons. And then in a way you don't.

But you just can't throw everybody that commits a crime in a prison, you know? Because there are guys out there legally committing crimes every day. And they get away with it, you know. But, ah, you know, this, this system we live in. . . .

Man, you know—I mean, like before, man, when I was handling good, when I was handling good money. Sure, the police know I took off a lot of sting. The police know I ripped. They knowed what I got out. They knowed when I made a good play. But yeah, they'd come to me and say "Uh—uh, Carl, we heard you got on today, man. You got on with such and such amount."

And I say, "Yeah."

"Well, kick over, baby!"

You know, you kick the bread over and they'd remove your mug shot from the book, and when the person comes down to look at the files, or to look at the mug shots to see if you're there, well—your picture's not there. So therefore, you never in there. But that's when you got the money. You got the unbrella.

There were cases that I should have got prosecuted on where I paid off. So you could say it's the system, man. It's the capitalistic system. You know. And maybe, like those cats was saying in Attica, maybe we are political prisoners. Maybe all of us are.

□ □ □

Because I certainly, for one, can say conditions, circumstances made me what I am today. I don't believe I had a choice in my making at first. And when I did have a choice, it was too late, because I had already turned out bad. When I did become, when I was thinking for myself, I was too late because I was turned out bad, you know.

So the system made me this way, man. I mean, I don't really have the answers. I wish I did.

[*Yeah, It's—it's, you know, it's easy to say "system."*]

Sure, it's easy to cop out. I was discussing this with another person. I think it was this doctor here. And he said, "Well, that's copping out, Carl. That's saying the system is the reason for your downfall."

Well, who *can* I blame? Who can I blame? I mean, I'm part of the system. Who can I blame?

I mean, I wasn't, I don't think no individual's just *born* a criminal.

Or—or—or—you're not born with, just the wanting to steal or take, or mimic, or—or—or—or—do wrong. Essentially you're all born the same way. But there's certain circumstances and conditions that can turn an individual to make him take a different path.

It's just like you say, there's one kid that came out of the ghetto that made a Congressman. While the other one came out and made a great prisoner. And they always use this; that's the first thing that comes up in any discussion. "Well, Carl, there were those who was raised in the same environment you was. And they made it." Yeah, but you know what? They had somebody to help them. They had a different person that channeled them in a different direction. You see what I mean? Whereas my—people that helped me channel me in one direction, they got channeled in another direction.

So therefore, you still say it's the system, man. It's the system and it's the way it works. Or the society that we live in. What are you going to do? Tear down the system?

[*I'm trying to think whether I really think—I'm trying to think of whether I really believe—*

[*I guess the way that I feel about it, it's not like*: "*Why does this single person do this single thing, why does that single person do that single thing?*" *If you look at anybody why does he do something—first of all you'll never understand him. I don't know why I do what I do. Okay? And I'll make up a different reason every time. But—*

[*See, it's a confusion. The issue isn't really, who do I blame? You understand? Like a* personal *thing.*

[*Like, I* know, *if I'm born middle-class, what's going to come* natural. *What's* built *there for me to* use. *Okay? What's built there for me to* use. *The* odds *are it's not going to get me anywhere near Jackson prison. And I can do some mean things to some individuals. But none of that is going to get me near Jackson.*

The odds are in favor that you're not going—

[*Yeah. It takes some peculiar circumstances. And, and . . . I think what I don't like about the way it is, is that: By the same token, if I'm born poor, what's around for me to use. Whatever I do that's* natural *for me to do using what's* around *for me to use, I have got a lot of good chances of getting involved in something like the police or with Jackson. Okay?*

[*And it's like I don't really think people are real different from each other. Okay? People seem very much alike each other. They just kind of do what's around to do.*]

So then you're saying essentially the same thing I'm saying. It's environment.

[*Well, I stopped because I thought, hell, are we just copping out here? It's easy to say. But it does seem. . . .*

[*You know, people, people don't seem that complicated. It's not like you have to invent a complicated story of why did somebody do something. It's more like: Aw hell, it was there. Why they do something? It was there to do.*]

Why does a hungry man steal, steal a piece of bread?

[*Yeah, well, we know that.*]

'Cause he's hungry. So this is the same thing when you're in the ghetto. Why does a child in the ghetto do certain thing? Because just like you say, because it's there for him to do and that's *all* he got to do. So he's going to do it. And chances are it's going to lead him in, as you said, to contact with the police. And chances are, his chances of going to Jackson is *way* better than the middle class.

[*Okay. Now look here. I don't want a soap opera. I mean, is he hungry? Is that why he's trying a B and E? Yeah, I know there are kids hungry. Okay? Well, let's get into that anyway, we might have some different feelings there. I know lots of kids, I think, they're going to do a thing, not because they're hungry. It was there to do.*]

Oh, I can understand, I understand what you're saying now. Just like when I used to go in Kresge's and steal little things not because I needed them. Because it was a dare. You know kids: "I dare you to do it." Well kids are going to be kids. And kids are going to do kid things. We realize that. But I'm not talking about the kids. I'm not talking about—kids like this, who'll take the dare or something like that. Or a lot of dares have ended kids up in the penitentiaries, I grant you that. I'm talking about a kid who *seriously* is *hungry*. His—his mother and his father. . . .

[*Okay now, how many kids are really hungry like that?*]

Oh, man—it's a tremendous amount of them.

[*You tell me.*]

There's a tremendous amount of them. Tremendous. If you went down on John R. Street today and walked the streets tonight, right tonight, you could see them out there, hungry. And they'd be asking you for nickels, "Mister, you got a nickel? You got a dime?" They ain't kidding. They want to go buy some candy.

[*It's not jive? They're really hungry?*]

No. They're hungry.

Their mothers done gave their money away to some pimp, or some guy. This is not society's fault. Of course not. This is the woman's fault. . . . And then again, you can say again, it's society's fault that she's got to give the money to the pimp. Because why is a guy pimping in the first place? Because society made him like that. You see, so you got the big circle again. Where you going to wind up at?

[*I don't know, but it's got to be thought about, hard. It really does.*]

Yeah, it does. And I believe it begins with the children. You begin a society with its children. You channel them in the right direction. That normal middle-class child, he's channeled in the right direction. He's got the mother influence. He's got the father influence. He's channeled in the right direction, so therefore he goes in the right direction. According to the society that we live in, he goes along. Somewhere along the lines he might rebel, but generally he's going to go along. He's going to be accepted in this society as a substantial citizen.

So this is what you're going to have to do down here in the ghettos. Before you go down there preaching that bullshit about, "You can come out of here, you can come out of that." I think you're going to have to go down there and tear down a lot of them tenements. You're going to have to get a lot of them rats out of there. You have to put some food in some stomachs. And you are going to show some of them ADC mammas where it's worth their while to get off of their asses and go to work. They can sit at home collect three hundred dollars a month, for having babies. So you got to give these people an incentive to want to get out to do something.

Now a kid has the incentive. He has the motive for stealing. Sure, there's a lot of kids down there that steal, that they're not hungry. No, they're not hungry. But every day they look at TV and they see the beautiful clothes on TV. Every day they walk down the street, they see the beautiful clothes people wear. Every day they see the nice cars.

You wonder why the kid steals a car. He's sixteen. He sees the nice car. But he sees those middle-class people got it. He ain't got it. So he goes and steals it. So what is it, man? You know, society puts it there and then says everybody's supposed to have this kind of car for every motherfucker in America. That's bullshit, you know.

I mean, maybe it's a cop-out, man. Maybe it is a cop-out in a sense, because you blame it all on society. But I can't just blame it on an individual, I can't put it on an individual.

I wish I could. I've evaluated myself. I've tried to put myself and say, "Don't feel sorry for yourself, Carl. Look at it realistically. Who made your downfalls? Who made your path like it is?"

Okay. I could say realistically, a lot of my trouble comes from me. Because I got old enough, I realized right from wrong. I know right from wrong. But I'm talking about, in order to start doing that, there had to be a beginning. There had to be a time when somebody channeled me different. You see what I mean?

[*Yeah. Now, see, there's two very different things. One is, okay, when you or I, when we look at ourselves—first of all, this whole thing: "Whose fault?" If I'm talking about myself or you're talking about yourself, that doesn't do any good. So what?*

[*What difference would it make if you said either: "Well, I'm an evil man," or you said, "It's an evil society?" So what?*

[*What's that got to do with anything? If you're talking for yourself. Because for yourself, where it is, whatever the world is like: Here you are. And, you're grown. So, like you're saying, use your five senses.*

[*Okay. And you figure, "If I do this thing, that's what's going to happen; if I do that thing, that's what's going to happen. However I got to where I am today, doesn't really make much difference. I'm here."*]

And so I'm gonna make the best of it.

[*Yeah. Or: Also, "Where do I want to be?" Okay. You know, you know nobody's going to give you—take you—carry you, right?*]

Right.

[*It's going to be your thing. Okay. But that's just if you're talking to yourself about yourself. It may do some good to try to understand the past. But it seems to me that basically when you're talking to yourself about yourself, and where you want to go, in a way the past is irrelevant.*]

I don't think so, I think in order for one to know himself, he has to know something of his past.

[*Alright. You're right. But . . . still . . . it does seem to me after you've looked at it some . . . the only thing you can control for yourself, you know, is yourself. . . . Suppose—suppose one says, "Well, that's society." Alright. You know, so what? Does that mean, "Well, I'll let society do to me . . . the next thing, like the last thing?"*]

No no no no no no no no, but see, see, Professor, that would be beautiful if we lived in a world where it was . . . how can I put it? A individual world. Where each individual could just live and do his thing.

And be left alone. Like you like to take tapes. Cool. You want to write books. You want to teach. Let you do your thing. Groovy.

But we don't live in a world like that. We live in a world where we're controlled by laws. Other laws are controlled by those laws, and other laws, and legislators, and all kinds of bullshit.

We live in a world that's conflicts. Okay. So, I can't do my thing the way that I want to. If I'm Black and I want to get out on the streets and I want to preach and I want to stand on a box and say: "Whitey is no motherfucking good, and here's the reason why he's no good." Chances are a white police car's going to come by and they are going to put me in jail. They are going to say, "Nigger, what's wrong with you?"

I can't do my thing. Actually no one in the United States can really. He's trained, man, from the cradle to the grave, to react a certain way. The system says, "You can do this, then this'll happen and then this'll happen and this'll happen and this'll happen."

It was already there when you was born, you know. I was born in the ghetto. The chances are from the minute I was started born you could see me coming to prison. Because step by step it looked that way. The chances are my kids, if I ever have any, you know, they're going to have it hard, too.

If we lived in a individual world where people could do their individual thing, or if you lived by yourself in the woods someplace, well, then, you could do that. But no, where we live, not in a teeming city like . . . *Detroit*, you know? You can't do your thing. Somebody always going to step on your feet.

You can withdraw, yeah, to a certain extent. And if you withdraw too far, then the people around you, they're going to say: "Do you know what? Ezekiel, something's wrong with him. He's kinda off, you know?" And if you go too much further, they are going to say: "You know, he doesn't keep control of those kids." You know? So they're going to go and try to take your kids. And the next thing they're going to judge you incompetent, and you are going to be in the nuthouse. They are going to say you crazy because you don't act like you supposed to act in this society, you see what I mean?

[*Yeah. I suppose that depends—*

[*You see the thing that I was trying to say was—I got to think, about what you were saying—the thing I was trying to say was that: for yourself, you use your senses and figure out, "What do I want?" Like I say, you can't go on that box, you'd be knocked off. Okay. You know that. So you make a choice. Okay? If you want to talk to somebody and say to them, "Well, whitey's no damn good," well, you don't have to stand on a box to say that. In fact, you'd be a fool to do that. Okay? Nobody asked you to be dumb. That was the thing I was trying to say, if what you're talking about is a grown person talking to himself about himself. Okay?*

[*What I was saying was, I'm not sure how much value there is for him to talk very long about, "Was this me or society that got me here?" It's almost like he has to . . . just, you know, so what? Decide for himself: What happens if I do this? What happens if I do that? And what do I want to have happen? . . . What do I want to have happen?*

[*That's one thing. It's a different thing if you're saying not for one man talking to himself, but, here, you're trying to find, how the goddamn hell do things work? So we're talking about my children and your children, you know, and a million children. And then you get to asking, well, what is going to happen with these children?*]

That's right.

[*To understand so we can begin to say "What the hell should we be—*]

Well, I think the first thing we can do is what me and you are doing. I mean if we talking in terms of racial thing. Black and white's got to learn to get together.

[*Yeah. But I think it's more than racial. It's got a whole lot about rich and poor, too.*]

There you go—well, you got—I mean— what are we gonna do? Rich and poor. If we tore down the whole system, tore it down and built up another one, we'd still have our differences. I mean, there's no utopia. At least if it is, where is it at?

[*Okay. But does that mean that they'll always have to be. . . . Look, today, a fifth of the children are in a dangerous place. I'm going to use those words: a dangerous place.*

[*It's a dangerous place because if you do what's around to be done, the odds are . . . unhappy things are going to happen to you. You are going to get hurt.*

[*You're saying to me, "Well, nothing's perfect." Yeah, I know that. Are we stuck with that, always going to be, one way or another?*]

No, I don't think that's always gonna be, because I think that, it's up to you, your kids' welfare, is your responsibility.

So here is where the individual comes in. You got your individual little kingdom right here. This is your little utopia.

This is the onliest place I can see a utopia here, is in my own house. I got my little utopia here. I got my little kids. I can channel, or I can—not make them just like I want them to be, but I can give them a sense of responsibility so that when they do go out to meet society, or get old enough to meet that world, they'll be able to meet it head on, and stand up and face the responsibility like men and women should face it. Accordingly.

And they'll still retain their own individuality in doing it. You know? And not just become a part or be a robot, like the one's that working at Ford's every day: *Knock-Press-Bang! Knock-Press-Bang! Knock-Press-Bang!* "How much do you make this week, maaan?" "Two hundred thirty dollars." "What you gon' do?" "I'm going get drunk tonight, maaan." "Why you come in late tonight, George?" " 'Cause I got drunk, woman. Fuck you." Okay. Monday morning; *Knock-Press-Bang! Knock-Press-Bang!*

He's a robot, man. He's a tool.

Okay, I don't want to see mine grow up that way. I want to see him grow up to whatever he wants to be, he can do it. If that's what he wants, that *Knock-Press* and that *Bang!*—then cool. That's your bag, kid, groovy. But give him the right to be whatever he wants to be, whether he's black, whether he's red, whether he's white, whether he's green— give him the right to do it.

[*Now—about work. Okay, what's real here? You got your children. I got my children. What about work—if you're Black. And it's nineteen seventy-one. What's the real story now?*]

I don't think actually that it's any different in nineteen seventy-one . . . than it was . . . in nineteen forty-one. You know. You still working for the Man. I mean, if you're Black.

Of course, now we got more technicians, we got more doctors, we got more lawyers, and lot of professional people. But essentially, the masses of Blacks are laborers, still.

So what's it like for a laborer? It's just like what I said.

He generally is a guy with a twenty-year mortgage on a home, that just beats the hell out of him because he's going to get *cheated*. 'Cause in the first place he didn't come up in this society that our kids is coming up—one thing about the Black children now, that's coming up, they're educated. You're not going to beat this generation. Because you're not going to beat him with figures, or you're not going to beat him by percentage points, because he knows about it. You taught him this. So you can't beat him that way. Like you beat my father. My forefather, my father, they were beat. They had to spend maybe, on a eight-thousand-dollar house, they wound up spending maybe nineteen or twenty grand for it. Not knowing what they were doing.

But right now the average thing is happening, as it was happening then. He goes to work five days a week, and he does it. And he works hard, the average Black man. He works hard out there in them factories.

Some of these jobs don't look it. People come by and look at him and say, "He ain't doing shit, man." But it's hard to sit there, because his mind becomes stagnant. He becomes just like a robot, man. So when he gets home, here he's got maybe four or five kids and they're shooting questions at him. They're saying, "Daddy, why?" And, generally, what's happening with the Black man, he isn't qualified to answer the kid's questions, "Why?" So the kid is going to go out in the street and he's going to ask, "Why?"

So what's going to happen then when the kid runs out in the street? The poor Black man works hard. And he's going to say, "Fuck it." And on Friday night, he's going to put on his good glad-rags. Get nigger-sharp. You dig? And he's going to go down to the place. He's going to get a whore someplace; he's going to get a bottle someplace. He's going to lay up, and he's going to have him some partying. Some fun. *To try to forget that he got to meet the Man Monday*. Again.

Of course now, you have other guys: you got artists, you got guys that's really doing their own things. This is seventy-one. You know. And you've got guys now that's doing their thing. Not exactly as they would like it to be, but they're doing something that they're happy at doing.

Ah, I don't know how to explain it. It's just like . . . you know, some. . . . Ah, my, my father, I used to dislike the cat, you know. Ah, because he never gave me much of a chance. And I blamed him for a lot of my troubles. I said, "Boy, this—that Black motherfucker." I said, "Man, if the cat would have had anything—" Now I realize that the cat didn't have much hisself to go on. He didn't really know which way to go hisself. And he still fucked up and confused, man.

He was a part of that, I guess, status quo, man. Whitey really made him, you know? He was just like them old-time whitey-made niggers. They made them just like that. To think one way: "You a nigger. You stay in a nigger's place. You gonna get what a nigger deserves, and that's all you can expect."

So I used to dislike the guy for that. Ah, when I had a chance to ever bring a problem to him, I'd bring it, man, and it would crack me up because he couldn't answer it. I'd laugh at him and say, "Wow, you don't know that, man?"

A math problem, a English problem, or anything. Well, the cat didn't know it 'cause he didn't have adequate education. So imagine the feeling; now I can see how he must have felt. Here was a kid, his son, coming to him with problems that he couldn't answer.

So now my old man's an alcoholic. Indirectly, I think I'm the result of him being a alcoholic. Indirectly, I feel as he's the result of me being a narcotic addict. You see what I mean? Because we preyed on each other. You see? But, again, whose fault is it?

□   □   □

So as far as what it is, being Black, it's hard to define, man. Because sometime it's beautiful to be Black. Sometime you listen to them spirituals, man, or when you see one of them pretty Black broads walking down the street, or when you walk down the street, man, and you see people, you know, they ain't got much, Jack, but they happy. You know. They laughing and they joking, and then you see the beauty in being Black.

And then sometime, it's hell to be Black. In nineteen seventy-one. When you look in the paper and you see pictures of dogs eating up Black kids. Or firemens shooting water on them. Or, Whitey's turning buses over, on kids. Or bombing buses.

When you go out to the factory, and you see that damn near every six men that come in there is Black, you start to wonder, "Damn, something's got to be wrong. Because it's all Black out here, man. Why ain't Whitey out here working?" You know? "Why is Whitey in the front office and I'm here? I got an education, I know I certainly qualify to be a foreman. See, I passed it too." You wonder things like this. And then it ain't so nice to be Black.

But nowadays, even when it ain't nice, I think more Blacks are becoming aware of their Black awareness. And they're becoming proud.

And they're beginning to say, "Either I'm gonna get what I want or else I'm gonna tear it down completely. And you can't take nothing from nothing because I ain't got nothing no goddamn way, so you can't *hurt* me, man. If you kill me, well, I'm mentally dead anyway. You got me working out here like a robot any fucking way. So mentally I'm dead anyway."

It's hell, man. It's hell being a Black man. In some respects. In some respects it's beautiful.

part three

excerpts

catherine foster

On a freezing December morning, Lame Catherine has run out of
money and food, her man is ill, the rent is due, they are plagued by rats,
and now the hot water doesn't work.

Catherine Foster

That's the truth! I ain't lying! I ain't got no water nowhere but in my
kitchen. And then that be cold. That be cold. I ain't had no . . . I can't
wash my dishes today! Because I ain't got no hot water!

He going to tell me something else. No, no! I don't live in a damn slum
like this! Never lived like this before. 'Til I come here. That factual
truth.

I ain't got no—now, how I'm going to take a bath? Tote water from out
of the kitchen sink! And I ain't got no hot water right now to wash dishes
in there. I can't wash my dishes!

I had to go to my sister's house to take a bath! It been cut off for going
on three or four weeks, a month now. I ain't got no hot water. In my
bathtub, in my kitchen, neither. Listen, I ain't got no water. What am I
going to wash dishes in cold water for? You can't wash grease off a plate,
can you.

My boss is Mr. Ricket. I got nothing but rats up in here. Now I got to
tote hot water? Naw, no, no! I mean, I pay him so much money a week.

□　□　□

But I ain't living in no slum no more! If I can't get no bath water in my
bathtub.

Rats come in my house! My man scared to get up.

Rats come here. Big old fat rats wander in here. I ain't scared of no

141

rat. But I was sitting here and that rat went 'twixt my leg. I said, "Wow!" Luther sat up; he said, "You scared of rats?" I said, "Oh, no, he just nothing."

He was soft. He felt funny, you know. Running 'twist me.

☐ ☐ ☐

And I fell down them damn stairs, and hurt my leg. Put my foot in that goddamn step! And Bernard told me, say, call your worker and say I ain't paying. Say, call your worker.

☐ ☐ ☐

Some of us in this world now dumb to the fact; we don't know what's going on in the world. Somebody got to come along and wake us up. Right? You come round, you wake us up to the fact, what's going on what we don't know.

You not doing that? Well, get out of here then! (She laughs.) Here is what I would say to you, I was just teasing then, here's what I was trying to say. So many white people now got colored people under their feet. They walking on us, Negro. We dark-skinned, they are white, you understand?

They got us under their feet; they walking on us now. We try to climb up to the fact of them and we got mother wit with that. You understand what I mean?

Mother wit, with this. Lot of men right now, they can't even not write their names. Why? They can't get no schooling. They . . . they . . . they . . . right now, people see their name on the wall, they don't know it. You understand? Why? When they come up here they didn't have no schooling. They didn't have any sufficient clothes to wear to school. They couldn't go to school. Right now I know, certain people right here, you write their name over on the wall, I bet they don't know it. And I know a man and I feel sorry for him today. I can read and write, but I really feel sorry that he can't do that.

You understand what I'm talking about? You understand what I mean, don't you? I think that's pitiful, because they didn't have nobody to tell them things. They didn't have sufficient clothes to wear to school.

☐ ☐ ☐

It's wintertime now; it's sleeting, it's snowing out there. Shit. And I ain't getting no motherfucking heat in here. And they going to charge me rent?

Now I mean the factual of the truth now. These are wrong here. And now he going to want a dollar more from me. Yeah. Rent going up. And look here, look up the side of the wall. These roaches be walking tall, these roaches and rats.

Can't be on them at night. Ask Luther. Luther say, "Give me some water." Hell, he scared. I'm scared, too. He say, "Go get me a little water." I said, "Luther!" I lay right back down.

These rats come in here.

I'll show you the rats that are dead. He killed them.

Why do I stay here? I ain't got no choice. I ain't got nowhere else to go.

joanne

JoAnne came over one afternoon to talk with Catherine. JoAnne is a bus driver for the city, one of the first women in that position, but she didn't want to speak of that; rather, she wanted to talk about the disturbances on campuses, which made her anxious.

JoAnne

Now I have a son in college. And I'm really interested in what they're doing in college today. It cost quite a deal of money to send your kids to college today. It's not just like getting a high school education. It costs you money.

I'm sending my son to college. I'm not married. I'm a single woman and I work and I'm trying to send my son through college because I'm trying to make him responsible. I'm trying to open up things that could happen today, the ways of life and the ways that people should live regardless to whether they do live this way or not.

I have a very open heart. And I'm Christian-hearted. My mother raised me. My mother was a very Christian woman and she knows nothing but Christianity. And she raised me in this respect. Respect. And do unto others as you would have them do unto you. And this I was raised with and I respect that as of today. And I teach it to my son the same thing down the line.

Now, my son is nineteen years old. He graduated at the age of sixteen. And, I never had any trouble with my son. He doesn't have his name on police records as of today. And he's a very respectable kid around the city. And, as being a mother, working hard, doing the things that I think

144

a mother should do, I've given up very much for the kid. I try to teach
him the right way to go.

I was born in the state of Georgia. I was raised there until I was the
age of sixteen. And I've always been able to get along with the Black and
the white. I've never had no conflicts whatsoever. I've got along with the
Black and the white. So, therefore, it didn't give me no reason to hate the
white people. Right? I got along with those people. Did I have any reason
to think different? *No.*

The people that I worked for. . . . I worked for one particular family
that the lady wanted to treat me like a puppy. And she brought my food
out on this place, something like a front porch? She brought my food out
there. At my break hour, she brought my food out there and told me, she
say, "JoAnne, it's time for your lunch. You may have your lunch here."
And her name was Mrs. Clark and I asked her, I say, "Yes," I say, "Nice
Mrs. Clark," I say, "Why do you bring my lunch out here?" And I always
been used to fixing my own lunch whenever I want to eat. Always been
used to going in and fixing my own lunch and eating whatever I want to.
I say, "Why you bring my lunch out here?" And she told me, she said,
"Oh." This is what she told me. She said, "Ohhh, you eat what I bring
you or you don't eat." I said "Thank you, Mrs. Clark." I said, "Take it
back. I'm not hungry." And she took the food back.
  In the meantime I start to do her kitchen. Mop her kitchen. I had a
wet mop and I was mopping her kitchen. She came in there. She
screamed and she yelled. She say, "Oh, what are you doing? You're
ruining my baseboards! I never had this to happen before!" And I
jumped back with the mop. I said, "What do you mean, Mrs. Clark? I'm
only mopping the kitchen."
  And she said to me, "Oh, JoAnne, you don't do it like this. I'll show
you how." And she went back somewhere and she got two or three pads
of paper and she brought it back with a sponge. And she got down on her
knees. And she start going all around the baseboard and on the floor and
what not, show me what to do. And I said, "Mrs. Clark, do you expect me
to go over your whole kitchen this way? With that sponge—on my
knees—and this piece of paper?" She said, "Well, yes, JoAnne." She
says, "I'm sorry about everything. I know that you're young and everything. I usually use elder women. And I know that you're young and
everything, but this is the way I always have my work done—by hand.

You go over the baseboards and the kitchen and you mop it with your hands and you wipe it with your hands."

I said, "Well, you pay me now." I told her—this was in Georgia—I said, "You pay me now. I am not going over this floor, mopping it and wiping it on my hands and knees. I'm not going to take that, I'm sorry. I'm not going over this floor." So in the meantime she took me in, and she pays me this little bit she brought me. And she said that she was sorry. She said, "I'm sorry, JoAnne, and everything." She says, "But in the meantime, since you can't do my work the way I want you to do it, I have to let you go. Because, this is the way I'm used to getting it done." And she paid me, smile, and shake my hand. And she let me go.

The house was splendid. It was nice. And the lady was nice. The lady was nice. But, she didn't want to respect me.

Now all the people that I worked for thereafter, they treat me as human. You know what? I worked for people after that that I used to sit with at the table. When I got the breakfast ready, fix coffee and what not, I sit to the table with them. And have coffee with them. I took care of their kids. But I sit to the table, had coffee with them and what not, and then the family would go out to work and leave the whole house to me. And I did all of this housework in my own way, which I went in every corner, crevice, and crack, cleaning dirt, dust. And I got on my knees— but I wasn't asked to do it. I got on my knees and did this because in a house, you have to do this. I got on my knees and went in every corner, crevice, and crack and got out all the dust, used vacuum cleaners and everything was real great with these people. They used to go off from one to two weeks at a time and leave me in their house with their kids and I used to take care of the kids—

[*That was in Augusta?*]

Augusta, Georgia. I used to take care of the kids and their house. This woman's husband was a liquor salesman and she was a drunk more or less. She stayed drunk most of the time. But she was nice to me. She was nice to me. Mrs. Balow. She was nice to me.

[*How much did they pay you for that kind of work?*]

Ten dollars a week.

I got ten dollars per week. But you know what?

[*That was about nineteen—*]

Nineteen forty-five.

[*You made ten dollars a week.*]

Ten dollars per week. But you know what I liked about it? As I told you, I didn't have no conflict. I was, just like I was at home. And we never had no conflict. I never had a conflict in my life down south.

And, my son, he don't know anything about the southern states. Only thing he know is what he hear. And what he can read about. And what I talk about. And other people talk about. But my son don't know anything about it.

My kid didn't know what a pig was until nineteen fifty-six. We taken him on a trip there. And he met this pig through the fence and he start to poke his fingers through the wire and I told him, I said, "Don't do that. That's a pig. He might bite you." But he don't, he don't really know. But, I *know*, I *know*. But, you know what? I have no hatred. In my heart I have no hatred against the white man because the white man really never did anything to me. But they have did something to my foreparents. I . . ., I've had people to get killed by white people. I've had people to get killed by white people through the Ku Klux Klan. But, I was so young I really didn't know about it. Only things my mother told me about it. And I really don't know about it.

Maybe I got carried away and I talked too far. By getting off it, by getting off the main subject that we was on, which was colleges. But in the meantime I got quite a distance off of that conversation.

But the college business is really what I was interested in because, as of today—I mean my young life doesn't mean too much about what's happening today because, I have lived a marvelous life and my young life, in the southern states as well as the northern states. And I haven't had any conflict and—but the conflict that's happening today I guess this is why I can't understand it because, I just can't understand it. By me being a southern-raised woman—I was raised southernly. I've dealt with the South. And I've never came in any conflict and this is where the prejudice are. And I never came in any conflict. And so why? This is what I don't understand: Why why why why why? Why is it that this thing have to explode so much that it takes effect on my kid and bring on such a great conflict in his life that didn't happen in mine and I'm older. I don't know, understand why. I just wish somebody would just tell me why because it, it didn't happen—to my—

I have always heard of the Ku Klux Klan. I saw some of the work of the Ku Klux Klan.

[*Well, What do you mean when you said you saw the work of the Klan?*]

There were a friend of mine who's named Bobby and he—they couldn't tell him from, they didn't know whether he were white or colored. But he were color. He were a Negro—

Accordingly to his complexion in many places he went, he passed for white. They didn't ask him for no identification. Because he passed for white but he was colored. I knew him personally.

In the end—

When they found out on his credentials that he were a Negro, his father owned many places. But when they found out that he were a Negro, he was killed. And he was dragged.

But I could see. I'll tell you what: I happened to be in a car that was on this highway during the time of that night. Bobby's body was chained to a car on a gravel road. And they dragged his body until it was unrecognizable. In Georgia. This is the only thing that I've held—I've seen that happened among the Ku Klux Klan and the only thing that I could say the reason why it was the Ku Klux Klan because all the people had their heads covered with white sheets. And since I've been able to study and see anything of the Ku Klux Klan, this is the way that they disguise themselves—through white sheets or white pillowcases or what not. And so Bobby had to be killed by the Ku Klux Klansmen because these people that unchained his body from the car, had these white things over their head.

[*What year did that happen?*]

Oh, this was way back 'cause I was young. These things were happening in about the year of nineteen forty-two.

[*How did you feel about it?*]

You want to know from me, truthfully? I did . . . I did . . . I did . . . I didn't have no opinions whatsoever about it because—The man that was behind the car being dragged, I didn't know who he was; I didn't know what color he was. The mans that had the things over their heads, I didn't know who they were. I didn't know what color they were. Only thing I know, only thing I said, "Oh, something terrible is happening." And this, and we went on about our way, because, you know, okay, you better not stop. Or you are going to get the same thing or worse. And so I had no feelings about it. And later, then it came out in the paper.

And when we read about it and then I thought to myself, "Oh," I said, "We saw this happen." You know. I said, "We saw this happen." But you know, when you see something happening and you in the deep South, you afraid to say anything about it, so you are going to hush-hush. (She whispers.) I thought: We saw this happen. And so we never said nothing about it. We read about it. I went to the funeral home; I viewed his body. And I seen the condition it was in and I knew him, and everything. But I don't know who did it. I don't know who did it to him because the people were unrecognizable because they had these white sheets or pillowcases or what not over their head. And, we couldn't see who they were. And you don't know whether they are Black or white, because they've got these things over their head. But we could see them dragging him. We saw this man.

We know they were dragging this man. But you know, like, what they call young lovers be out riding and what not? We saw this. And, and we saw them drag this man down the gravel road. And so this is why I say that this is the only thing that I've seen happen with the Ku Klux Klan. And after I read about the Ku Klux Klan, I say, "Well, this had to be the Ku Klux Klan that did this." But as far as me knowing it, I couldn't say that, well, I know the Ku Klux Klan did this—I couldn't say that because it could've been somebody that disguised themself as the Ku Klux Klan and did it. And so I don't know whether it was the Ku Klux Klan or not. But as far as me reading about the Ku Klux Klan, since I been here, I say, well, the Ku Klux Klan killed Bobby, because they had their heads covered over with white sheets or pillow cases, you know. And they killed him and dragged his body. And this is why I say it was the Ku Klux Klan but as far as me knowing it, there was no signs, no evidence or nothing to bear the names of it. I were only going by this white thing over the head and, ah, at the time, ah, it was a Negro that was killed and they didn't have any investigation or even if they had had one, I guess I'd a kept a hush-hush. Because I was in the South and I wouldn't have wanted to get killed myself. And I never would of said nothing and I never did say nothing until now; but this is the only thing and the only action that I really can give that I saw with my own eyes that happened—that would indicate the work of the Ku Klux Klan. And from the way that they really do their work. But, ah, as far as I'm concerned, I never had any trouble. Just like I said, I never had any trouble among the Black and the white. And my son, since he's grown up, he never had any trouble among the Black and the white. He has as many white friends as he do white. As many white friends as he do Black, I mean. And, he's never had any trouble. And I don't know why this is all going on, but it's going on today. And it's only one question, just like I asked you: Why? I'd like to know the reason why. I can't give my son an answer if I don't know.

Yeah, I mean truthfully speaking. There's quite a few Black that's gonna be prejudiced. And there's more or less a number of whites that's gonna be prejudiced because the stuff has, ah, recently been broken down. And there's some people go for it and there's another that don't. But what's the reason? What's the difference? This is what—I can't look no individual in the eye and get a common question answered with common sense. Why? What's the reason? If there's a Black woman in love with a white man and they both love each other, what the hell anybody else got to do with it? Why not let them people live their life and go ahead on? And whether it create millions. And if the same thing happening with a Black man and a white woman, why not let it go on? Huh? Why you gonna stir up something and destroy blood? Why not live for yourself? Huh?

Now I wouldn't feel good over this even through I'm slaving, I'm working like hell to give my son a college education. I give less than a damn whether it's white or Black.

I don't want him to marry a tramp. I don't give a damn what color it is. And it's on tape and I don't care.

I don't give a damn what color it is, white or Black, I don't want him to marry no tramp. Because I think within myself, I work hard to give him this education. Something that he will be able to support and care for a wife and raise a decent family when he have kids. So why marry a tramp? I don't care what color she is. But just don't get a tramp. Yeah, this is what matters to me. I don't, I don't want my son to marry a tramp.

matthew

Matthew came up from the South years ago. He works in the auto plants to support his large family. The following passages come from a long discussion of work in the plants, when Matthew, two other workers, and I were sunning ourselves on the sidewalk on a bright March afternoon.

Matthew

Look here, you-all have done got more money than every damn body. The Jews done have everything.

You say they pay you twelve thousand five hundred to teach school. Well, that's a thousand dollars a month. The average working man, the average factory worker, he earn from six to eight thousand a year. A skilled worker might earn ten. You *could* make ten, it would be working seven days.

Working seven days! Get up and go back to work, get up and go back to work.

Made one hundred and forty-two dollars and eighty-eight cents. Seven days! Double time.

Shit! I went to the foreman and said, this goddamn check ain't even right. And he cut this out and put that down and he cut that out and put that down. And it went seven dollars up. But then he got to adding it up, motherfucker, it come to forty-three eighty or some shit along there.

They done took damn near all that money from me. When I left I wasn't going to come back no more. I said, "You compel the worker with Sundays and Saturdays, I ain't coming." He said, "You know they can fuck with you."

I said, "I don't give a goddamn. When I do my goddamn five days, tell them to kiss my ass."

I make more money doing that! I get the same damn thing, five days as for seven days, with tax. Hundred and forty, hundred and thirty, working overtime! I'm not going to work a whole seven days, ain't even got to have relationships with my wife, so damn tired. Wake up, she got out of the bed, "Wake up, it's time to go, baby." Get in the car, run to Ford. Fuck that goddamn shit!

You can't make this money. You cannot have no money, goddamn it, and be honest!

Now you say you got this little money in your savings account. You make more money than I do. Alright now, look at this, now how can you save? The son of a bitch got all that goddamn money to him over there. Now if you running some dope or something. But you can't save no goddamn money. I never save a quarter in my motherfucking life.

I tell you one damn thing, a man work all his goddamn life, they done gyp the motherfucker out there in the factory, talk about loop-tee-doop and all this. All of them old motherfuckers out there. The man think he's great, god dog it. He ain't shit. And all he's got is a home and a car.

'Fess, you know, it's better not to have that house, you know, it's better just to pay some rent and go ahead. You know what I'm talking about. You ain't going to go in debt.

Your old lady going to tell you, we need a new couch over in this corner. What about that chair that's set over in this corner? And your head's still to the damn grindstone. Well, the kids done broke the mirror. This and that is busted, that's ten dollars. The water pipe in the basement, it's busted. Leaking. Basement's full of water. Man got to put on his boots go down in the basement. Shit! But it's going to be a reckoning, everything going to be all right. Hey, the furnance wall is broken. Goddamn, the furnace losing water; go there, tighten that goddamn shit up. Ain't getting no heat!

You going to go and try to save for a car when you be saving on a home?

Some of these is five thousand dollars! Five thousand dollars is too much to pay for a car. I wouldn't spend five thousand dollars to see Jumping Julia jump the moon!

Shit! The best a son of a bitch will get from me for a car is six hundred dollars. If that is a Ford. Five thousand? No sir! This Mark Three and all that.

I mean, I am on the way to know what it cost to build a car. I know what it cost to build a Ford. A car ain't that goddamned expensive to make.

Like the man said on the news last night, you look at all these new cars in the junkyard. New cars, sitting up there in the junkyard. And you still have to pay for it! Some poor man is fucked up.

Man, when I was born . . . you know, you could buy a car, you could get a car for a hundred and some. Five hundred dollars was the highest car in the world. And that was a Cadillac. And that other old big son of a bitch, what do you call it, a Lincoln.

Five hundred dollars! Now a pair of mules cost as much as that did. Shit, for six hundred dollars, you could get the biggest car in town. But you don't get no mules out there a year and a half old. They're a thousand dollars. For a pair of mules a year and a half old, a thousand dollars.

[*Yeah. But tell me one more time, I really want to understand it. What people are making in the factories. How much you can make there, whether you can live on it, what the work is like. Okay?*]

Well it depends on what job you get in the factory. Now the guy's working at Pontiac, he's making more than we do. I'm making three twenty-three an hour. Know what he's making? Three fifty-five an hour. And he's working on the same thing.

Now he's been there longer than me. But goddamn! That's why I'm telling you, when I worked those seven days, I told that honky foreman, hell, he can have this overtime too. Shit, my wife just sitting at home with seven kids.

[*Can you make a living, just from that work?*]

It's tough. With seven kids. It's tough. A single man, like one of these here, yeah, he can make a living. 'Cause when he eat, his whole family done ate. But I have electric light bills, gas bills, rent, kids that go to school, shoes, clothes, and all that. Naw! Anyone going to make it at Ford's, boy, you got to have some help. Ford's will work you till your eye-teeth drop out.

□   □   □

You know what's the matter with the goddamn people? Not you, you're a Jew; I'm talking about the honky: Ford and all of them son of a bitches, Chrysler's and all of them. Work me all my damn life for nothing, goddamn it!

You see what's getting the money. You can see! Their kids coming up.

The motherfuckers never picked up nothing but a broom. Their father picked that up. *Pick up a pencil!* What's that motherfucker know about *hard* work? *Nothing!*

He can't go out there right now, there by the street here, and turn that rock over. See? I work for that motherfucker all my life and kill myself out there in the goddamn factory like this! I need it a little longer, then let me go, I'm through! I ain't *going* to make it too much longer, you-all motherfuckers forget it, 'cause I'm getting my four or five more checks and retire, he's through, motherfuckers never work me like that!

Son of a bitch, my daddy worked all his life on a goddamn farm. And never did even own a brand new bicycle! Motherfucker honky, boy, I ain't bullshitting you, they ain't going to do nothing for you.

My daddy, goddamn, it took my daddy *five* goddamn years to pay for *six* mules! Every time my daddy go down to Mr. George's, that motherfucker have a goddamn pencil: "You're damn near coming out of debt this year. You know all you end up owing me is five hundred dollars, man; you sho' getting ahead." All that goddamn shit!

[*He's working for the man every day and he's in debt to him.*]

That's right. Normal, a kid. . . . My daddy a man just like you. He say, just like you, my dad say I'm going to get me a bicycle when Christmas come. I don't get a goddamn thing!

In my young days, sixteen, seventeen, I didn't get shit! When I got grown—I owned seven cars since I been grown. I didn't have shit when I was young. Nothing!

Brand new pair of overalls, a pair of shoes, and ship my raggedy ass to school. That's all she wrote. And you better not tear those overalls none. "Look out how you shoot those marbles; stand there, don't get dirty." "Come on in here, young man! You been shooting marbles!" And all that shit. Fuck it! But I *know*: my life, *my life is as good as theirs are!* Any goddamn man in the world, I got the same heart and the same blood. As another son of a bitch. I don't care who he is, where you get him from.

I am not going to kill myself. I ain't playing.

[*What kind of farm was that? Your father's farm.*]

That was in Alabama.

[*What were you raising, cotton, corn?*]

Cotton. Corn. Watermelon. Sugar cane. The main thing is eating . . . hogs.

[*Did the farm belong to the guy?*]

Belonged to the *white man*!

You know what I'm talking about?

[*So, sharecropping or what?*]

Yeah. Working for the man's money. Goddamn, the man had Daddy fucked up. Every year. Goddamn, he had him fucked up. *Putting that pencil in the goddamn air*! If he get three dollars, goddamn it, it be four.

Yeah, messed up! Really got him messed up. Worked all my life. . . . I tell you one goddamn thing, though: if Ford can work your goddamn ass and if you be waked up when you wake up and get your lunch bucket, you alright with Ford's. Had a old man there putting a goddamn twenty-gallon drum. Man old enough for my granddaddy. A twenty-gallon drum! Talking about he going to retire next year! I said, "Mister, you just barely *can* go now!"

He says, "Got my home paid for!" I said, "How much money you got?"

"I got three dollars in my pocket; I got a car."

I said, "That's good."

Shit! The *white* man! "Get you a job!" The whole damn town a bunch of shacks and shit downtown. "Go pick some damn cotton!"

I said, "I ain't planted none." This is down home.

"Go pick some cotton!"

I said, "I ain't planted no cotton."

"What you mean you ain't planted none? How they going to get it out?"

Well, *goddamn*! Let *them* get it out! *I picked cotton all my life, plowed all my damn life, and I ain't had shit! Damn the damn cotton*!

You want to make some clothes, tell them to make their own. Worked all my life and all I got was shit. But you just don't know. Lot of people ain't come through that shit, they don't know.

[*That's what the hell I'm trying to get you to talk for. As you know. You understand?*]

I understand what you're talking about.

[*That's why I'm trying to get people to talk.*]

By the time you get all the records down, what *good*, now *what good* is that going to do, 'Fess?

They ain't going to give a goddamn what you do out here.

They going to pay you. Well, so what?

People want to see how people feel about the world, right? How the wrong son of a bitches done did people. How dirty they done been. Then they look at theirself, say, goddamn, they shouldn't have did that. Because they ain't no more of that damn shit no more.

[*I didn't know if it would do any good. I thought when I started it would, but you know, I didn't even know anything when I started either.*]

They don't give a damn neither: "It's alright, just another nigger talking." Go on about their business.

But, the time is catching up. They will try to kill all the good people that restored respect from them. Well, nobody is going to stop nothing. Everybody going ahead. They killed President Kennedy: they went on ahead. They killed Martin Luther King: but they still going ahead. They fucked around and they killed Robert Kennedy: but they still going ahead. They can't stop them!

☐   ☐   ☐

And these jive-ass police got their little precinct job running around and people say, "Hey, hey, hey, Pow!" They getting killed. They better fool around with the wires, get them a job on the telephone poles, or fix signs—get them a job! 'Cause people laying for them! Everyone you see now has got a gun. That doggone little kid right there by the sidewalk, bet he's got a gun. He's barbecuing. Watch him grab it, shoot the shit out of you. Everybody.

"Police." It's not no police! The honky is what took all this money a long time ago. *When* he took all this goddamn money, he say: "We going to make a *law*!"

They had laws in Texas, didn't they? I come to Texas right now, everybody you want to see got a gun on. Go down to Arkansas right now and go to Texas, everybody you see has got a gun.

"We going to make a law!!" The honky got a law to save his money! He done *took* and *stole* and *robbed* and worked people to *slaves* and *branded*, branded Negroes, "that's my nigger this ain't none of your nigger this is my nigger here, this is my nigger, gimme"—all else—NOW the mother-fucker's SCARED!!

The man's through. He's through! He's through.

He ought to know that. He should realize: "Well, I'm through now." 'Cause God didn't put no one man right and no one man wrong. He know that. He's through.

He should know he's through. He don't think about it. "I got the *law*!"

Old motherfucker, he got all that shit out here, guy still going to kick him in the ass. "Get the National Guard!" Goddamn on the National Guard! "Send the Army here!" Army my ass!

That's from the White House.

It's not no law! God said, "Judge him not, I am the judge!" My Father in Heaven said this. You can read. That sonofabitch, everytime I get downtown, this motherfucker on his ass: "Give him three days!" "Give him five days!" "Six years!"— How *can* a motherfucker sit up there and give somebody some time? God said, "Judge him not, I am the judge." It's not no law! The honky *took* all the money, *took* all the money there, and *took* and stole, *worked* people *for nothing*, and going to say: "I got a Law. You do that you breaking the *law*." WHAT LAW?? Tell me where it came from—I done read till my eyes hurting. *LAW*!! Shit!

cement man

He was on the Corner one sunny day playing blues songs on his guitar. He improvised in a deep, gravelly voice: "I love my woman so well, so very well." I played the songs back for him from the tape, and we talked. Everyone knew him, but I never saw him before or after.

Cement Man

I was born in nineteen and twenty-two. You can tighten that up, please. You want to know my name? My name is John's other brother, Paul's cousin, Peter's son.

[*Where do you work at?*]

I'm a cement finisher.

[*What's that like?*]

I make five dollars and seventy-six cents an hour.

[*What's it like? How's it feel?*]

Bad. Everything you walk on, I makes it for you! As long as you walk on the face of the earth, my job never expire.

[*Do you want your kids to have that job?*]

You know what? I do not, because it's a *hard job*. You understand? You see that out there? I crawled twelve and thirteen hours a day on that thing. On my *knees*. I do that.

[*You crawl with the thing and level it off?*]

Yes. That's me.

[*How many years you been doing that?*]

I've been doing that for eighteen years. I make eighty and eight, nine dollars a day, that ain't too bad.

[*Winter?*]

Winter, summer, all the year around. I works inside, you know,

158

pouring basement, that stuff. I make four and five hundred dollars a week. That ain't too bad. I got a little money, got a little money saved up. So, that ain't too bad.

◻   ◻   ◻

Listen. Now I got an allergy, and then I cannot find out what it is. See, I went to the Army, and we got over there, I went to Korea, and they got some weeds over there, if you get in one of them, they will not turn you loose. They give you some shit that will not—listen, I got stung with one of them and partner, right now, and that's been—that was in fifty, fifty-five—shit, I ain't got rid of that shit yet. It itches me all the time now. And that is bad stuff, bad stuff.

I got two children. I got a girl and a boy. What kind of work do I think they'll do? Well, I think my kids will, my boy will come up to be like, just about like I'm doing, because, see, my work can never expire.

Never. As long as you walk on the face of the world, there's always going to be concrete put down.

So that's what I do. Now, he tries it, and then, my daughter, she trying to do practicing nurse. Because my wife is a nurse. And I think that's the way they are going to come out to be. I hope so, anyway.

And I hope she'll be a nurse and I hope my kid be a finisher. Because, see, I'm getting in bad shape now, because, see, you know what? I was born in nineteen and twenty-two; I'm *old*.

Forty-six years old!

But I tell you what, I can finish as much cement as any man in there. I crawl all day long. That's what I have to do, crawl, and it's hell. But I make eighty, sixty, seventy dollars a day with it.

[*Lot of money.*]

Yeah, but look at the work! It's hell. You think I'm joking, don't you. My knees just as sore! Shit. I tell you what, I go through so much hell, it ain't funny. But you just got to go through with it. You got to take care of your family. What the fuck. And I'm buying a house and it is going to take me a lifetime to pay for that motherfucker.

the old man

One morning in June 1970, one of the men took me to see his new apartment. In a little hallway at the foot of the stairs were seven men, sitting on chairs or leaning against the walls. The men had thought that they might be able to go to work at a construction site, but the heavy rain meant that there would be no work today. The men were all middle-aged or older, worn from years of labor. Some conversation about the President started up, but an old man took the floor and held it with his intensity.

The Old Man

I'll say we had three presidents: that's my father, that built this pretty project, Roosevelt . . . (*interruptions*: "He's dead," *etc.*) . . . We wouldn't have all these slums if it hadn't been for them cheap politicians. You show me a politician today, he's a thief! But when my father, Roosevelt—I'm a Black man, but Roosevelt one of the best presidents, and I'm seventy years old . . . (*more interruptions—*)

(*The old man by now is shouting.*) . . . A *poor* man, anytime a *poor* man, *anytime* a poor man like myself vote for a Republican, he's taking bread out of his baby's mouth! (*Another*: I have to agree with you about that.)

For the Republicans is a rich, old party. And they want the poor people to humble to them.

Ike Eisenhower one of the greatest generals that our country ever had in life, but he didn't know as much as I do about political . . . (*Interruptions—*)

(*The old man tries again.*) . . . Our President Johnson, he tried out Kennedy's program, but they split it on him (*Interruptions—*)

(*The old man presses on and prevails.*) I can talk history now. I like talking to a young man like you.

Now, that's the money the Democrats left to us poor people, and the Republicans going to get it. Nixon's gonna get it, and you'll be in a soup line by November, shaking just like a skeleton. You tongue, your tongue will even look like *this*! (*He flaps his tongue and gibbers.*)

Well, let me tell you, we have had—I is, nationality don't mean nothing to me, I know good people from bad people, for I had a good mother and a good father—*but anytime* a poor man vote a Republican ticket, he just putting another nail in his coffin. Putting another nail!

But the Republicans just balance their budget. They take what *you* got, they don't want to see; they want you to come by and by, and put your knee on the floor and everything like that— (*He mimics a patron speaking in an affected voice.*) "Oh, poor so and so! He's alright, take him in the kitchen and give him some coffee and some bread."

You understand? Or a doughnut, or something like that. But the Democrats—I hope this country will go Democratic *all the way*. I want these people like me, I want us to go hungry from today until the next election time—I don't know when it's gonna be, why, I don't care nothing about politics, I ain't got long to be here yet—but I'm telling you, I'm telling you, I'm telling you: the *Republicans*, that's a *rich* party, that's for *rich* people, not for common people and poor people like I am.

□   □   □

I didn't express it, by words, like I know it. I been to school, and I'm an old man, well striked in age. No, I didn't say nothing; you got a vocabulary, but I could never speak, I know I got sense I never used yet. I can remember things when I was three years of age.

[*Alright, but let me ask you this . . . who started that war, what's going on?*]

Politicians started it. The politicians. That's all it is now, them young boys getting killed over there for nothing, don't know what they're fighting for.

[*Well, what are the Democrats if they're not politicians?*]

He'll look out for the little man!

He gon' make his now, he's no angel, he'll make his, but he will look out for the little man!

□   □   □

There's enough for fruit and food and everything in this world for everybody on the whole face of it. Look at it, they done whupped Germany twice, and gone back over there and build the country up, and feed them, and have to fight them again, same damn thing. And they're going over there in Vietnam right now. North Vietnam is going to surrender. And, you know, build the country back up and give them the milk and honey and stuff like that. But that don't bring *your son* back! Or *your daughter* back.

You got to have nurses. A nurse is like an angel. And a soldier is the staff of life. Just like bread. So what them young boys dying for? For the *Big Man*, that's making a *profit* off them! That's all you can make out of it.

So—God has been good to me. And I figure somebody don't believe in a Supreme Power, he's nuts, need to be in a nuthouse (*several interruptions*).

(*He presses on.*) They're trying to go to the moon. And they're telling a damn lie about that. And they ain't been up there. They may be up there in Alaska someplace walking on that ice or something up there. Millions and millions of dollars. And here's little kids running up and down the street.

This should be the . . . the land of Heaven right here. But these politicians won't let you do it.

I'm just talking for—I don't have nothing to talk about. And they'll say I'm a Communist. What in the hell I know about being a damn Communist? I been here all my life, working like hell.

Working. And ain't got a damn thing to show for it. And I go through Bloomfield Hills— I works all out there, all out in Grosse Point, Palmer Woods. I say, "Why can't *I* have something like this?"

Goddamn it, I ain't had the chance! I would have it, I know how to *live* and keep a *beautiful* place—

(*Another tries to join in; the old man deals with him.*) *You* older than I am, and you ain't got *nothing*. You—you don't have a cigarette—but you want to *impress* people. I don't believe in impressing people, I believe in action. If I had *my* way about it, let them people—they want to fight and kill each other over there, let them do it; bring them boys, them mother's sons, back home!

And give them a job!

Getting them wounded and killed, hell, them kids don't know what the hell they're fighting for. *They do not!* But—I don't have no boy—

War is, is—I'll put it like this. Now you know more about history than I do, you or this gentlemen, either one, or the lady sitting here. But let me tell you this:

A-a-a war creates profit for the Big Man. Not the *little* man, the *Big Man*.

It mean *death* to you and I. And this man next to you; he ain't got nothing.

But—Uncle Sam got his finger pointed. "I want *you!*" But the *Big Man* sitting back there in his den or someplace, you understand. And the best of drinks and the best of everything. All right. You got to go jeopardize your life, for him to make a profit.

Here your mother down on her knees. In a corner, praying, "God, please bring him back home, please." That's the instinct of a human being.

maggie

Maggie, twenty-nine years old, was living in an upstairs flat that was the home of a beloved great-aunt. With her were her three sons: Jonathan, ten; Andrew, four; and Davey, three. She was in the last month of a fourth pregnancy. She was quite playful with her children.

The following passages are taken from the beginning of our first interview, and deal primarily with child-rearing. I then include a section from a later interview.

Maggie

Since the birth of Andrew, I haven't really worked, other than baby-sitting or doing some little small jobs like that. I've always preferred to stay at home with my kids. I don't guess there's anything wrong with working. But I feel that when children are small like that, if you don't get to know them then, then you can't handle two jobs; you can't take care of a home properly and the children properly and then work on a eight-hour shift. Particularly when you're by yourself, you and your husband aren't together.

Davey and Andrew, sometimes they give me a run for my money. They really do. But, they say that this is the new generation. So, why should I upset myself by screaming and hollering and trying to chastise and show my power of authority? When I find that, most of the time, I get no results—but nervousness, being upset and the children just as calm as they were before I started whooping and hollering.

But, if I sit down, and I say, "Well, why don't you do such and such a thing"—*many* times this brings more results than it does by me grab-bing the strap or the cord, getting ready to tear them up.

And, they're inquisitive. They ask very many questions. Andrew, he will want to know who everybody is. He'll run to the phone. You can't speak to anybody in this house until you let him know who you are. He will ask you, "Where do you live?" "What do you want?"

And my oldest boy, he'll wonder. He doesn't say any too much. He'll look at you as if to say, well, what are you, who are you? And yesterday, he even went so far as to ask me, "Your stomach has gotten mighty big. Is that where the baby's coming from?"

And with kids nowadays, I find with my own—I can't think about everybody else's, but with my own—you cannot sit down and lie to them. You just have to just come on and tell them like it is.

Because if you don't, when they get a little older, they are going to go out there, and they are going to find out what it is. So you tell them just what's what, lay it on the line to them. Then when they get out there, it's not so hard for them. They'll figure, "Well, my mamma said it was such and such a thing, it was this way—and it *was* that way." Kind of pacify their minds. I find that just coming on, telling them like it is, it saves a lot of wear and tear later.

So my oldest boy asked me, he said, "Well, I used to hear that the birds bring the baby." I told him, "No, the woman brings forth the baby."

"Well, that's the baby in your stomach?"

"Yes, it is. The baby is in my stomach. Right."

This is *my* view of how I want to raise *my* kids. I am going to tell them how it is.

Because they *don't* have a father around up there. And you're trying to be both mother and father to a child, you're trying to be ninety percent feminine, ten percent masculine. In order to try to keep them under control. And also let them know, well, this is Mamma, who we can go to when we're sick. Mamma's going to be here. Mamma's going to this, Mamma's going to do that.

And it's a load. It's a heck of a load to carry. When you're raising kids by yourself.

Now in addition, I try to teach them to be independent.

Independent. Don't be the follower. If you got to be anything, be the leader. Always keep in your mind that regardless as to what this one does, that one does—if it's not your thing, or if you really don't want to do it—don't do it! Go *your* way! You may get talked about, and nasty things said. But you are doing *your* thing.

And this is the way I talk to them. Because nine times to one, I'm doing *my* thing.

And this is what Andrew told me about a month ago. I say, "What are you doing?"

"Sitting down, writing on my cards. I'm doing my thing." That's what he said, "I'm doing my thing." So I said, I see right now what *I* got to cope with!

I got to go along with this. I have got to be a *mother*, I have got to be a *brother*, I have got to be a *friend*.

Because if you don't be a friend to your kids, then you can always expect them to run out to outside people, pouring their troubles out to them, or whatever it is that they are going through. But I always want to feel as if my kids can come to me with whatever problems they have.

"You know you are mine, you know I'm your mamma. You know I'm going to stick by you. I'm going to be your friend as well as your mother. Talk to *me*. Tell me if you don't agree with something that I say or something that I do; come to *me* and talk to *me*."

See? And this is where a lot of parents have *failed*. They are always holding that dominating hand. But they never give the child a chance to speak their mind.

[*How were you raised?*]

I was raised, my mother raised me, to respect older people and to always do as I was told. When she told me to do something, she meant it. She meant for me to do it. And there was no *ifs* and *ands* about it.

And when I was coming up, you didn't give Mamma no lip. You didn't disrespect an older person. A lot of things you didn't do. Or you get tore up.

But this is a different age. A different date. And this is the way I feel.

This is the way I feel. And this is the way I'm raising my children. I want them to be independent in their minds. Be independent. Now, I'm going to tear them up sometime; I'm still the authority until they get out on their own. But *I* can be *wrong*.

I go along with my kids on a lot of things. They can change my mind. They can make me look at something again, and really see some small, little small error that I've made. And then my mind can be changed.

A child can be right just like an adult can be right. And nobody knows it all. There are some things that a little child like that can tell you that you may not know, maybe something simple that you overlook. Something like that.

A lot of times I'm told that I am wrong. But this is my way of thinking. And I don't intend to have anybody step in and trample my way of thinking. Because I was raised to have a mind of my own, and to use it for whatever purposes I saw fit. And this is the way I am going to raise my kids.

☐   ☐   ☐

[*Where did you get these ideas?*]

You know what? Sometimes at night, when they're in their beds, I sit up and I think. I just look at people. I hear other people talking. For a while I began to feel sort of . . . inferior. Because *I* felt *this* way, you know, and so many parents now, they *don't*. They still trying to live into that thing where you chastise them and everything has got to be a beating.

This is what is in my mind. Maybe it's because it was pushed into my mind from a child, but I knock on wood and thank God that I had the kind of mother that had a strong mind that we could see. Regardless as to where we lived, here was a woman that we had to look upon who was *strong*.

She might have been weak inside, but she never showed it, and that's the main thing. Because you've got kids you can't afford to weaken. Believe it!

If I ever weaken, I may as well throw my hands up. Because everything I'm striving to instill into them and to teach them—just go down! I can't afford to weaken under any circumstance, under no amount of pressure.

Because they are leaning on me. And I know this. And if some time you just feel like, "Oh, forget it!" or something like that. . . . Can't afford to. Can't afford to!

I know I'll get over. I feel as if I have a pretty strong mind. And whatever problems present itself, if I can't cope with them, then I go to somebody that has the teachings or the knowledge that can tell me certain things. I'm not afraid to ask.

But, it's a hard-down, knock-out world, honest to God!

□ □ □

I don't try to instill in my children's heads too much of anything except independence. Always be able to be independent. And whatever you want to be, try your best.

Whoever, whatever, they want in life—even if they be bums—whatever they be—for God's sake, be *independent* bums. And be the best. *Be the best!*

This is why . . . I don't love boys any more than I do girls, but I prefer having boys. They are going to get into trouble, you know. They get into trouble and everything else. But, whatever they do, at least, God knows, if something happens to me, they *will* to a degree be able, a lot more able, to take care of theirselves than a girl.

I think it would break my heart if I was to have a girl. And I became a little sick or something. Where she couldn't make it other than turning into a prostitute or something like that.

And this is the only way that she could make it if she was under age
and hadn't finished school. And I know this. This happens, it happens a
lot.

[*It would really come to that?*]

It may. I'm looking at the strong possibility, of it happening, of her
becoming involved in something that . . . would tear her status down as
a lady. To nothing than a common everyday woman.

And . . . I don't think I could take that.

That's why I love the boys. They will get in trouble. A lot of them get
in trouble, go to jail, anything. But I think I could cope with it better,
because I try to keep an open mind. I don't never think that my kids are
so A-number-one that "they will never do this" or "no, my child won't do
that"—oh, no, no. I don't know what they will do when they leave my
eyesight. And I try to keep my mind open and not narrowed. That way
you don't get hurt by children. You don't really become so shocked until
you have a heart attack, at anything that you may find out.

This is the way I am. This is the way I think. This is the way I believe.

I could be wrong. In society's eyesight. But I'm not trying to raise
society, and I'm not trying to please society. Because society is not going
to give me a quarter. Society is not going to help me raise my kids. So I
give less than a damn what society thinks. That's the way I feel about it.

[*I want to hear about your mother. Who you feel she was. But first, how
many of you were there?*]

Just three. Two girls and a boy.

This is a picture here. That was my sister, baby sister. But she died.
And . . . my brother was older, he's the oldest. And now there's just two
of us left.

She was twenty. She died of childbirth. She was twenty when she
died. . . .

It just happens like that sometime, you know. Tomorrow is not
promised to anyone.

[*. . . And your mother—*]

Well, she was just like . . . any other mamma. Hard, firm, and strict.
And she meant business. Wasn't any speaking and asking twice. As a
matter of fact, there was no *asking*. If she wanted you to do something,
she told you. And you moved. At that time. There was no second telling.
Because if it had to be like that, then the next thing you know the strap
was on you. And you better not run!

She was just firm and strict and more or less hard. Very hard. But she was a person really to be admired. Because of her strength.

I admired her myself because of her strength. As a woman now, I admire her now. But as a child—naturally, at times any child resents a parent that chastises them or demands certain things out of them.

But I admire her now because I'm a woman myself. And I'm raising my children myself. And I know the difficulties. And the things that can present themselves that you may want to strike out at and avoid, but they're unavoidable.

And when you've got children, you run into some walls, believe me. There are some pitfalls as well. You have to do a lot of bending. Whereas if you didn't have those kids, you wouldn't have to do it. And you wouldn't do it.

But I have heard quite a few women that said, "Eat shit and go to hell for your kids!" And you do! You have to eat a whole lot. Chew it and swallow it!

And this is the kind of woman that she was.

□   □   □

. . . How do I feel about the police? Well, I've really only had a couple of contacts with them. You know, the one incident that I told you about?

[*You didn't tell me about it. You were going to talk about it.*]

Oh. When I went to the NAACP. . . . And I got me a couple of lawyers? Concerning these two policemen?

I was involved in a car accident. And it was myself and two other girls. We hit the guy's car, he pulled out without looking, and we hit him. And they sent out a police car, and these police were just going to state that we were in the wrong and were going to use profanity and everything else.

So I was just telling it like it was; they asked me, so I just told them what had happened. And then this policeman told me that I thought I was too smart. And he got out of the driver's side, opened the door on my side, because they had all three of us in the back seat. And when I stepped out, he just *snatched* me, and turned me around and slapped me! And when he did that, well, I just forgot about that he was about six feet five and weighed two hundred and fifty pounds. I just *ran into him*, that's all! I just fought him like a dog!

[*What do you weigh?*]

Then I was weighing around a hundred and ten.

Hey, but wait a minute, you haven't heard anything yet.

[*Now, what . . . wait a second . . . now, what did you do to aggravate him? To make him start that?*]

I was trying to tell him. He was asking us questions, asking what happened, and I was trying to tell him what had happened. And, okay, the other guy, the one with the car, he was Caucasian. And the two police officers were Caucasian, and they were hillbillies. They were *hillbillies*! And I guess I talked too much, and because my complexion was as light as it was . . . "I thought I was white," "I need to go back to Africa," and all this talk going around. Telling me I need to go back to Africa with the rest of my folks, that maybe my skin was yellow but I was still the blackest nigger walking the street, and all this and that and the other, you know. And using profanity.

Like, if somebody speak to you like that, you are going to come back on them the same. Those people, you can't talk intelligently to them, so you got to get all down to their way. So I just told them like it was, you know.

And that's when he politely removed hisself out of the driver's seat and opened the back door for me to step out. And then instead of getting on back out of my face, he just want to take it on hisself to grab me and slap my face! And when he did, I just ran into him!

You'd really call it, in a way, self-defense. I'm not going to be struck down, you're not going to when you know you are not in the wrong. And he had to call for another police car, to restrain me. One-hundred-and-ten-pound me. But he had to have me restrained.

It took two of them to hold me. Now you know, that don't even sound right. Now does that sound right? And he took that thing, that night-stick or whatever it is, and played it up and down on my arm, just played it on my arm. And the only thing really that got me, that really got me, when he threw me down, he put his knee in my throat. And his, what is it, blackjack? That black thing with that big thing on the end? He was getting ready to bust my head open with it.

Now these other two girls, they were too scared, they didn't bother to try to help me. Any kind of way. But he called a police car, another police car. And when they took us downtown, this just goes to show you, when we got downtown to be booked, there was two other policemen. They were Caucasian. And I began to tell them about it. You know what they told me? "We know you're right, but there's nothing we can say. We know you're telling the truth. But there's nothing we can say."

And then to top that off: after they put us in our little cells, they called us out of there about two o'clock in the morning into a little room. And this guy down there had a form, a little form. "Now if you tell us that it happened *this* way, we'll just send it on over to the prosecuting attorney's office, and we'll forget the matter. Forget the matter totally. Say, now, didn't it happen this way?"

I said, "No, it *didn't* happen that way."

But if I had been fool enough to fall for it, and if I had put my signature down on that paper, I would have been sitting up in the House of Correction somewhere.

And when we went in the court, that was the most comical sight. We went to court three months straight. That was the most comical sight. I was standing up there, hurt, bruised, bust my lip. And this judge, I'll never forget that sucker 'til the day I die. I hate that so-and-so. *He* going to *sit back* and *roll around* in that chair.

He gave this policeman the respect of sitting like a judge, like a public official. And listened to his story. When *I* began *mine*, he had to *rear* back in the chair, and fool around with a pencil in his mouth, and that kind of carrying on.

And this policeman stands up there and tells him, "Your Honor, I had to defend myself, because this woman attacked me like a vicious tiger." And he showed him all the cuts on his neck that I put on him, all down one side, and show him where he had to have a couple of stitches here and a couple of stitches there. And say I tried to bust him open. I did. I tried to bust him open. And he is going to stand up there and tell him I attacked him like a vicious tiger. And the people that were in the courtroom busted out laughing!

I'm telling you God's truth, they actually laughed. Because I can imagine what was running through their mind, here's this little skinny woman, poor and frail, and this big hunk of a man, but yet and still she attacked him and nearly beat him to death. Nearly beat him to death!

We went to court three months. Because this judge really thought he was going to railroad me. But, see, what I did, I went to the NAACP. And I had two lawyers. Because I knew I wasn't wrong.

When everything came to a climax, ended up with six months probation. But I would have been in the House of Correction, if I hadn't went down there to the NAACP. Because he asked me, how would I like to spend Thanksgiving, Christmas, and Easter in the House of Correction. He didn't have to say no more. Because that's when I went right down to the NAACP and got me two lawyers.

I don't even remember his name. He was half bald. But I'll never forget him, he just kept reeling and rocking the chair. He gave this police officer *respect*. But when I got to tell my story, I had to see all that rolling around.

hawk and his brother-in-law

When I crossed the street that first day, Hawk was the person I met. Many months later I came to the Corner with a young woman from my office. Hawk ran into us and insisted we walk over six blocks to meet his sister and brother-in-law. Hawk decided that the time had come to raise some isues with me. When Hawk had finished, his brother-in-law took over.

Hawk

Alright, 'Fess, you say this book is going to be read by middle-class people, white people. And I ask, what does that consist of, what do you call people, what's the definition of people? Who are humans? *Why*, I will ask you this, *Why*, does the whitey want to make us look like we are not humans?

[*Because they can get away with it.*]

Why can they get away with it? That is our problem. Why do the whitey want to dominate us so much? We and him are humans. We are living creatures, the same. We are something that God created. Our blood, it runs just like yours.

You know, think about it. Think about it! Why do you want to dominate us?

You know what, I'm going to tell you something. I was intending to tell you this before, when you was at my mother's house.

The white man—the white lady—you know why? Bring that damn thing over so you can hear! You want me to talk, bring that tape recorder over here so you can hear! I don't want you to miss nothing!

My mother—my mother and my father—my mother and my father was always good enough to serve the white man's babies, but she wasn't good enough to eat where he ate at. She could have poisoned the son of a bitch. That's what she should have did. There wouldn't have been no whitey if it hadn't been for the Black sisters. You understand what I'm talking about? Well, then. So why did they abuse us so bad?

I'm the one that made you exactly what you are. Today. So why are you abuse me? I haven't been enslave you; you went over there and get Black people for slavery and brought them over on damn ships, chains and shit on their heads. Damn! If you really want to know, see, you really don't want to talk to me. You don't want to talk to me. Look here, you chained my people down. And my people, my poor parents were good enough to feed you and make you be what you are. But you, after you get up and be such an age so you can smell your piss and shit and wipe your own ass, now my peoples is no good! You understand?

And if it hadn't been for us, there wouldn't *be* no whiteys. Frankly speaking, if there was no whiteys, didn't have no Caucasians . . . I don't see why they didn't try to blow your goddamn honkeys' head *off*. Now, do you want any more?

Shit, if it don't be for the Black man, there wouldn't be no United States. It wouldn't be no states, period. The Black man save the United States. Are you hip to this? Just about everything that, in the United States, that you would say, "I have progressed something, accomplished something?" The Black man, *he* accomplished that! But the whitey, he snaps it from him and put it in progress. So! You can't compete with him. You cannot compete with the Black man. So that's it. 'Fess, that's it, nigger, and you can cut that motherfucker tape recorder off 'cause I'm gonna shoot you some pool! And that be it; right on, brother, right *on*! Now we gonna do our thing and it's gonna be good!

Hey, you and me, we know a hustler on this corner used a tape recorder on people, done like you're doing. But I don't do it and I can't get paid what *you* get *paid*, baby! You know why? The *colors* . . . are a little *different*. Yeah. If my mother had of *snowed* on me, maybe I could! (*He laughs.*)

It might would have been a little different then, brother. But I'm not bullshitting, boy, it's a hell of a thing. But I'm going to tell you something, now you know what? You can't keep your brother down. You know what? Did you ever go to school? Well, maybe you might of went to school. But you know, 'Fess? I mean, it might seem like a laughing matter, but you know what? Whatever I learn, I *know* it. I know it *ten* times better than you do. If you know two and two is four, I know it fourteen times better than you do. Because you know why?

Because I had something to hang onto it. But see, it would just slip through your mind. 'Cause you know why?

Because you're *flakes*! You're snow white! But see, I've got *this* flakey-assed color, thank the Lord, I'm proud of it! 'Cause this will forever stand.

See, yours is gonna fade away. But mine is gone be forever, he will not go nowhere, I'll always have this. And see, you lay out there on my lawn and try to turn this here color. You know why? 'Cause it is beautiful. This color is beautiful and it will forever stand. This will not fade.

See, I'm going to tell it like it is. You would like to be my color, you would like to be this color. Brown.

[*Okay. Listen, Hawk, if you can talk to these people, what do you want to say to them? What do you want to say to those white people?*]

Well. You know what I'd like to say to the average whitey? You know what I'd like? If I could make a speech to the white man, I would put it in this category, I would say: Mister man, mister man, mister man—it's no laughing matter—the colored man. . . . Now, you believe this. I will soon be forty years old. I've been employed around, and in the Army and the Air Force. I've been in places for months and months, for forty-seven months I didn't know what a colored woman looked like. But I came back to my soul sister. But you know what? I don't want your lady. This is the fault of the white man, this is his fear.

He fears that if a—nigger, if that's what you want to say. "A nigger" has passed, it isn't no more of a "a nigger," it's a "Black man" now. That if a nigger, a Black man, get next to your woman, you have lost your woman.

Why?

That is the only fear that a white man fears the Negro. Because you know why? A Negro know how to love. A Negro is a lover, and a white man, he don't know but one thing, that's how to go to a job.

And like if you remember when President Roosevelt was the president, it wasn't nothing in the Army but white boys. A nigger wasn't good enough, the average Black boy, to soldier? Well, we got two generals now. They have got three more up for a rating. You understand? Well, see, the black boy, he is *going to move! He got to go!* It's no stopping for him now. That's the reason *you* got to come on this corner, find out what the hell we are doing. And you all try to get with this soul bit. See? They couldn't turn Black so see where they went: *hippie!* So all that consist of, all them kind of do whatever the hell you want to do.

So you go ahead, 'Fess. Talk to someone calm and good. But give me the pool stick, give me the pool stick. But I'm telling you like it is.

□ □ □

Don't stop me now, you asked me to start! So I'm going to finish, and then you may have your say. But this is why the white man seem to be afraid of the colored man. He feel like the colored man can make love better than he can. Now why is that?

See, that's why the whitey is afraid of the Negro. He thinks he going to take his lady from him. But we don't need her. You know what we need her for? Just to be happy. You see this lady sitting here, your friend? I could love her just as well I could love my sister. And there would be no complications. Whatsoever. "This is my lady." And think nothing of it! She is a lady, she is a human.

But as I was saying, that's all the Brother want. In other words, brother, I break it down, the Black man, that's all he want. He just want love. If you work on that box, and I work on that box, well, hell, if you make two fifty, let me make two fifty! I pull as many bricks as you pull, or more.

And you not going to pay me but so little? You going to think I'm a damn fool. Hey, that don't work no more! *It's all over!* Don't work with whitey no more! Get rid of that whitey! Get rid of that shit.

[*Okay. Now look, suppose you give me this speech, to take to my students. They are going to say, "Now hold on, I never did anything to you. What did I ever do to you?"*]

Their foreparents. Their foreparents are dogs. You take the young generation that's coming along now, they are wonderful. You can't beat them. They're wonderful. And I got, oh, my goodness, I can't call the number of ah, Caucasians—I won't call them whiteys. No, I'm not going to say honkies. I'm not going to say whitey. I'm going to say Caucasians. Associates of mine.

And they sit down, sit down, and have—just like we here now, we have some hell of a conversations, man. I don't know why.

[*My students will ask, did my people hurt you? Not your grandfather, but* you?]

Wait a minute, 'Fess. Wait a minute. You have to think. You don't teach from today. History, it comes from years ago. See, now, you teach. Okay. Where did you come from? You don't come from—today is the twentieth, right? Do you start your class off from the twentieth, May the twentieth of this year. Do you start your class from this day?

I've never had my rights. Sing the national anthem. Sing it now. You look back through it—now have I had my rights? Tell the truth.

Hey, every time I run up into one of you white sons of bitches I have to shoot you. Every time I stand in front of you white motherfuckers we got to shoot you. That's why we come up with Black Panthers. Because you whiteys are not doing right. Now you ask me. So I'm going to say.

You know goddamn well what you been doing wrong all your life.

And because you've been afraid of your woman. Hey, we don't want your woman. We don't want your woman! You know what the Black man want? He just want to make him a *promising living*. That he can make from day to day.

A promising living! But good God, help me Jesus! One of you whites always block the path. You know that. You know this.

You take Kennedy—naw, not Kennedy, God knows. Before God! But you take your goddamn Johnson! That bitch and him own every damn thing down south, while the poor-ass niggers is living, today— They own all the plantation, this little bad little old antique—and then, all *my* poor people is living down there in *slavery*! You might as well call it slavery. Because Johnson, motherfucking fool, drop this, like you do the *cows* when the shit freeze up, drop the cow some motherfucking hay.

I mean, the younger generation, they do not know. But you ask me something about the older generations, I got to tell you. That older generation has done this to my peoples.

The elder peoples is the one that made this, the elder people; it's not the younger generation. The younger generation is so beautiful.

I wish today that I was back in Alabama. That's my home. I wish today I was back in school, Alabama, going back to school. Because . . . everybody seem like they have settled down, and the younger generation have, all this old fear, it has been swept aside. You know. And this is lovely.

We *can* live together. You know? We go over there and fight together. I'm going to tell you, mister, I laid over there for twenty-seven months. Yes, this was in Korea. Twenty-seven months.

I laid up in the mud for damn near a year. Up to my ass, and this ain't too far; ain't too much mud to cover my butt, pardon me. You understand?

You know what I had? The best friend I had was a whitey. He was a white boy from Tennessee. Him and I. Then I had got my leg all fucked up, and it still hurts me right to this day. And this eye—you know when I sent that picture home— Well, maybe you don't recall, but mamma had it—this eye here, I didn't see out of my eye, man, for six months, six months and twenty-one days, I couldn't see nothing. *But* you know what helped me? I had a good white friend from Tennessee. "Heyah, *boy*," he says, "you going to *make* it, *boy!*" I was still "boy," but the bullets is flying at our mess gear and shit. So I mean, it just goes to show you.

Myself, I live all over, 'Fess. Different places. I live near these peoples, we associate, I'm pretty well content.

You know, the only thing that's lacking now. I need . . . a thousand dollars in my pocket. That's all. I'd buy my brother-in-law here a present; I'd buy my sister a present; and since I met your friend, I'd buy her a present; buy you a present; and say, "Let's go out of this." It's made us so very happy. And that's all of it.

That's all. And my mother—she is going to fly to New York. But I would just like to send her some money; to say, "When you get to New York, just keep flying, honey."

That's my life. Really. Lift my hand to God; that's all. I don't want no awful lot of money, you can't be happy.

I would like just to have me just enough money here to go through the block, to go through the Corner. And I would just buy a case of whiskey, buy a case of beer, and sit it out there for the fellows. And say, "This is for you all."

And I'm going to be dressed. Good God! And my lady. She going to be dressed. Me and my lady, dressed alike. And just ride, ride, ride! God knows in Heaven, you can't do much more than that.

□ □ □

That's all in life, baby. You know. That's all in life. You don't need too much money; you just need a little bit of money, man.

And with your abilities and mine, shit, we put it all together, and good God! If you knew what I know, if I know what you knew, shit, we'd own *all* that!

But, see, you don't want to do anything. You're afraid. You want to take something, but what you going to take? Some of that shit these folks say like what I'm talking about? Now you going to go back to school and you going to write all that shit down, and you going to have a special class. I know what you're going to do. I know what it consists of. Am I right or wrong? Hey. And now you going to talk like a big man in front of everybody—and every student you got, you *could* bring a truckload of them down there and pick up the same thing, that is being recorded as of now.

Like I told you before, why don't you get your students, get all your students and bring them around and experience this. Experience. Anything that you experience sticks with you. You can talk, you can talk, you can talk for the next ten year. They have to experience it. You cannot carry this back to no college. You cannot take this on a piece of paper.

You take, like . . . my mother. Okay. My mother. Told me when I was a small kid. I can't forget it. Said, "Baby, there's no other mamma now." I had two pair of pants. I was trying to make it to school. Said, "Now, you

about the oldest boy, baby." Which I was, I was the oldest boy. Mom is
. . . kind of whipped; we ain't got no dad. I didn't have no father, my dad
. . . my old man and my mother, they didn't . . . they had some misunder-
standing.

There was four boys and four girls. And my mom. So, I . . . I . . . left out
of school in the tenth grade. Joined the service. And put my age up, and
joined the service.

Anyway, wasn't no old man. So we had to go along, man. And it's just
rough.

So you just put yourself in a different category. You just have to make
it or let it go.

But I mean, what I am saying is, this is the real thing, 'Fess. You
know? This is the Black and white downfall. Frankly speaking. The
white man—you know what? I love you just like I do my brother-in-law
here. But, there is a flaw. You hear of this, the fine print?

This is the fine print. Do you know what the fine print consists of?
"Don't mess with my lady!"

I mean, you know what I'm talking about. See, you're no fool. Because
I know you've been around. I mean. Frankly speaking, this is the way I
see it, man.

Hawk's Brother-in-Law

Hawk, why do women have so much to do with it? Why do the women
have so much to do with it?

I don't know about the younger people that are coming up today. I
don't know, we figured wrong, what I know about the younger people
coming up today, they're not like I was when I was coming up.

I went and I stayed in the Army for ten years. Korea, I spent four
years. Okay, I get all messed up in Korea. Shot up, cut up, pain and
everything, and burnt also.

I gets out. You know. They tells me this, they tells me that. You can
go and you get all these kind of rights, you go to the VAO. But when I go
to the VA Office, they don't have time to talk to me today. Years in
Korea, and I can't even go to them and get a loan or nothing. Can't get
my home— No, cannot. No, hell, you cannot! Don't tell me, I done tried
it. But I'm the guy that went over there and caught hell, you know. For
them.

Okay. When I went in the Army, it was really hell. I go into Korea. I
catches hell in Korea. I stayed in a concentration camp for nine months.
Okay. I weighed a hundred, about a hundred and forty-two pounds;
came out weight ninety-eight pounds.

Still catching hell today, you know. You go in a job today, you go in a job today, to get a job— Well, the same people that go to all these bars, you say hillbillies, yankees, or whatever you call them—okay, you go to one of these place, like one of these factories to get a job today, and they look at you like a *fool*, you know. They want to see your discharge, they want to see everything. The next train up that come, this guy can come from Tennessee, Alabama, Georgia, Mississippi, hillbilly, they call them, he can come, they'll move *him* right in.

They don't give a damn about you, you know. Okay, go over there and this is a part of your life. Which has been taken part of. They done taken part.

Now, that's the part I got against them. That's the part I got against the white man, that's the only fault I got against the white man. Because we don't—we can't afford, where we never had the opportunity to own a factory like General Motors, you know. And Ford. Well, we can't own these kind of things. 'Cause we ain't had the opportunity. Because, well, you understand how it is, we came to this country, we came to this country as slaves, you know.

I mean, that's the way it was in the olden days, when we came to this country. What fault I have against him, 'cause we can't walk into the factory, where the government say equal opportunity, all this kind of stuff. But it's not. That's a front.

□　□　□

The way I feel, it's a front. You can walk in, they would hire one Black man to five whites.

It keeps on; it's the same way today. Okay, if Chrysler or Ford . . . over the time. . . .

The common laborer, the common laborer, the average colored guy, he don't have a good education. Because his parents, really, when he was coming along, they didn't have the money to send him. Like my parents. When I finished high school, I could have went to college. But no, my people didn't have the money, see. My granddaddy, he was working on the WPA, they just didn't have the money. We was just barely living. Wearing one pair of shoes the whole year. So we had to go in the Army to make a living.

Okay, when you come out and get a job, and, man, it's the same; you go through the same hell, year after year, day after day, week after week, hour after hour, everywhere you go. The same . . . crap. You know. Over and over.

So, that's one thing the Black man really feels. It's not these ideas— the Black man want the white man's woman, want to get his, ah, move into his neighborhood. It's not—the Black man don't want this. The Black man want the same thing as the white man got. To make a better living.

I *want* my children to be able to live like the kids in Grosse Pointe or Birmingham. That's what I want. I want my kids to get a good education. I don't want my kids to be a dropout like I was. I don't want, I don't want my kids to have to go to Vietnam or Korea, Indochina, catch the hell I caught. Okay, get their fingers split, shot in the leg, and burnt. *Then* come *back* home and walk in a factory to get a job, stand on the line three hours, fifteen whites ahead of him and two colored, the old woman come, point, say, "*You*, come in the office." Well, this is a whitey.

This is how they do it. I done it, I'm tell you what I've experienced myself. They will point over me and they'll point at the next guy. They say, "*You* come in the office." This white guy go in the office, may be small as anything, they will hire him.

When *I* get in—they do about five whiteys and then maybe they'll point and pick me out—like it's happened to me, to pick me out—*I* go in the office, and they say, "How much you weigh?" I tell him how much I weigh. He say, "Well, you don't weigh enough; we're looking for a man at least weighs a hundred seventy-five to a hundred eighty or a hundred ninety." Well, I looked; I looked at the guys going in. But there's nothing I can say. These white guys, they smaller than me. Some of them weigh a hundred thirty-five; they much smaller.

Okay, why in the hell couldn't he call me? Instead of calling five of them, call me. Yet and still, these guys never did nothing. Never fought, never went out and cleaned up the alley and things like that. You know, that's what the Black man really feel. All the Black man really want.

And, it gradually moving in. We got more Black kids in colleges, we got more Black kids in colleges and universities than ever have been in history, today. It's that the white man—now, not all whiteys is lowdown. And not all whiteys is mean. It's some whites is really beautiful. Really. The reason why I love them is because they're trying to help. You know, they're trying to help. And keep things moving. And they realize what we going through and what the Black man really have went through.

But now, to me, I don't know how the rest of you feel, I don't feel that the white man owe me nothing. As far as I'm concerned, he don't owe me nothing. Just give me the opportunity to make it on myself.

I'm willing to work. I have—like, man, you take, I never been in jail, never been to prison, never arrested in my life. All I want to do, I'm forty-one years old now, all I want to do is get out there and make a honest living. To bring my kids, to keep them from growing up like I was in the ghetto; you know, in the ghetto with a bunch of hoodlums out there, begging, stealing, robbing. I don't want my kids to do that. Prostitutes and all that stuff. See, I don't want my kids to do that. See, I don't want my girls and I don't want my son to call theirselves pimps and all that. I want it, to be brought it to a way, to get a *decent honest job.* You understand? So they can go out in the world and their kids can keep going.

It's not the idea . . . see, I, I have the feeling that the peoples out in Birmingham and around, Grosse Pointe, different places like that, they have the idea that we want to move out, live in their neighborhoods, their area. I definitely, I never want to live there. I'm happy right where I'm at. That's why I'm trying to buy my place. I'm happy right here.

And, I want, I feel I can help my peoples more by living here than by moving out there. There's some, just like whitey, they make a little money and it go to their head. Then they pull away, they think they too good. On both sides, the white race and the Black race. How many Black man you know that has money that would speak to you? It's the same way in both races. When the white man get a little money, he down on the hillbilly. When the Black man get a little money, he down on the southern Black man. That's the way I feel about it. And that is true.

nathan

One afternoon Nathan Coolidge and I drove up and found Dog Man standing over Runner, who was lying on the ground. Dog was holding a knife and threatening Runner. Nathan picked up a brick, walked over, and faced Dog down. The next day I found Dog and his girlfriend both badly scraped up; they had been hurt in a fight with Nathan. A week or two later, Nathan gave me his version of that fight, in which he beat the two up with a shotgun that Dog was firing at him. During Nathan's description of that fight and others on the Corner, he spoke at length about the crucial issue of standing up against threats, lest you be constantly harassed. Then he began to describe people who are prone to harass the weak, beginning with a discussion of Dog, leading on to a discussion of Haskell, and then to a discussion of a bully who had recently been killed by one of his long-time victims. I quote the discussion of Haskell.

Nathan

See, Runner owed Dog a quarter from a couple of weeks ago one Friday night or something, I don't know about it. Anyway Dog just decided, well, I'll jump on me somebody, and Runner just as good as any, he owe me a quarter, I jump on him. Know what I'm talking about? Same thing was with Haskell. About two weeks before he went to jail this last time. He was sitting out there on Luther's porch, you know. And Easy, you know Easy. Easy come by, and Easy owed Haskell two dollars.

Easy had paid Haskell the two dollars the day before though. But he owed Haskell the two dollars about two or three weeks. And Haskell decided, he charge Easy some interest. He didn't tell him in the beginning. Told him to give him two more dollars. Easy said, "I don't have no money." He said, "You ain't got no two dollars?" Easy said, "No." He said, "I'm beating your old grey ass today." And, he push, you know. I told him, I say, "Haskell, don't push that old man around like that." I said, "He can't fight you. Only thing you can do is just jump on him and beat him and hurt him, or something. He's too old to fight you." So Luther's wife, Catherine, she come out. She gave Easy a five-dollar bill, and told Easy to go and give him two dollars. Haskell snatched that five-dollar bill and throw it on the ground. He said, "I don't want her money, I want your money." He told Easy. He just wanted more or less just take advantage of him.

He's gone now in Jackson now. He got eight months to two years, they gave him. And this was, what Haskell had, five felonious assaults. With a weapon. Now, he was on probation for two of them. He had two pending in court. He was out on bond on those. And they got him again. You know that guy, that kind of old guy they call Spider?

It was about three days before Haskell went to jail. Haskell shot him in the leg. With a twenty-two. He told him, he said, "You don't believe I'd shoot you." You know, just like that. And Spider said, "For what? What you going to hurt me for?" And Haskell pulled a pistol out. Boom! He shot him right in the leg.

He limping around now. Shot him in the leg. He said he never got that bullet out of his leg yet. He said every time he reach it, it drops or moves and he can't get it any way. It didn't hit a bone, but it's in the leg, you know.

Just no reason at all. Just like me and you sitting there talking, I tell you, "You won't believe I shoot you," and, boom! People like that suppose to be in the penitentiary, they ain't got no business to be walking around the street free.

raymond stone

Although I spent relatively little time speaking with children, I am including one short interview, not to suggest some serious issue, but to remind the reader that there were children around. The respondent is Raymond Stone, the oldest child of the Stone family, and the only boy in it. He is eleven and likes baseball.

Raymond Stone

What could I say?

[*Why don't you tell me what you do in the day, like from when you get up to when you to go to bed. What are the different things you do?*]

Go to the ball games, ride bicycles, look at TV.

[*Yes?*]

Play horseshoes. Play baseball. Listen to the Tigers' baseball game. Watch them play basketball at the basketball court at school.

[*What about on school days?*]

Play baseball in the gym. Sometimes when it's rainy, we have free play to shoot basketball. Then we go to our other classes: arithmetic, science, and art. In art we draw things and we paste paper on the colored paper.

[*What classes do you like?*]

Gym. Art. Arithmetic.

[*Are you good at arithmetic?*]

Sort of.

[*How are your teachers?*]

They're good, too.

[*Yeah?*]

They never paddle you unless you do something real bad, or keep talking. They only warn you twice.

[*Do your friends like school?*]

Yes. Most of all, they like to go in gym and play baseball.

[*Uh huh. They play hookey?*]

No.

[*Let me see now. Do you go up here to the school on the corner?*]

Yes.

[*Uh huh. Do you ever sing in school?*]

We sing in music. Our music teacher name's Miss Baldwin.

[*Tell me about . . . let's see now, you're eleven, now . . . pretend that you're a grown man already, okay? Tell me what your life would be like if you were a grown man now?*]

I'll probably get me a job at Chrysler's.

[*Well, tell me all about your life. Pretend you're telling me all about your life when you're a grown-up, all right?*]

I'm married, and get me a car and buy me a home.

[*Would you be happy?*]

Yes.

[*Why? Why would you be happy?*]

I have a car and a home.

[*What kind of work would you do at Chrysler?*]

Make parts of cars.

[*Would you like that?*]

Yes.

[*Why?*]

I like to build cars and make parts, too.

[*How do you know you like to?*]

I be practice on building little model cars.

[*Plastic models?*]

Yes.

[*You do that now?*]

Yes.

[*Is that the work your daddy does?*]

He's a janitor. He used to make parts of cars, but now he a janitor.

[*Uh huh. . . . If you work in Chrysler's, would you have enough money for your family?*]

Yes. Probably get about two dollars and seventy-five cents an hour.

[*How many hours would you work?*]

Probably eleven.

□   □   □

[*I see. . . . Can you remember back to a couple of times that were real nice? Describe a couple of times in your life that were real nice, Okay?*]

When I was ten, I went to a Tigers' baseball game, and I got a free bat.

[*Can you think of another one?*]

When I was ten again, I went to a Tigers' baseball game, and I got me a ball.

[*Can you think of another time that was real nice?*]

When I was ten, I went and got me a hat.

[*What kind of hat?*]

A baseball hat.

[*I see. Can you think of a couple of times in your life when you felt bad?*]

Yes. When I couldn't go to the baseball game.

the death of
robert kennedy

On the morning that Robert Kennedy lay dying in the hospital, the Corner was in a mood I had never seen. All was tender silence. People were gentle and close. We brought a radio outside and listened to the newcasts. People drifted by and spoke of their love for Robert Kennedy, and of the assaults on the Kennedys and King. The next morning Kennedy was dead, and the Corner was drenched in bitterness.

The fragments that follow swirled about my microphone as I sat by the horse-shoe stakes that morning.

The Death of Robert Kennedy

No, I don't like it. But it's nothing I can do about it right now. It takes time for everything. It will be straightened out. That's all I have to say. I hate to have it to have happened. I mean, as well as I loved the man. I mean it will be straightened out. But that's all I can say.

◻   ◻   ◻

There ain't going to be no voting now! You just have to make your way now. You don't need no president, they won't let a man have a presidency, you don't need no president no more! You just need a world to live in. *Live for yourself*!

So that's the things like it is now. Don't need no president no more. Just live for yourself! That's the way I'm living from now on. Me and a lot of other people.

We just live for yourself from now on. Whatever come, you take it, and do whatever you can do about it to solve your problems. And keep it going. Keep the world going.

You don't need no president. There's no more people that would . . .

187

stand up for you. Because, they think that they will get killed. That's the thing you got to look at. No one wants to take the responsibility of getting killed. How many wives would let their husbands go out and take the responsibility of getting killed.

See, this is the thing that he'll think: everybody that go out there gets killed. Unless he's a Democrat. And if it's a Democrat, it'll bring you right back to the Hoover days. I mean a Republican. You'll be going back to Hoover days. Going to soup lines and different things. So we don't want that. We don't want that no more. See, I was born in those days, I know about it.

☐ ☐ ☐

Brother, let me explain to you. You know, a *long* time ago them dad-blame hillbillies was down in Texas with them git-tars, singing, "Get them Kennedys out of there, get them Kennedys out of there." And they trying to get them out of there. Playing them old git-fiddles down in Texas, "Get them Kennedys out of there." And damn if they ain't getting them out of there.

☐ ☐ ☐

Johnson and Nixon, them's the one they should have got!

☐ ☐ ☐

Humphrey alright.

☐ ☐ ☐

You ain't going to have no peace in the world!

☐ ☐ ☐

Look here, if Nixon or Wallace or any of them get in there you might as well just to pack up and leave and get you another set of mules. Haw and Gee!

☐ ☐ ☐

I ain't going no motherfucker where; I am going to stay right here.

☐ ☐ ☐

Let me tell you something, Republicans get in there, they are going to suck up all the money. You work six months, next six months you are going to be on your ass.

☐ ☐ ☐

Republicans are not going to let you have no money. That's what it's for.

□ □ □

Democrats let you have some. Republicans going to suck up all that money. You work for Chrysler six months, next six months you be out on your ass.

□ □ □

People that I know say they ain't going to vote for nobody!

□ □ □

I know three words now: Stick 'em up.

□ □ □

Now the white man, he need the colored man, he need him.

□ □ □

My forefathers, he built this land while the white man was back on their ass, he built this world. Just like the man last night on TV: They got all that land in Mississippi, the government rather build a fifty-million-dollar jet and send it to South Vietnam and kill them innocent people over there, than give a Negro a dollar to buy a little piece of land.

□ □ □

The poor people. That's why they killed him! What has the poor man got? *He got to go for himself now!*

□ □ □

Whitey can kiss his motherfucking ass! Killing all the good people! Boy, this is going to be a motherfucker!

□ □ □

There's going to be some changes!

□ □ □

Do you know the Bible says: Before the end of time, the bottom going to be on top and the top going to be on the bottom. The white man knows his goddamn time done come, but he's still holding on. His string is going to break!

□ □ □

That's why he sleep with all his pistols. He got all the guns. He got all the money. He got so much money he worry all the time. He can't sleep. The man can't sleep. It's worrying him, he'll do anything to stop somebody from getting his wealth.

But Robert Kennedy didn't buy no kind of games. All this racketeering shit. He didn't cut or fool. When he got ready to do something, he put his foot on it. Just like he told my boy Hoffa, "You going to jail." He say, "You are going to jail." He meant it.

We going to do it on our own, man!

That's right. 'Cause *ain't going to be nobody vote for nobody, man!*

Who going to let the Republicans in there? They'll be running their ass back to the thirties. Everyone will be killing to get something to eat!

It won't be back in the thirties, 'cause people, the Black man, have been advanced, they ain't going to take that shit. He will not take that shit no more.

Do you know the white man know he can not put that shit back where it was. *He's through!* He knows he's through. But he's still trying to hold on, like a spiderweb hanging down and a spider come down that pole and somebody has broken it here at the ground. The white man know he hanging on a string, boy. He done did, he done did, he done took, he done killed, he done did this and done did that.

He took it! Everything he ever had. When he took what *he* wanted, he got him a law: "Put the motherfucker in jail!" *I* go take the money, put *me* in jail.

It's no man, it's *no man* in the world, *ever* got rich, if he didn't *take* nothing.

There's no *honest* money-making nowhere, without you go out there, like I did, go to Ford's, goddamn it, and kill yourself, for a little money. And then you're too goddamn tired to enjoy it. And then you don't get nary cent cause the motherfucker going to take it as fast as you make it.

Every son of a bitch got all this damn money sitting on his ass with his tie on, he *took* it! He's in some kind of racket to get it! And the honky, he know it. No brag, goddamn it, that's just fact. He *took* it. And then he got him a law: "Alright, don't let them bother me! Don't let them bother me."

Only one thing leads this world today, that's money. Any son of a bitch got money can do anything. Like some son of a bitch has the money, he can pay to have the President killed. That's right. You got to have the money. And poor people can't do it. Like that mother fucker like me, you, we can't do that. And you got to get for *yourself*. Now.

Do you know another thing? Them judges sit on their ass give a man all this time, but he must have didn't read the Bible. God said, "No man should judge no man; I do the judging myself." Now the *judge* going to sit on his hind part, like this: "I cut your pecker, your freedom, I give you twenty years in the state penitentiary." Son of a bitch! He don't know nothing, he said, "I heard" that "he told me"—he wasn't nowhere around! Goddamn little pop-gun police be so big with a gun. I can shoot good as any damn police!

Well, my man, I tell you it's a bad thing to happen. But it just happen. So whatever the outcome be, that just about what it is. You know. That's three times this has happened, and its about to get to the end now. It can't more, three strikes is out.

Four times, brother. Four. Malcolm X, that's the first one. Kennedy. Two Kennedys. And one Luther King. That's four.

Malcolm X was the first, man. And you ain't heard no shit from that, did you?

Well, this done come to a end now. Something's got to be done.

Every motherfucker and his brother don't want to die. And who is going to get up there and say, "I stand for this." And say, "Here I am, shoot at me!" Everybody's scared, to get up there, to speak. Everybody. All people, all nations, needs a speaker. Now who's ready to get up now to be a speaker, behind Kennedy.

That's what I'm saying. That's why I say we don't have nobody else.

□   □   □

That's what I'm saying. You think I'd get up there and say. . . . I would, I would, but I'm saying I'm not qualified. I'm not qualified for that. You can't talk. You can't talk to a police, to the judge, downtown, unless you are a lawyer. You can be in court and the judge downtown, if you ain't got nobody to represent you, you can't say a goddamn thing. You cannot talk. You can't say, I defend myself. They give you one of those lawyers for seventy-five dollars, that come to you and say, "Well, I know you did this, I can get you two to five." You say, "You mother-fucker, I didn't do a goddamn thing. You tell me 'I can get you two to five!' I don't want *no* motherfucking time, because I'm innocent!" And then when you get up in the court the judge tell you to sit down, them bailiffs got you, wham-bam-bam, you ain't got a chance to say shit. That's what I don't like about this world, boy. If I'm the one that did it, let *me* ask that man questions. Find out who lying. You tell the lawyer something, you tell the lawyer, "Man, ask this motherfucker this ques-tion." And then the judge, they don't talk to you. Naw, the lawyers go back there in chambers, get things together, and come out and tell you what they going to do. And you ain't said shit! What can you do now? And you get more time, the judge just run it on up the tree, boogedy-boogedy-boogedy up the tree goddamn it 'til you can't go no further. By you opening your mouth.

□   □   □

Well, man, ain't nothing for you to do but just hope you can do and get through with it. Let me tell you something, man, do you know, he got a time coming? Do what you got to do and get through with it. If you can get through with it, I mean if you can slip by with it, then well and good. If you go to jail, just go ahead on and forget it. 'Cause there'll be some more out here doing the same thing. So just forget about it.

□   □   □

Ain't no telling what it's going to come to now. People are angry all over the world.

□   □   □

Who going to vote for any damn body? You can forget about a vote. You don't need to vote no more. When you vote one in, they kill him. What you going to vote for?

□   □   □

If he do anything for the poor man, they are going to kill him. What you vote for? Yeah, that's what I'm talking about.

□   □   □

They are going to have their own president anyway. So let them get what they want, and you do what you want. Let them put their own president in. You talk about going to start a gun law, can't nobody have a gun. That's a lie. They can get them a president anywhere, they can go to Mississippi and get one. But then don't come fucking with the man that's trying to protect himself. 'Cause see, that's when they are going to start trouble.

□   □   □

Ain't nobody going to vote no more! You can get a gun.

□   □   □

The one that had him killed gonna vote. Do you understand?

□   □   □

They talking about white people got all the guns. You don't need no gun. Just let them be laying up there sleeping with them guns. You can get rid of them. You burn up enough of them.

□   □   □

Man, we have fought with spears, sticks, and rocks.

□   □   □

You don't need no gun; the worst weapon in the world is fire! Fire and water. You don't need no gun.

□   □   □

Just one thing, man, let me tell you, ain't no use in no man going around saying he going to collect all the guns. His toes going to be just like Bobby Kennedy's, coming into somebody's house, looking for a gun. That's right. And everybody, I think everybody, loved him. Bobby Kennedy, everybody loved him, man. 'Cause I prayed for the man to live.

□   □   □

Forget about that gun thing. Don't nobody need no gun, but people not going to give up no gun. I don't care what they got, but I mean they don't need it. Guns ain't no big thing.

□ □ □

When you get ready to do something anyway, they going to call the troopers. They got all them machine guns, all them fire weapons.

□ □ □

And they don't have a colored National Guard in Michigan. They don't have one. They don't have any.

□ □ □

Hey, you see them police right now, just cruising by here, going to circle and take another look at us right here. And I bet you a dollar, I tell you what I do, I ain't got a dollar, but I bet you anything in the world, that nary one of them police live in Detroit. They don't live in Detroit. Ain't nary one of them live in the city of Detroit. They live out there in their land and come to Detroit and run over niggers. That's what they do. That's their thing. If you do enough dirt, they transfer you to another station. Out there in the white neighborhood. That's right, where you won't never see them no more.

□ □ □

Well, they ain't going to do it to me 'cause I'm going to take care of me as long as I live.

□ □ □

Boy, I don't understand the world. I can't understand the day, man.

□ □ □

Well, I know I ain't voting for nobody else no more as long as I live. 'Cause ain't nobody to vote for. Who you going to vote for? Who you going to vote for? There's nobody to vote for!

□ □ □

Man, I saw a lot of people, that people say they don't need no voting papers. Throw them away! Besides, who you going to vote for?

□ □ □

Don't nobody need them Republicans. What them Republicans ever did, ever since the world began? Republicans ain't never did nothing! Just as long as I can remember, way back in the thirties, man. Twenty-five cents a day! President Roosevelt, he got shot at two or three times, I think. He told them all, them guys had that money: "If you don't turn this money loose, I'll counterfeit it, I'll *make* some more money!"

Johnson run again. Yeah, Johnson glad he dead, Kennedy. He glad he dead hisself. Man, you know Johnson, let me tell you something now: If Johnson be in there another term, be all over for him. Ain't nobody going to have Johnson. They all talking about, "If ya'll help me, I can help ya'll." He on his ranch, barbecueing, riding horses. When he over here and try to start the war in Vietnam! Who want him? He's a Republican his dadblame self, really, that's what he is! Who want him? Don't nobody want him. Let him go on back down to Texas, down there somewhere. He ain't did nothing since he been in there. What have he did? He ain't done nothing! That's all he did, started a war. All he did. He ain't got no business over there, them people fighting. That's what's the matter with the world today.

Stop this war! Why don't you stop things over *here* what's happening? Here we are messing with somebody else's damn business. Ain't got nothing to do with them people over there. That's *them* people's damn business!

My nephew just went to Vietnam. My brother-in-law just came back from Vietnam. And you talking about mean shit, motherfucker, Vietnam is right here! He went to jail three days after he came back. Taking the gun to get it registered, and the police stopped the car. He just back, glad to be back, celebrating, going to get the gun registered, brand new gun. Taking it in to get it registered, do right, and here is the police fucking with him. I mean, now, he get out of it, because that was his intention, and right's right and wrong's wrong. Never had no record. But what they're doing is trying to get every Negro a record where he can't get no position. Fuck 'em. Why don't they attend to their own motherfucking business?

nell

One night Hawk took me to a little one-story house that he was using some of the time. We stopped to pick up a man about forty whom Hawk knew and a young woman of about twenty-two. I had never seen them before. The man got bored and left, Hawk fell asleep in an old armchair, and Nell and I talked.

Nell

For the kids, huh, you going to make a book. You going to make a book for the students to read. Okay. Let me tell you a story.

[*Tell me a story.*]

Okay. About a little girl that was born in Mississippi way back in the woods someplace, and came to the big city. Her parents brought her there when she was about two years old. So she grew up here in Detroit. And you talkin' about good livin'? In the ghetto? I had the best. Nice house. Coal stove sitting in the middle of the floor. And if you weren't by that stove you were cold. And if you let the fire go out in the morning, when you woke up, you were cold trying to put your clothes on. Okay. The rats would pay you a visit every so often. I had a room that was in the front of the house. And it had a long hallway, to the kitchen and then the back door. And there was a couple of rooms off of that. And these rats, every night, they would make a game—I think they were playing or something like that—they would start at the kitchen door and run straight through the house and over the foot of my bed. On my bed. Over the foot. Down up under the bed and back to the kitchen door and round and round all night 'til they got tired. Then I could go to sleep. Now I had to go to school in the morning too, you know. Scared to death. So I finally told my father about it, and he got some rat poison to put around there.

You know. And roaches and all that business. The roaches would drop off the ceiling *in your food.* You hear me? Talk about the ghetto.

That was a little place across the street from me, too. The man wouldn't keep the place up or nothing like that. It was a firetrap. And it caught on fire three or four times. That was right down two blocks from right here, yeah. And the man didn't do nothing for it and there was an invalid guy up there. He was in a wheelchair. And was three or four kids. And I remember, I was a kid then, I remember that the place caught on fire. And it was late and nobody went up there. And you could smell the flesh that had burnt for *days* after that.

And all this is what you have to live with. This is the thing.

I tell you one thing. I been here all my life, but the first time I ever found any prejudice I was in Kansas City, Kansas. And I had checked in a hotel. And they didn't have a coffee shop, so there was a drugstore down on the corner so I went down there and ordered a cup of tea. So, I could have the cup of tea, and they put it in a container. Yeah. And I said, "No, I don't want it to take out. I want to drink it here." "No, you got to take it out." I said, "No, I want to drink it here!" "Well no, you got to take it out." I said, "Why?" "Because you can buy it, but you can't drink it here." You know. And you supposed to love everybody and all that kind of old stuff.

david wainwright, luther, and robert scarlett

We have already met David Wainwright and Luther, who lives with Catherine. Both men served in the Army in Korea and were seriously wounded. The following pages present brief excerpts from interviews with Wainwright, Luther, and a third worker named Robert Scarlett.

David Wainwright

I leave here in the morning, I'm ready, that's for sure. That's for sure. Every morning, I don't care how it is, rain, snow, or sleet, or snow, I hit that road. Ain't nothing stop me. Don't nothing.

If something stop me, I'll tell you what, the world know it. 'Cause I live *here*, at this house. And my wife lock that door when I start to leave. I hit that road going clean up to the bus. I don't give a damn, or snow up to my . . . up to here. When the big snow was out here, the bus, some buses didn't run, but I went over to where a bus was running. I went to work. I did.

I walked. I've walked in snow, sometimes, up higher than my boots. *But*, I look at them kids. I have to take *care* of the kids. That's what I went out there for. And right today, I thank the good Lord for— That Man up above, people don't believe. I tell you one thing: He will hear! *Ask* Him to. Why, He will show you. I've gotten so, I mean there are things, changes coming to me. . . . Why, I believe in Him up above, I've went through things that I didn't believe I was . . . but we made it.

I mean, I thank the good Lord. I'm working every day. And I know I drinks my liquor, too. And I know I got my kids to take care of. I have to get out there and work to get that, right?

That's right. You know, we got a whole lot of people, they ask me, say, "What in the hell are you doing living up here?" I got people coming cross town, say, "Why you here?" That's not the idea. I live where I want. Now he ain't got no business over here, that's bullshit. I live where I want. Look, I'm going to respect you and you respect me. What th— I got time to move, I can move whenever I get ready, but look, otherwise than that, damn. 'Cause long as you don't mess over me, I'm not going to mess over you, that's for sure. You can bet on that. 'Cause long as them kids satisfied, and I can get out there and hit that road every morning and come back, I ain't got no complaints. Yes sir. Me, right today.

But just don't, you know, if somebody is going to come around and aggravate me and everything, I ain't . . . I can quick get that off my mind, I'm just going to go on and tell them the truth. But they keep on aggravating me, I know what to do. First thing that I pick up in my hand, I just knock the hell out of you and go on about my business.

[*I have never seen you quarrel with anyone. Come on.*]

No! No. I hope the good Lord that I never will. 'Cause that's the reason I pray to that Man up above. You might not believe in Him, but I do. I do. I seen a time when I was in Korea. I seen a time . . . that I didn't see no survive. I have asked the good Lord, have said, "Where you at?" Damn. He . . . He showed me. But it cost me. Them bullets in the leg. Stab. And every damn thing that a son of a bitch can get. But He was with me. And still, I'm still just like I am, nothing but a regular man.

Listen, I don't . . . I mean, right now, I still don't have no complaint with nobody. How *can* I have complaints? Huh? When I'm going to work every day, and putting eight hours in. I come back here, and I sit up there and read the paper and talk with the kids. Come back out here and get me a beer. I still don't have no worry about, ain't nobody got no business messing with me. No. Not, not like that. No, you know.

[*Now, you spent six months in the hospital after Korea, right?*]

Six months? Yeah, about that. Might be more than that. That was that grenade, and that bayonet. Everything. Ain't no trick bag. You know, sometimes, you may notice how I walk, sometimes my leg kind of messed up and I have to walk a different way to keep my leg in balance. Sometimes I have to *throw* that leg, you know, to make it fit right.

I had six boys in my family, six boys and one girl. Every one of them went in the Army except one. That was in Mississippi.

It was a little town. We have plenty of stores, had plenty of stores, you know. It was a nice little old city, too. You know, people over here talking about all that shit, that down south the white man did this, the white man did that. That's bunk. I mean, maybe that's right, some of them did. My daddy down there, he worked on the railroad. He worked on the railroad and when he was off, he'd go down and do these little jobs on houses and buildings. That's where I learned how to do those kind of things.

I'm working maintenance now, at the bakery. And I make three dollars an hour, supposed to be getting more after next month. Anything what have to be done around in that plant, in my department, I do. You know, they got a whole lots of machines. Now, some, they are special made, you know, they check on them theirself. But minor things, in that building, they come and gets me.

But, like I said, all I ask for—you know, me and my family. Me and my family. Long as I take—I'm not trying to get rich. I don't want to be rich. All I want to do is just take care of my family. That's all. I take care of my family, I'm satisfied. I ain't ignorant acting. I got my beer and I got my liquor. If I want any liquor, I can go to the store and it still ain't not hurting my family.

But, you know. You know. When you drink that liquor and wine and all that stuff mixed together, you can't control yourself. Little arguments comes up. I tell you one thing. I wish everybody . . . you, everybody, I mean, the way I looks at it. . . . If you got to be . . . you know, uh. . . . Long as you take care of your own business. That's what I try to do.

Otherwise than that, if I try to take care of my business and your business and everybody else's business, I ain't getting nothing but get misused. Otherwise than that, long as I lay in there and take care of my kids, what *they* do outside, on the streets out here, this is not—uh, uh, no, that's the city's problem. What they do, I don't know.

See, I walk in my house, go on in and talk with them kids, they play a record or they looking at the tube. Go on inside. . . .

□   □   □

Otherwise, I'm just a working-ass man. That's all. And when I'm not working, like on my day off, I enjoy myself and my beer. I wants a shot of liquor, I go and get it. Otherwise than that . . . like me, I go back in the house. . . .

And I wish . . . get rid of all this old damn. . . . When I see a joker, or you or me or anybody, start an argument or something. . . . First thing that I do, I cut you loose. That's it. Otherwise I don't have no complaints. Period. They can be arguments, fighting around here, arguing and killing each other, long as they don't interfere with me, I ain't got none of it. But I might say to somebody, well, you know, "You-all might cool it, you know, talk to yourself, you know, help yourself without all this . . . *bull*." So I rather, you know. . . . Long as they don't mess with me, I don't have no complaints. Just like we are right now.

[*Do you work overtime at the bakery?*]

Oh, yes sometimes I do. But I quit that though. I went to work one time at six-thirty. Six-thirty Saturday morning. You know it was three o'clock Sunday morning I was leaving! But I told them, I said, uh, uh, I never do that no more. I couldn't sleep! I couldn't sleep, I couldn't sleep, everything that I know is on that plant out there.

Working. I'm talking about working. I'm not talking about just sitting around. I'm talking about working. . . . The money looked good, but damn the money, I'm looking at myself. My health means more to me than that damn money means.

I bring in about a hundred and fifteen dollars. And, then, we pay sixty dollars on the place. Then, I got them little bitty little ones. That's where the money goes! That's where the money goes.

Right, I can go, now, me and my wife, I got to get her a loaf of bread and that stuff and spend about five or ten dollars on me and her. But I got three, myself makes four, my wife makes five. . . . How much in the world that. . . . Shoot, she get through buying food, paying rent, how much do you think I got!

[*Yeah. Hey, David, how far did you go in school?*]

I finished, I finished eleventh grade. When Uncle Sam tooken me.

I could have stayed on, but no, I might as well go on and get it all over with.

Nineteen fifty-one. I wanted to go on, but, look here, I mean, when you look at them things, either way I do, I have to go. I went to school, I still have to go in.

Oh, shoot, all the children in that school, about, there were about a hundred of them, they give us a going away, what you call a going-away party. Preacher and everything, man, you know.

Luther

Where I been, Professor, I been at the hospital. And I got to be back. I drank too much. I guess. Too much booze. Just had one too many I suppose. I got to be back on Friday; supposed to be back on Friday. To have an operation for one of my kidneys. So I supposed to make it back. I can't make it then, but I be there the day after, around the weekend, anyway.

I don't know how long I am going to be in the hospital. Who knows? Maybe a month. Maybe a day. Maybe two days. Maybe I don't come at all.

But I will not have time for you to teach me to read. I got to go back to

Rhode Island, to the Veteran's Hospital. I wouldn't have time to do anything, really. All, all I can do is sit, till I get straightened out.

I was not supposed to be drinking. But I took a drink.

It started at the toes, and went way up to here. Way up to here now. It just—chill. The leg. From here all the way up to my thigh, it's cold.

And, when I take a drink or smoke a cigarette, I feel it right here inside. I feel it inside. When I take a drink. What I believe, I have to have an operation. Once in a while, I get hurt in my chest. I don't know, it's just one of those things. You know.

He told me, don't smoke or drink. So, I done both of them. And like I say—what's gonna happen is just gonna happen anyway. So, what the hell.

You time is gonna come one day. So now, I just don't give a damn. You know. What gonna happen just gonna happen. I may be able to come back down and I may not be. It's just one of those things. That's all.

I'm thirty-one years old. And so, this is the first time I've ever been in a hospital. First time. I never seen a doctor, or, you know, but just only check-ups. And so, this time they got me in there for *good*. (*Long silence.*)

☐ ☐ ☐

[*Luther, what were the happiest times in your life?*]

Happy time? What years were a happy time in my life? Well. To tell you the truth, I don't think I had no happy time.

I don't think so. Not so I can know it. I can't remember.

I never had a happy time.

I left home, because of bad treatment. They beat me up. My father. Everybody else, too. Everybody old, around my father age. I took unnecessary whupping.

We lived in Georgia. There was three boys and one girl. My mother. Father. And—I hoboed. Hoboed into Detroit. Freight train, to Detroit.

I met a lady, down here. On Lomont. And I asked her, did she have any work could I do around her house? Told her, sweeping leaves off her lawn and everything, rake off the lawn and everything. So she asked me in, and was I working and all of this. So I explained to her. And I explained to her and I told her what's what. She said, "Well, do you have any place to stay tonight?" Nope. She said, "Well, where you figuring on staying?" I say, I don't know. She said, "Well, you can have a bedroom and you can sleep here tonight, anyway."

So, she reared me up. Until I was sixteen. And then, I volunteer for the Army. I went out and then I come back to her. She kept me until I

was sixteen years old. I volunteer, went into the service. I come back out.
. . . Hell, I'd rather not talk about that no way.

A good time? If I did . . . I can't remember.

□ □ □

In the Army, I worried. Had troubles.

Friends? Yeah. I had friends. So-called friends. A lot of people say
they have friends, they don't have 'em. Everybody who say he your
friend is not your friend. You can laugh and talk with a person all day
long, and say that's your friend— No, it is not. I feel like this here: I had
one friend and that was my mother. That's in my book. That's the only
friend. Otherwise, the hell with the rest of 'em.

My mother is in Rhode Island. She had an operation on her neck just
before I left, she just come out of the hospital two days before I left. My
dad, he's sick too. Well, both of 'em stay sick. He's . . . sixty-five. She's
sixty-three.

I tell you something, I have had some hard times in my life time! I
been shot, cut, beat up, and everything!

Had a couple of hard times.

I had times, I think I wouldn't be living today. Because of what I have
been through. I have been through.

□ □ □

I'm staying with this woman right here . . . that's old enough for my
mamma. She old enough for my mamma. So, I'm staying with here for
. . . 'til I just get together. But, she don't know it. I don't tell her. I
shouldn't. . . . Which, I'm not married to her. Staying with her, over the
moment, as I feel. I mean, I can go out and get somebody that's my equal
or my age or something, you know. I'm not. But which, I can't work right
now. Until the doctor release me. Which, I love her, and her worth, what
she have did to me, here. And she would never forgive that. Never
forgive that.

If I live to be happy, I will turn that same thing over. What she did to
me.

I had a wife and a family, over here on Rampion Street. I had two
boys, and a wife over there. And I *love* all of 'em. . . . Nothing for it. . . .
When I was working my wife messed up on me. By going and giving
some kind of prophet all the money I come in here and give her. Giving it
to the prophet at the church. So. I done get tired! Yeah. I just get tired.
He told the money gonna be doubled, and get it back, and this here. My
kids hungry and all this here, you know. And I mean, I just couldn't

stand it anymore. So I left her and stayed by myself. And I runned up to this here.

□   □   □

[*Seems like you were a lot happier when I met you than you are these days.*]

Well. It's the way I carry myself. I try to make friends with everybody. I want to be happy with everybody. So I have more good than . . . white, black, blue, red, yellow, or nothing, I been this way all my life. I treat you just like I treat anybody else.

What I used to do, I work on building the tunnel. The tunnel to Canada. I work in the tunnel, so far under the ground. You know, digging. You go so far down.

□   □   □

See, I was married to my wife thirteen years. And I married my wife when she was thirteen. Thirteen. That's right; I hope God may kill me. I was eighteen.

I took her out of school. At thirteen years old. I was traveling at the time. When I met her. We talked, together. Spoke. So, her mamma wouldn't—well, she didn't want me to have her, and so, when I'm getting ready to leave, she said she better not promise to run with me because she's too young. She said she was going anyway. So her mamma drew a twenty-two-rifle on me. Her mother. Said, "If you don't leave my daughter alone, I'll kill you." I said, "I'm not bothering your daughter; your daughter come to *my* room." She did. Always did come to my room. I didn't ever go to her house because I was afraid.

So, one day, Lenore came up to the house. Seven o'clock, Saturday morning. Say, "Mamma said, come on and go fishing with us." Okay, I think, that's real good. You know, I like that; I say, well, Mamma getting on my side. You know, go fishing with her.

Well, it was a lie. I got halfway to the courthouse. Her sister say, "Lenore just lying. What did she tell you?" I said, your mamma wants me to go fishing with her. "No," she say, "Lenore want to get married."

I say, no, well, uh, her mamma gone have to sign, or her father, one. You know, have to sign. She say, "Don't worry about it. Don't worry about it. We'll get Elder Jamison."

He married us. Got married there. Without no signature or nothing. Just four of us, with the judge.

So, I got married. So I come down, have my arm around her, going around the house. Everybody standing around in the street there. Wants to know, what's going on. You know. Because her mother didn't allow this, you know, her daughter running with mens and all that, the time she drew a rifle on me.

And, I say, "This is my wife." I say, "You have anything to say now? This is my wife."

So. I stayed away from her two weeks and a half. I didn't even stay with her; she stayed with her mother. *She* say, "We'll see if she's yours." When the license came back, showed it to her. I say, "Well, I'm taking my wife home." So, I went to my mother's house. Took her there. . . . Her father knocked her around the head. So much . . . that's it, I mean what happened.

□ □ □

But, I'm still making it.

Everybody, around, surprised to see me here today. . . . Once upon a time . . . my brother and I . . . we did something wrong. . . . And it's worrying me today. Only time I got some rightening.

I had been to the service and come out. I was twenty-four years old. I went and did some time. What you call a chain gang out here . . . My brother and I both did time . . . for torturing a guy. We took him. Tied him to a tree out in the woods. . . . Set fire to him. . . . I had a reason.

Robert Scarlett

You take it no one can see you, Professor. I'm the only one on the corner got your position. You still sit and listen and play dumb like you something stupid. And all the time you're playing yourself for a fool.

You play like you don't know nothing. You see, I listen to many of your conversations. I know that you maintain that that is so. But then you have this position? You got to be kidding! That's your job. You're the same as the detective. You can listen to a person's speech, you can listen from what he talk, what he say, and you can determine what he really and where he's at. Which the average person can't do.

You can tell the most of it. Don't say no! You wouldn't have the job you have. Don't kid me! What you want to try to kid me for? I don't know much, I don't know much, but I know that. . . . I'll say this: I was raised in . . . I came from a . . . family. . . . I had to work and support my . . . sisters and my mother. My father, they separated, see. And I didn't have the opportunity to attend school. And *so*, what little bit I did learn, I *know* this. And can't *no one* take it away from me. Cannot take it away.

I know the sketch of it. Just like, if somebody rob you, and you might not know the direct figure of the face, but you can give a sketch. And you get the artist, and they'll finish it for you.

See, you need help any place you go and any bracket that you go in, I don't care how good you get. There's someone that's always a little bit higher than you.

See? But, I never got to that stage. Because I came from a very, *very* poor family. Down south.

I tell you, I'm not going to come in here and try to put myself here, there, every other place. Because, it's the idea, why should I pretend? It don't make sense. I mean that's the way I see it, but a lot of people see it different. But that's their prerogative. You understand that part of my point?

I am *just what I am*, and that's all! If I say, "Professor, come in and have a drink?" Well and good. I say, "Come in, you can spend night!" Well and good. If I say, "No, you can't spend the night!" *Still* well and good. You see, I'm just a plain-spoken person. Tell you where it's at, and that's it. Ain't no seconds, ain't no "after" behind it. If I don't like you, I don't associate with you.

[*All right, let me ask you a question. Look here, you trust me, you asked me here, into your house.*]

True. Right.

[*Okay. Think about this. Why do you trust me? See if you can pin it down.*]

From your appearance.

[*Can you get it closer?*]

Your appearance . . . and . . . your negotiation. I put it to you that way. . . . I'm going to leave it up to you. Define it the way you want to.

Even though you could fool me. But, I believe it would take a hard man to fool me. Mother wits is a hard thing to hamper, or to misuse. I don't have the education, which I'll admit. It's no secret to be hidden; because, down the line someplace, you'll find out. So no point in me kidding myself. That's where I get further in life; people, they help you, when you don't try to hide behind things. Am I right or am I wrong? That the way, the whole situation, that's the way the ball bounce. Actual.

[*Hey, listen, how far did you go in school?*]

Fourth grade.

Fourth. As I first said, I came from a very poor family. And they was unable to . . . support . . . support me. And so I had to drop out . . . work . . . and take care of them.

[*How old were you?*]

Oh, about nine.

[*Really! . . . what were they doing?*]

Oh, farming. Grew up in the country. Twenty years old when I left there and I went and served two years in Uncle Sam's Army.

All my sisters and my brother-in-laws and all of them, they graduated from college. A & T College. But, I'm the black sheep of the family. Which you don't believe, I can tell from the expression on your face. You think I'm telling you something wrong, but it's not true.

They stayed on, all of them. All of them. I'm the only boy, out of six. They completed, but I didn't. I was the black sheep of the family. Because I could plough mules.

[*Your daddy and mamma were separated?*]

Oh, yeah. You know how rough *that* is. My dad, he got a couple of farms down there. He's . . . a big wheel, you know. My mother, she has nothing.

My mother raised me.

[*Yeah. . . . Did you resent it, the fact that he wasn't around?*]

Well. . . .

[*Tell the truth.*]

The . . . the fact is, *never*. Because when he . . . presented himself as my father, I was at the age to respect him as a father. And I loved him. And I still do.

And she talked to him. I talked to him. Matter of fact, my brother-in-law, he gave me his car; he said, "Go down, see your daddy." Which was twenty-six miles from here. He got two farms, twenty-six miles from there. He told me, "I build you a house, anywhere you want." I didn't want to live in the country. I don't. . . . See, he really could . . . we. . . . Let me tell you something, Professor: when you put the tit . . . the tit in the baby's mouth, and then you take it out, it's *hard* to get it back in! You understand what I'm saying?

I drove a tractor and I ploughed a mule. Twelve hours a day. I was a kid; no shoes to wear; I was only a kid. My daddy deserted my mother, and why should I love him? Why should I love. . . .

But I have nothing wrong, I have no harm in my heart whatsoever, *against* him. Know why? He is still my father, even if he didn't treat my mother right.

But I still love my mother. I'm going down for the Fourth of July to see her, I don't give a damn what Daddy or no damn body say, I'm going to see my mamma for the Fourth! I told her and I told my boss.

catherine foster

During a discussion between Catherine, her friend Elizabeth, and myself, Catherine described the attack of polio that left her with weakened legs.

Catherine Foster

You know how I walk like this. Let me tell you about my life, now. You gonna tell part of your life, Elizabeth, I'm gonna tell part of mine.

Did you ever hoe cotton? Darling, my father, we hoed the cotton seed. I had to hoe for fifty cent a day. Two day were one dollar. Where I caught the polio at. Why I'm crippled now. You want me to tell you?

I went to this woman's well. She had dug a well. You like to let the bucket down and draw water out there. I drink the water. (*Elizabeth says*: That's the best water you ever had, help me.)

No! No, no, no! When I drink that water, I took with a headache.

I took with a serious headache. I laid down. In the bed. I told my sister, Lorraine, I say, "I don't feel good." She said, "What's the matter?" I say, "I got a headache."

I lay on the porch. She say, "Get up, get into the bed." I walked to the bed. And I told her—they had the bathroom outside, not inside like now. And I said, "I have to go to the bathroom." She said, "Get up."

Well, I got up. Dropped on the floor. I said, "I can't walk." (*She sobs.*) Never could walk.

And she ran to the field and got my mamma.

They quarantine me. They kept Lorraine away from me. They went, the doctor, the state doctor went to that well. And draw water out there. They inoculate that water. My daddy say. "Get up!" I say, "I can't walk." Every time my daddy would pick me up, I would fall. Both my legs weak.

208

They put two twenty-five pounds of sand, sand bags, on each one of my legs. They flop in the air like balloons.

That evening— Never again— At six o'clock my head was hurting me so *baadd*! Lorraine ran, my sister Lorraine ran to the field and got Mamma, say "Catherine can't walk!" My daddy throwed his cotton sack off and my mamma, they ran to the house. Say, "Get up!"

Everytime I get up, I drop down. I say, "I can't walk."

I couldn't walk. I couldn't walk. My daddy went and got a state doctor. I had the state doctor. Where I went, I was in Mississippi hospital. They say the marrow in my leg was gone. So they couldn't do me no good. Say the marrow was just like—my bone, right now, just like a child's. You could take your fist and hit me, my bone would break. My bones'll break. They're no good.

I was seven years old. And my sister was six, Lorraine. We went to the well that day to get some water. We draw water. We draw water at the well. I want some water. I could ladle it out. The lady's name Miss Roger. I said I want some water out of that dipper. When I drink that water I took deathly sick. And the doctor told my mamma and my daddy it was jaundice. They didn't have no good doctor down in Mississippi then. The doctor didn't know.

They quarantined the room where I live. They put— My sister— Couldn't nobody could come in there but my mamma. She'd always have that mask over her face. She fed me. And they had to write on the door: No Visitors. I'll never forget that as long as I live.

And, when my mamma used to go back to see—my mamma had to change me. Like change a baby. I couldn't get up. I couldn't walk. Sat back on this leg, my leg'll flop down. Tie my legs to the bed. My mamma know the time I had to be changed. She come and change me like a baby.

That no lie. My sister tell you the same thing. I went through death. People talk: "My Life"! I had a hard time. I did!

When she come down, she has a mask over her nose. To see me. Said they would catch it. I asked, "Mamma," I says, "What's she wearing that wet thing on her face for?" When she fed me. . . . Couldn't come in there but my mamma.

So, twelve o'clock, my mamma used to have to take my water. I couldn't tee-tee. My mamma took my water from me. My mamma had a little rubber hose. She had to take my water from me. She is eighty years old. She be eighty now.

She took my water from me. My water had stopped on me; my bowels had stopped on me. She took everything from me.

And I used to holler. I used to holler, Elizabeth! You talk about you had a hard time. You did not. But I did.

So I had the polio. I suffered the headaches for three days straight. I was nor but seven years old. Mamma went to the fields that morning, me and my sister jumped up there to play. And I fell. I said, "I can't walk." She said, "Oh, yes you can." She say, "Get up." I say, "I can't walk." Ask Lorraine. I said, "I can't walk." She said, "Yes, you can, get up." Everytime I got up, Elizabeth, I fell. She ran to the field and got my mamma and daddy. Said, "Mamma!" Said, "Catherine can't walk!" My daddy come and pick me up. I fell.

part four

separate peoples

I remember a morning in Africa in the summer of 1962. I was a graduate student. We were doing research in Ghana; we had returned from the countryside to the capital city for a few days. I was having breakfast in the open-air eating room of the Star Hotel, a modest establishment. Since there were only a couple of customers at that hour, the staff had little to do. The young African woman who had served me was chatting happily with her friends in the cool morning air. She stood behind me, laughing and talking with several other waitresses, as I sat and ate. She put her hand on my shoulder and casually rested her weight on that hand.

I was surprised. Not that she had touched me, but that the contact involved no hesitation or fear for her. I had come to expect in America that Blacks who were near me would betray by some small sign a discomfort and a fear—not because I was a fearsome person, but because my people had destroyed assurance in a way the British had never achieved in their colony. We had taught Blacks, in the America of my youth, that any white might bring to bear the power of his white world.

The assurance of that young woman, the assurance of Ghanaians on many days, taught me by contrast what America had done to her Blacks. I was shaken to realize that my culture had been more destructive than a colonial culture.

I grew up in a small, segregated town in Texas. Texas, as viewed on television, is now rich and wealthy, but when I lived there, in the thirties and early forties, it was a poor and dusty province.

Our county grew cotton and peanuts. Our town was the county seat and had two commercial streets with six blocks of businesses, banks, and stores. The drugstore sold sodas for a nickel. The movies cost a dime.

There were three movie houses, the Palace, the Queen, and the Dixie.

213

The Dixie showed cowboy pictures, each preceded on Saturday afternoon by the serials. Up in the balcony somewhere there was a section where Black kids could go. Out front there were parking meters and a number of old iron hitching posts.

The story books tell it that white folks in the South had good friendships with Blacks, especially when the people were children. Perhaps our town was different. But I was born and lived in that town twelve years and I spoke with a Black child once. Segregation was total. J. C. Penney's had two water fountains on the ground floor; the placard above one read "WHITE," the placard above the other read "COLORED." There were four bathrooms: white men, white women, colored men, colored women. Years later we moved; a bus carried us from Texas; groggy from travel (it was wartime and there were no seats), I came out of the bus at our first rest stop in the North, walked through the mist and fog of an October dawn into a coffee shop in West Virginia. There were only two bathrooms, and the doors read only: "MEN," "WOMEN." I felt in a direct and physical way that a weight had been lifted. I straightened. Yes, thank God, *North*! Men and Women!

In my years in our town, I had learned little. Outside of town in the country, I knew, were a large number of shacks where Black people lived. The shacks were unpainted, appeared to be made of one or two rooms, looked grey, old, and falling apart. They had no front or back porches. I had never been inside one. If Black people lived inside the town itself, I did not know it. Somewhere there was an elementary school for Black children. I did not know its name or its location. There may have been a junior high or a high school; if so, I knew nothing about them nor wondered about them.

A sad comment; I was being raised by northern, liberal, Jewish parents; I shared their dislike for the language, customs, and values of segregation but it did not occur to me to wonder where Black children went after sixth grade.

It is not my intent to portray America as a society that is unusually cruel. First of all, the land of opportunity and hope to which my mother emigrated from Russia does exist and is a reality for many of us. And, second, the cruel aspects of America are not unusual features. Our society is much like other large Western societies. Indeed, it probably is less cruel; our rich resource base has let our struggles take place in a context of easier margins than are found in many nations, and the struggles have taken place in arenas governed to some extent by the careful limits on power that were institutionalized by our Constitution.

But while our nation has not been unusually cruel, it has had its own particular form of cruelty. Despite denial and despite inattention, one central truth of American society is that it is a society in which the whites dominate the Blacks. Whites and Blacks live in two separate worlds; whites and Blacks fear and hate each other; not all whites have power, but the power that exists is held almost entirely by whites and is used, consciously or unconsciously, in a way that is sensitive to race.

People often say today, "Race doesn't matter anymore, it's just people." My answer is, "Good, friend, go try it. Spend the afternoon walking in the Black slum." And, indeed, perhaps one should make that walk. One could begin to absorb some certainties of Black life. Don't count on anything, one hears, things don't stay together. Poverty cripples a person. When you try to put something together, soon enough a new emergency takes your energy to a different front, and the bit that you have pulled together begins to crumble away, like sand held in a fist under water. Poor people (Black and white) live in weary frustration. It is an unending struggle, just to keep a decent roof over your children's heads, just to see that they have good enough clothes to wear to school. People work hard in the poor neighborhoods, in their houses and at their jobs.

"Whitey wants to hold you down," Black men say. "Any time when he sees that you have got things to where you are a little better off, to where you are getting somewhere, sure enough you look up and he will be there, pushing you back and taking what you have got. No way do he want you to be able to make it up to where he's at."

I have heard this more times than I can count.

Parents lived in fear and resignation: a daughter might fall in with some drunkard and be left with children, a son might run with hoodlums and be shot. The Corner lives close to death. Family histories were scarred with lynchings in the South, fatal quarrels in the North, and accidents. Death was part of what was accepted. You tried to raise kids so that they could take rough breaks; you worked to give them and yourself a backbone, but you couldn't shape the world they lived in—the whites shaped that.

Walking in that slum, the white sojourner begins to meet his or her white nature. The watching eyes, with their wish to hold you at a distance, tell you that you are white, not just an individual. You begin to sense the whiteness— the fraction of yourself that does feel Blacks are different, that does react with fear, the fraction that is in all of us, that can be mobilized into hate when we are in danger, but that in relaxation is still enough to hold back change. You feel the part of yourself that mistranslates Black needs (the result of socially produced poverty) as an expression of Black nature: needful Blacks seem *by nature* less bright, less competent. (Just as Blacks translate unthinking white complicity as an expression of the essence of whites: whites seem *by nature* cruel.)

The least successful Blacks flee that demeaning evaluation. They huddle together, as at the Corner, exchanging acceptance without examination. Anything can be said at the Corner; no one will question it (because no one listens). This is the function of the Corner; it is a refuge in which to give mutual solace.

But beyond the Corner lies a much larger Black world of sturdier families. As a white, one has not been raised to imagine Blacks as competent, as real agents on the earth. We attend to images of sad families without fathers, but ignore the millions of men who came North, found work in heavy industry, bought homes and raised their families through the sweat of their toil. The working Black father does not exist in our imagination, only the (less threatening) mother. Thus we preserve the image of the Black who is, by nature, less a force, less entitled to that which should come to all who can ask for it seriously.

The ultimate lesson of this sojourn among the Black poor is separation. I express the lesson in several phrases: "us and them," "the invisible Blacks," and "Whitey is cold." These phrases refer to ways that Blacks and whites think about themselves and each other.

"Us and them" refers to a portion of minority identity. I am white, on the winning side of the split. The benefits of being white come to me automatically, without struggling for them. It never crossed my mind that someone gave me a job *because* I was white, or was polite to me *because* I was white. *White* never occurred to me as the reason. But at one time I lived on the losing side, the minority side.

When I was in grade school, we did Christmas. All of us—three hundred and sixty celebrants of the birth of God's son, and three Jews. The day that we finished coloring pictures of jack-o-lanterns, we began coloring pictures of Santa Claus. "And now we will sing the songs," the teacher said. "You better watch out, you better not pout." I sat and squirmed, wondering whether it was OK to say the word "Santa Claus," since that was not a religious word, but before I figured that one out we were into the hard stuff. I knew that if I sang the word "Jesus" or the word "Christ," I would be a turncoat and a traitor. But I knew also that everyone in the room could see that I was singing and would think I was crazy if I sang every word but stopped when the word "Jesus" came or "Christ" or "Savior." I knew they all were looking at me and laughing at me.

That was how it felt to sit in the room, grades one through eight, and sing Christmas carols. We sang them an hour a day, Halloween until Christmas.

The twenty-nine other people in the classroom were simply singing a song. Probably most of them paid little attention to what they were doing, and did not think of themselves at the moment as people who belonged to a group called Christians. They did not see the successive days of carol singing as being primarily devoted to that activity and all alike. *They* were just living, while I was having a particular experience.

I was experiencing intense conflict and what it means to be on the minority side of an occasion. One of the odd parts of such occasions is that the people on the majority side usually are not aware that an occasion is going on. This is an eerie experience for the minority person. The obliviousness of the majority person is a signal to the minority person that he or she, the minority person, is *crazy*. If I keep feeling that something very upsetting is going on, and twenty-nine sane-looking, ordinary people keep acting as though nothing at all is going on, I must be crazy.

I can deal with this by withdrawing from the experience and avoiding it in the future. Or by deciding that they are *not* ordinary people (but, for example, devils). Or by embracing craziness and pursuing it. Alternatively, I can go berserk as an individual and force the stone-faced people to admit that something is going on. Or I can carry out some organized confrontation that forces that same admission. (Thus perhaps the importance of confrontation in group relations—the minority person's need to have the Other share the realization that something is happening.)

The moments of isolated awareness which I describe here, these moments in which one passes through a tense encounter to which the other participants are opaque, became for me seed moments in the formation of my identity, and gave me a sense of a world composed of us and of them. This sense of "us and them" lies deep in the identity of every member of a minority group.

That profound sense of "us and them" arises for Blacks from special circumstances like this one and from the general circumstances of everyday life. Black children experience a world of enacted separation; a line has been drawn between the races by whites, and it has been drawn with hostile intent, and it has been maintained. "Us and them" is necessarily the beginning point of Black thinking about whites. Whites, generally, miss this learning; they seldom experience themselves carrying out the acts that create or maintain the separation. The separation long ago became part of natural-seeming and inevitable-seeming events (that is, institutions).

Since whites seldom notice themselves creating the separation, they seldom think about it. Since Blacks live within the effects of the separation, they think of it often. "Us and them" becomes a fundamental part of their lives. Whites ignore it, and, in the ignoring, badly miss the point of Black experience. In missing the point of Black experience, whites seem to Blacks to be either insulting or foolish.

The second phrase "the invisible Blacks," refers to the white perception of Blacks.

"What do whites think of Blacks?" Whites don't think of Blacks.

White or Black, when we brush our teeth, when we walk down the street, when we are at ease, our minds are occupied by and large with the simple necessary issues of our lives: the job and the family. Whites, like Blacks, think about whatever, or whomever, is important at *that* level. Obviously, there are other thoughts during periods of duress, but day in and day out, the questions are: Whom do I have to satisfy to get a raise? Who is important for my family getting along? For me getting ahead?

As a consequence of our history, Blacks are not the people whom one has to think about at that level. I do not have to please a Black boss to get a raise. I have never had a Black boss. I do not have to get a Black banker to agree to give me a mortgage on my house. I have never seen a Black banker.

Thus it is the Blacks are invisible for whites. They control little that we need (since they have been held from power). They can offer us little, so we do not think of them. They exist for us primarily as a nuisance. Periodically they pose a threat to our safety, or our self-esteem, or our sense of peace, and then we have to think of them. Reluctantly. Why don't they go away? Why don't they disappear?

We make them disappear.

We make them disappear with freeways. I drive a sunken freeway and cross the West Side of Detroit every Tuesday without seeing one Black person who is not in a car.

We make them disappear with suburbs and beltways that link white suburbs to each other while avoiding Black areas.

We make them disappear with rotting cities that are legally no concern of the surrounding Whiteland.

We make them disappear with the evacuation of finance, advanced jobs, and basic jobs from the abandoned cities.

We make them disappear with a callous indifference to the assault on the soul that is poverty. We leave them to look at the walls and the hopelessness. We leave them to make themselves disappear in boredom and alcohol, anger and work.

The third phrase, "Whitey is cold," expresses the fundamental Black perception of whites. As a white, I am still surprised, must always learn it afresh. How can this be the starting point for anyone looking at me? Certain that I am a sensitive person, I presume to demand to be seen as an individual. But the person passing me on the street sees only the skin, sees only a member of the group that has written about its sensitivities but that has left his mother to scrub floors, has left his father to curse as he sought work, will leave his children to soak up the new insults. The Black passing me on the street sees the true history of his family and my membership in the people that has made that world; he assumes my nature from the actions and the lack of actions that he knows.

□   □   □

What then? From these voices, from these several reactions, what follows?

What can follow, but, again, the necessity to dig in, to come to know oneself, to attempt to be open to knowing by the Other, to attempt to work, together, in sober acquaintance?

Blacks with little money, we see, perceive themselves to live outside society and perceive the white world as a hostile force. White thinking, we see, is not grounded in any sense of everyday Black experience.

An understanding in depth would require a sharing of vulnerability, but the structure of our society works against whites and Blacks coming to know one another in settings of shared risk.

The self that liberals bring to bear in thinking about intercultural life is an artificial one within which one imagines that one has no self-interests. This odd construction induces distrust, as well it might, since it must lead to unreliable postures. Part of knowing oneself is learning to understand what one does gain within the social order and coming to grips with questions as to how much one is willing to lose permanently. We rather tend to hide from ourselves and from others our personal agenda. In pretending to have no agenda of our own, we re-enact the conversation that goes on at the welfare desk, where the unknown white lady invites the supplicant Black lady to bare her soul.

This hiding is a perversion made possible by differentials of power. One overcomes it by achieving a sense of self and then permitting knowledge by the other, entering a dance of learning and becoming learned. Then perhaps one can create settings in which common striving would be possible, and deep understanding could arise.

Beyond this level of psychological consideration lies a brute world of economic development. Its course and direction are not mysterious to those who watch. Industry and finance are leaving the inner cities; corporations close the plants inside the cities while leaving open those in the suburbs. It is increasingly difficult to see where the Black communities inside the cities will find enough economic resources to protect themselves. The Blacks are being starved out, while everyone pretends that not much of anything is going on.

The outlook could not be more perilous. In that dangerous world, the structural forces that discourage understanding and trustworthy alliances must weigh heavily.

The outlook could not be more bleak. "Impartial social forces" are intensifying the threat of life-long poverty for new generations of Black children. Our genteel white acquiescence rests on our ignorance about the other—whose life we have not shared—and about the self—whose hungers and fears we have not admitted.

The painful and death-haunted struggle by Blacks to construct lives for their families has been enacted on a stage that is empty: Where are the whites? Mounted on the side and back curtains of that stage are pale ceramic masks with empty eyes.

We must bring eyes and voices to those masks.

I must inhabit my mask, let it become a face—with eyes that meet eyes, voice that inflects to voice—so that my brother and I learn each other, so that my sister once more leans upon my shoulder in trust.

The children are at stake.